D0272142

The Thatcher Decade

To my mother, and to my godchildren and other young friends who are the children of the Thatcher decade.

The Thatcher Decade

How Britain has changed during the 1980s

PETER RIDDELL

Basil Blackwell

Copyright © Peter Riddell 1989

First published 1989

Basil Blackwell Ltd
108 Cowley Road, Oxford, OX4 1JF, UK

Basil Blackwell Inc.
3 Cambridge Center
Cambridge, MA 02142, USA

British Library Cataloguing in Publication Data

A CIP catalogue record for this book is available
from the British Library.

Library of Congress Cataloging in Publication Data

Riddell, Peter.
  The Thatcher decade : How Britain has changed during the 1980s /
Peter Riddell.
    p.   cm.
  Bibliography: p.
  Includes index.
  ISBN 0–631–16274–7
  1. Great Britain—Politics and government—1979–. 2 Thatcher,
Margaret.   I. Title.
DA589.7.R53   1990
941.085'8—dc20

Typeset in 11 on 12½pt Sabon
by Footnote Graphics, Warminster, Wiltshire

Printed in Great Britain by Billing and Sons Ltd., Worcester

Contents

Preface

There is now such a vast literature on Mrs Margaret Thatcher, Thatcherism and her administration that any addition needs to be justified – as much perhaps to the author and publisher as to readers. Many accounts, including my own *The Thatcher Government* of 1983 (updated and revised in 1985) have been overtaken, if not I hope entirely contradicted, by subsequent events. For the Thatcher revolution/phenomenon has been a continuing one. Radicalism rather than consolidation has remained the keynote, requiring frequent reappraisals.

In *The Thatcher Government* I attempted a tentative, interim assessment after the administration's first term, measuring its achievements against what Mrs Thatcher set out to do in 1979. It focused on the problems of government. A different approach is now required. Far-reaching developments, such as privatization and popular capitalism, were only beginning to be established in 1983, with little indication of their subsequent significance. So this is a wholly new book.

Moreover, the book aims to cover different ground from most of the other recent studies. There have been several biographies, even the occasional memoir by a retired or sacked minister, numerous attacks or defences from particular standpoints, as well as countless monographs on specific policy areas or episodes, such as the Falklands war or the miners' strike. There have been a few broader studies like those by Dennis Kavanagh, Peter Jenkins, Andrew Gamble and Hugo Young which have looked at the evolution of Thatcherism and the impact of Mrs Thatcher on British politics.

My aim is also distinct from most of these studies in that I do not look primarily at Mrs Thatcher herself or her impact on British politics. Instead I examine how Britain itself has changed during the Thatcher decade – its economy, industrial structure, labour market, society and place in the world. I discuss how far these changes have reflected the intended or unintended actions of the Government itself, underlying changes which began before 1979 and trends common to other industrialized countries. I also consider how deep-seated and irreversible these changes have become. In short, how far has there been a Thatcher revolution?

Any commentator, let alone anyone aspiring to contemporary history, faces numerous problems. There is, first, the inherent constraint of personal standpoint. Even those of us accustomed to a detached perch like the one I occupied in the parliamentary press gallery from 1981 to 1988, have views and a vote, even though not a partisan commitment. Paradoxically, some of the allegedly academic studies proclaiming their scholarly detachment have produced the most partisan accounts, on both sides.

My own viewpoint is that I have sympathy with the redirection of economic and industrial policy which began in the mid-1970s and developed a new energy and momentum with the arrival of the Thatcher Government. There was a need for a new approach after the failures of the 1970s. As a result there have been undoubted gains for the economy, though these stop well short of the miracle trumpeted in early 1988. But there have been clear costs and I am critical about many of the social consequences of Thatcherism, as reflected in the divisions which grew during the 1980s. But I do not share the widespread, and often snobbish, disdain in which the old establishment and the chattering classes hold Mrs Thatcher. By any standard she has been a remarkable political leader, not only because of her electoral record but also because of the extent to which she has changed Britain's political agenda. She may be disliked by many, but she cannot be patronized. Many of the results of the Thatcher years may be vulgar and philistine – the 'loadsamoney' culture – as well as socially divisive, but there has been something refreshing about her challenge to previous assumptions.

Like most others in the political world my views have changed as a result of what has happened since 1979. Obviously it is hard to offer lasting conclusions at a time when Thatcherism is still unfolding. There is the danger of extrapolating into the future trends current at the time of writing. Depending on the standing of the Conservatives in the opinion polls, Thatcherism has appeared either about to founder or set to remain dominant for the foreseeable future, as on her tenth anniversary in office in May 1989 when a common theme was 'she's gone too far.' The direction of this determinism depends on when you write.

Mrs Thatcher has undoubtedly been a personal phenomenon as Prime Minister, but she is not immortal. At some stage the Tories will falter under either her or her successor, and there will be a different pattern of politics. But when this happens there will not be a sudden reversal of all that has occurred since 1979. Instead, there is likely to be a shift of emphasis. The changes in the Thatcher period will be built upon and new political, social and economic priorities will be asserted. Consequently, my aim is to attempt to distinguish the underlying from the ephemeral, the secular from the cyclical.

It is none the less inevitable that the title of this book, like so many others, should include Mrs Thatcher's name. Unlike any other post-war British politician, she has left her personal mark upon Britain since 1979. While other ministers, notably Sir Geoffrey Howe and Mr Nigel Lawson, have played a leading part since 1979, it has been her interventions at critical points that have determined the outcome. Her resolution, energy and resilience ensured that the Government regained its momentum when faced with crises such as those over the economy in 1981, the Falklands in 1982, the coal strike in 1984–5, and the aftermath of the Westland affair in 1986.

Until the end of 1988 I was closely involved in observing Mrs Thatcher and her administration, first as the economics correspondent of *The Financial Times* until the summer of 1981, and then as its political editor. For such a privileged vantage point I thank the paper's editors of that period, Fredy Fisher and Geoffrey Owen. I am also grateful for the insights provided by many politicians, fellow journalists and other observers of the endless fascinations of the political scene. They are far too numerous to mention, though they will no doubt recognize some of their views as interpreted by me.

I am particularly appreciative of the advice and support of a number of good friends, notably the invaluable comments on several chapters offered by Roger Liddle and Ben Stoneham, as well as the perceptive insights over the years of Elinor Goodman, Michael Cassell and James Naughtie (and their families). As ever, I am grateful for the encouragement of Martin and Helene Hayman and for the stimulus offered by their sons Ben, Joseph, Jacob and David, who in time will be better placed than I am to provide a lasting verdict on Thatcherism.

Sean Magee of Basil Blackwell has shown considerable patience during this book's lengthy gestation. He produced the most charming postcards as gentle reminders to effort as well as suitable editorial support.

I have drawn much, both consciously and unconsciously, on the thoughts of others, to whom I am grateful. But the judgements, conclusions and faults are naturally my own.

Peter Riddell
June 1989

1

Introduction: The Nature of Thatcherism

There are dangers in consensus: it could be an attempt to satisfy people holding no particular views about anything. It seems more important to have a philosophy and policy which because they are good appeal to sufficient people to secure a majority ... No great party can survive except on the basis of firm beliefs about what it wants to do. It is not enough to have reluctant support. We want people's enthusiasm as well.

> Margaret Thatcher, Chief Opposition Spokesman on Power, Conservative Political Centre address, Blackpool, 10 October 1968

It became the accepted wisdom, not merely that we were, as a nation, in a phase of relative decline which might soon become absolute, not to say terminal; but that our social cohesion, our political institutions, our very governability and even national integrity were in an advanced and probably irreversible state of decay. From Michael Shanks' *The Stagnant Society*, in 1961, through the special 'Suicide of a Nation' issue of *Encounter* in 1963, all the way to Sir Nicholas Henderson's valedictory despatch of 1979, the grimness of the diagnosis was unvarying. It was a theme which offered irresistible temptations both to the purveyors of gloom and the peddlers of glib solutions.

> Nigel Lawson, Energy Secretary, Patrick Hutber Memorial Lecture, London, 22 June 1982

The Conservative Political Centre lecture at each October's party conference is intended to be a prestige event. An invitation to deliver it confers the mantle of promise on the aspiring middle-ranking politician concerned. But that is all. No one then pays much attention to the platitudinous and safe comments generally uttered. October 1968 was no exception. The speaker was the most junior member of Edward Heath's Shadow Cabinet, and the lecture attracted almost no notice at the time. Yet the ten pages of the subsequently published pamphlet contain the essence of what has become known as Thatcherism.

With an ice maiden photograph of the author on the front, the pamphlet offers as clear a guide to Mrs Thatcher's approach to politics as any she has subsequently given. More than 20 years later little has changed. Under the title of 'What's wrong with politics?' she sets out her distrust of government: 'What we need now is a far greater degree of personal responsibility and decision, far more independence from the government, and a comparative reduction in the role of government.' There are passages urging greater concern with control of the money supply, with increasing personal responsibility for social provision, and with giving people a measure of independence from the state. There is the first appearance of her familiar argument that the Good Samaritan 'had to have the money to help, otherwise he too would have had to pass on the other side.' And, as the quotation at the beginning of this chapter shows, there is the dislike of consensus and a belief in firm and clear alternatives.

The pamphlet is interesting now not just as an illustration of the consistency of Mrs Thatcher's views, but more to show that Thatcherism is a personal, highly distinctive, approach to politics rather than a coherent set of ideas. Mrs Thatcher is not a great political thinker or theorist. Her inspiration is personal experience and a view of Britain. She is not a consistent free-market advocate, not an out-and-out libertarian opponent of the state – far from it. Mrs Thatcher's attitudes and actions have often been contrary to free-market theories. In particular, she has always been sensitive to the interests of owner-occupiers in staunchly defending the retention of mortgage interest tax-relief against the views of the Treasury and of most economists who believe the subsidy artificially distorts the housing market and inflates house prices. She has also taken a distinctly mercantilist view of industry and trade, championing British companies rather than adopting a purely free-market approach. Similarly, she has reacted to middle-class concerns over violence and pornography by balancing her support for the deregulation of broadcasting by also setting-up a body to monitor and supervise standards. The nanny state lives on.

As I have argued previously (1983), 'Thatcherism is essentially an instinct, a series of moral values and an approach to leadership rather than an ideology. It is an expression of Mrs Thatcher's upbringing in Grantham, her background of hard work and family responsibility, ambition and postponed satisfaction, duty and patriotism.' In one of the characteristically frank insights which tend to come at the end of her television and press interviews, Mrs Thatcher disclosed her underlying approach on the *Weekend World* programme in January 1983. She extolled Victorian values:

I want to see one nation, as you go back to Victorian times, but I want everyone to have their own personal property stake ... I want them to have their own savings which retain their value, so they can pass things on to their children, so you get again a people, everyone strong and independent of government. Winston put it best. You want a ladder, upwards, so anyone, no matter what their background, can climb, but a fundamental safety net below which no one can fall. That's the British character ... Of course, we have basic social services, we will continue to have those, but equally compassion depends on what you and I, as individuals, are prepared to do. I remember my father telling me that at a very early age. Compassion doesn't depend upon whether you get up and make a speech in the market-place about what governments should do. It depends upon how you're prepared to conduct your own life, and how much you're prepared to give of what you have to others ... It's the sincere approach born of the conviction which I learned in a small town from a father who had a conviction approach.

Mrs Thatcher stands for the values of the English suburban and provincial middle-class and aspiring skilled working-class. She is very much an English phenomenon, as shown by her lack of political appeal in Scotland and Wales. However, she is not a metropolitan establishment figure, partly because of her sex, but also because of her attitudes. Her style of conviction politics and self-conscious radicalism are uncomfortable for the established. Some of the greatest hostility to her has often come from representatives of traditional pillars of society like the universities, the Church of England, the Foreign Office and the professions. She is not a naturally clubbable person. Indeed, Mrs Thatcher has been in equal parts patronized and disliked by the liberal intellectual establishment. This was brought out by several contributors to a vivid collection of views in the *Sunday Telegraph* in January 1988. Producer and writer Jonathan Miller talked of her 'odious suburban gentility and sentimental saccharine patriotism, catering to the worst elements of commuter idiocy.' Others complained of a bullying style, her materialism, and her hostility to the performing arts, education and research work. In response, novelist Kingsley Amis said Mrs Thatcher brought out the latent snobbery in those no longer deferred to.

Her approach has revolved around a number of themes – a belief in Britain's greatness and the assertion of national interests, a prejudice against the public sector (at any rate in economic and industrial affairs), a backing for the police and the authorities in fighting terrorism and upholding law and order, a strong dislike of trade unions, a general commitment to the virtues of sound money, a preference for wealth creators over civil servants and commentators, and a support for the right of individuals to make their own pro- vision for education and health. In a moment of stark self-revelation during the 1987 election campaign Thatcher said she used private health facilities because she wanted to go into hospital on the day 'I want at the time I want and with the doctor I want ... I exercise my right as a free citizen to spend my own money in my own way' (quoted in Butler and Kavanagh, 1988).

Many commentators, notably though not exclusively on the left, have argued that this adds up to a coherent ideology – that Thatcherism represents the practical application of a set of theories, whose proponents are known as the New Right, which has swept to success on both sides of the Atlantic. There have certainly been similarities – as well as striking contrasts – in what has happened in Britain and the US, and to a limited extent elsewhere. But, as will be discussed later in this chapter, this reflects the circumstances of the time more than the ideology. There have obviously been ideological elements in the approach of Mrs Thatcher and the Conservatives since 1979 – for instance, the dislike of state intervention in the economy – but this has not produced a consciously pre-determined strategy. Too much of the analysis of the fashionable left (the school associated with the magazine *Marxism Today*, most clearly and subtly expressed in Gamble, 1988) has been based on an ex-post rationalization of what has happened. Hindsight often provides the coherence and clarity denied to contemporaries. To talk, as the new Marxists do, of a coherent hegemonic project, or of the Thatcher project, is meaningless, as well as absurd. It is part of the dire linguistic legacy of Marx and Gramsci which makes the work of many Marxist commentators so indigestible and so misleadingly determinist. The word 'project' conveys the impression of the Blue

Peter children's television programme and papier-mâché models – nowadays the world of Spitting Image. The new Marxists may be right to see the Thatcherism of the late 1980s as a deliberate attempt to replace the post-war social democratic consensus and to create an economic and political constituency for capitalist values and aspirations. But that has been very much a second and third-term phenomenon. That was not what the Conservatives were about in opposition or in their first term, up to 1983. The radicalism of the late 1980s has developed on the basis of earlier political successes. Or, rather, many of the most important new policies have been the result of the failures of initial policies and in response to circumstances. Mrs Thatcher's electoral and political dominance has given her the rare opportunity to remedy earlier setbacks and policy weaknesses.

There was no master plan. Mrs Thatcher won the Conservative leadership in February 1975 in what amounted to a coup d'état against Edward Heath. It was based on the dissatisfaction felt by a majority of Conservative MPs after the party had suffered two electoral defeats in 1974. Some senior Tories, like her original mentor Lord (then Sir Keith) Joseph had become highly critical of the economic record of the Heath administration. But her victory represented no conscious ideological shift on the part of most Conservative MPs. It reflected more their search for a clear cut alternative and the availability of Mrs Thatcher in that role. There was certainly a stirring of thought at the time among free-marketeers – with the Institute of Economic Affairs coming into its own under Lord (Ralph) Harris and Arthur Seldon after 20 years in the intellectual wilderness, and with new bodies being formed like the Centre for Policy Studies. The New Right enjoyed a heyday in both the UK and US during the late 1970s. Yet this was a diverse group – including supporters of reining back the public sector and of tax cuts, libertarians, and monetarists. These views were generally, though not invariably, linked. For instance, support for strict monetary control frequently overlapped with a belief in supply-side economics and tax cuts, but at times they could be in conflict. In the US, for example, supply-siders in the Reagan administration who backed tax cuts – even though they initially boosted the federal budget deficit – also attacked the monetary squeeze of the Federal Reserve Board. There were also contrasts, and at times, conflicts, between the anti-government libertarians and traditional conservatives who accepted the disciplinary role of the state. As we have seen earlier, Mrs

Thatcher personally embraced a number of these divergent views and she was in no sense the champion of any particular ideology.

Instead, the main concern of Mrs Thatcher and her close allies was more general: the decline of Britain. As reflected in the quotation from Nigel Lawson at the beginning of this chapter, there was a growing feeling during the 1970s that the post-war settlement – Keynesian demand management of the economy, agreements with the trade unions and so on – was no longer delivering the goods. In a retrospective assessment in January 1988, Nigel Lawson saw the problem of the 1970s as the pursuit of equality, which, he argued, 'led to growing discord and the exercise of big government led to the point where it was widely felt that Britain had become ungovernable':

Yet it was not until the final stages of this process, in the mid-1970s, as the tensions that had been building up exploded in a holocaust of inflation, a disease as socially destructive as it is economically damaging, that the tide of ideas began to turn. Not until then did it come to be realised that the problem lay not in the inefficient management of the prevailing consensus, but in the consensus itself: that the use of state power to run the economy and to enforce equality lay at the very root of our national difficulties, and had to be abandoned.

Mr Lawson talked of 'a decade of self-doubt and relative decline'.

There has been a large, and growing, literature on the issue of decline, both in Britain and, more recently, in the US. Two broad theses have been put forward. The first, most closely associated with the historian Paul Kennedy (1988), is that of 'imperial overstretch', which states that empires and nations have declined in power and influence because of their attempts to maintain overseas commitments which they can no longer afford. This view of nations 'living beyond their means' may have applied to some extent to Britain in the 1950s and 1960s, but was harder to sustain in the 1980s, when defence spending rose sharply in the first half of the decade. The main alternative view, most clearly expressed by the social scientist Mancur Olson (1982), has been that societies decline because of the growth of vested interests – of producers, trade unions and state bureaucracies – which over time impede change and reduce economic efficiency and the rate of productivity growth. What Olson has called 'distributional coalitions' develop to the extent that societies become inflexible, increasingly slow to adapt, and they lose dynamism in competition with their rivals. On this view a nation's maturity brings its own problems. Mrs Thatcher and her allies like Mr Lawson have implicitly accepted the Olson thesis (and domestic variations set out by Barnett, 1972 and 1986, and Wiener, 1981). As Professor Olson has himself more recently argued, the Conservatives during the 1980s have challenged this sclerosis in Britain by seeking to weaken trade unions, nationalized industries and establishment values and attitudes.

Mrs Thatcher explicitly saw key political issues in terms of Britain's past greatness, recent decline and the possibility of recovery. Her vision was never purely economic. In her final broadcast before the May 1979 election, Mrs Thatcher said: 'Somewhere ahead lies greatness for our country again. This I know in my heart. Look at Britain today and you may think that an impossible dream. But there is another Britain of thoughtful people, tantalizingly slow to act, yet marvellously determined when they do.' Similarly, two months after her election victory, in a lecture to the Conservative Political Centre summer school, she talked of a nation which had been 'in dire straits before' and had recovered. Decrying the move towards collectivism, she argued that 'the wanton expansion of the state's responsibilities had been accompanied by a great drop in public spirit'. Behind the election victory of May 1979, lay 'the need for renewal of our traditional craftsmanship and civic spirit; renewal at every level, and in every profession, of our old vigour, and vitality.' In the language almost of a prophet, she set out the Government's objectives:

The mission of this Government is much more than the promotion of economic progress. It is to renew the spirit and solidarity of the nation. To ensure that these assertions lead to action, we need to inspire a new national mood, as much as to carry through legislation. At the heart of a new mood in the nation must be a recovery of our self-confidence and our self respect. Nothing is beyond us. Decline is not inevitable. But nor is progress a law of nature. The ground gained by one generation may be lost by the next. The foundation of this new confidence has to be individual responsibility.

After talking of the themes of opportunity, choice, strength and renewal, Thatcher revealingly drew an imperial parallel:

It will not be given to this generation of our countrymen to create a great Empire. But it is given to us to demand an end to decline and to make a stand against what Churchill described as the long dismal drawling tides of drift and surrender, of wrong measurements and feeble impulses.

This essentially moral vision was reflected in the Conservatives' 1979 election manifesto. The document itself was short on specific commitments and certainly did not represent the deliberate start of an ideological revolution, or rather that of a counter-revolution. The main influences on the manifesto and on the campaign were the events of the preceding few months, particularly the 'winter of discontent' with its highly publicized trade union disruption. The Tories promised action to limit trade union powers and to reduce inflation. But as the chapter on privatization shows the pledges on what was then known as denationalization were limited not just by political caution but also by doubts about the extent of what could be achieved. The manifesto talked of working with the grain of human nature. The appeal was to the fears and aspirations of those disillusioned with Labour – skilled workers, especially those living in the suburbs, new towns and smaller cities of southern England and the Midlands. These were the people whose living standards had been squeezed during much of the 1970s, and many of whom were a ready market for one of the Tories' few specific pledges – to sell local authority owned homes to their occupiers. These people were also attracted by Mrs Thatcher's emphasis on law and order and strong defence, and in some areas by her tough stand on further limits on immigration. In any event, among the third of the electorate counted as skilled workers there was a swing of 11 per cent of voters from Labour since the previous general election in October 1974. There was even a swing of 8.5 per cent from Labour to Conservative among male trade union members. This compares with a one-point net switch from Conservative to Labour among the non-manual middle-classes. Indeed, a feature of Mrs Thatcher's electoral success not only in 1979, but also, subsequently, in 1983 and 1987, has been her ability to retain the support of skilled workers, who have in every sense become Thatcher's people.

The Conservatives also worked with the grain in the broader sense of taking up, and forward, a shift in macro-economic policy which developed in the mid-to-late 1970s under the Callaghan administration. As the next chapter explains in detail, it was from 1975–6 onwards that the emphasis on monetary control and public spending restraint was initiated by Denis Healey as Chancellor of the Exchequer, in part somewhat reluctantly in response to financial market pressures. Nevertheless, many of the themes put forward by Mrs Thatcher and her colleagues in 1978–9 were in line with the policies being practised by the Labour Government. Yet, despite its share in the parentage of the Thatcher experiment/phenomenon, the Callaghan administration at times seemed half-hearted in its commitment to this redirection of policy, while its broader strategy was fatally undermined by the destruction of its attempt to secure the co-operation of the trade unions on wage restraint by the disruption during the winter of 1978–9. So the Tories' call for a new start was in tune with both a wide spectrum of elite opinion – civil servants had distanced themselves from their political masters during the spring of 1979 – and it was in tune with popular opinion as reflected in the polls. Even the defeated Prime Minister James (now Lord) Callaghan was reported as acknowledging that 'there are times, perhaps once every 30 years, when there is a sea change in politics. It then does not matter what you say or what you do. There is a shift in what the public wants and what it approves of. I suspect there is now such a sea change – and it is for Mrs Thatcher.' At the time, the sea change was seen as basically negative – against the collectivism of the 1960s and 1970s and the failures of the Callaghan administration rather than specifically in favour of a capitalist/individualist blue-print.

Once in office, Mrs Thatcher's administration responded to Britain's problems by curbing the power of the trade unions, attempting to get on top of inflation via a tight monetary policy, seeking to cut public spending and taxes, rebuilding Britain's defence capacity and dealing with rising crime. In the social area there were some minor proposals – removing one tier of health authorities, cutting back on some social benefits and on education spending. After a couple of years few of these main goals were near achievement. Unemployment was soaring as output fell sharply, yet the money supply and public spending were rising substantially in excess of their targets. And there appeared to be little progress elsewhere, with serious inner city riots in the summer of 1981 and the Tories in electoral retreat in face of the newly formed Social Democratic Party and its Liberal allies. The Government's free-market supporters were disappointed. A series of essays published by the Institute of Economic Affairs in 1982 was entitled 'Could Do Better'. The free-marketeers argued that the Government had failed to develop a coherent political strategy to deal with trade unions and the welfare state, and had left the public sector largely intact.

Yet 1981, for all its troubles, was the political turning point for the

Thatcher Government and for Thatcherism. In the March Budget, Sir Geoffrey Howe, the Chancellor – and one of the under-appreciated architects of the administration's policies – raised the tax burden in order to curb public sector borrowing, even though unemployment was still rising sharply. This turned on its head the conventional wisdom of post-war Keynesian demand management, under which fiscal policy should have been relaxed rather than tightened. This budget underlined not only what later became known as 'the resolute approach', but also showed how the Government was determined to change economic policy, for all the predictions of a U-turn. Secondly, that September, Mrs Thatcher achieved dominance over her Cabinet by the removal from it of some of her critics, like Sir Ian Gilmour, by exiling others away from its centre, like Mr (now Lord) James Prior, and by promoting to the Cabinet allies like Nigel Lawson, Norman Tebbit and Cecil Parkinson. That marked the effective end of the traditional Tory 'wet' challenge to Mrs Thatcher. Her strong and successful leadership during the Falklands war in the following spring and early summer solidified public backing for her internal party dominance – and this was reinforced by the start of a recovery in living standards.

In domestic policy, Mrs Thatcher's political victories in 1981–2 enabled her to regain the initiative in a number of areas where previous approaches had not worked. In particular, the failure to get to grips with the large deficits of the nationalized industries led to the development of the privatization programme. As often during the Thatcher decade, what turned out to be a far-reaching initiative developed in an unexpected fashion in response to a particular problem, rather than as a result of some pre-ordained plan. It is certainly true that Mrs Thatcher and her close allies had an ingrained hostility to nationalized industries which they regarded as less efficient than the private sector. But even the most radical private thinking of the Conservatives in opposition – let alone their cautious public commitments – had not envisaged the sale of the major monopoly utilities, as happened in the second half of the 1980s. The programme which transformed the boundaries between the public and private sectors was in response to a policy crisis.

Similarly, in her second term from 1983–7, the proposals for the restructuring of the education system emerged as a result of a perceived crisis over standards in schools. This reflected concerns expressed during the lengthy teachers' pay dispute of 1984–6. Again, radicalism was the child of earlier failure. The Government's chequered record on local authorities provides other examples. Each successive initiative – rate-capping, the abolition of the Greater London Council and the metropolitan counties, and the community charge or poll tax – was a response to earlier failures to establish Whitehall's control over mainly Labour controlled big city Town Halls. After Mrs Thatcher's third election victory, the story was repeated when the chorus of protests over the funding of the health service during the winter of 1987–8 led to the announcement of a far-reaching review into the future of the National Health Service – contrary to the earlier intention to leave a fundamental review until a fourth term. On each occasion the Government's response involved a similar approach – a dislike of public sector solutions, and particularly of local authorities, trade unions and the like. The instincts of Mrs Thatcher and her allies have prevailed. In all this there can be detected a preference for individualism over collectivism – even though free-market economists have often despaired of some of the detailed proposals such as privatizing monopoly utilities without introducing sufficient competition. Yet the key point is that all these important policies have been a response to events rather than the execution of a clearly prepared and argued-out blueprint.

The most striking aspect of Thatcherism may seem in retrospect to have been its ability to renew itself, which it has done more successfully than previous administrations. It has done this through the application of Mrs Thatcher's instincts, values and, above all, energy to the solution of successive problems. For instance, when the Government faltered in the first half of 1986 after the Westland affair, with the resignation of two Cabinet ministers, followed by the rows over the future of Land Rover and the use of British bases by the US to bomb Libya, Mrs Thatcher and her colleagues quickly recovered composure and momentum. As Norman Tebbit, the former Conservative Party chairman, has recorded in his autobiography *Upwardly Mobile* (1988), a campaign was carefully prepared, with advertising consultants Saatchi and Saatchi, to change the public perception that the Government had lost its way by developing the idea that it had a sense of direction. So, at the Conservative Party Conference in Bournemouth in October 1986, ministers were told to include in their speeches statements of objectives which they aimed to achieve within the following three years. Mr Tebbit said his aim 'was that in 1986 the media should reflect the image I wanted – of a Government confident, united, clear in where it was going – and determined to get there'. It worked and the opinion poll ratings of the Conservatives recovered. But this was not just an exercise in public relations. There was, thanks to Mrs Thatcher's reassertion of leadership, a genuinely new sense of drive and direction.

Similarly, after many complaints over the thin and hastily-prepared manifesto in 1983 – and a largely wasted 18 months at the beginning of the 1983–7 parliament – Mrs Thatcher took a delight four years later in the ambition and radicalism of the Conservative manifesto and the packed programme for the 1987–8 legislative session. There was an almost manic desire to carry on the revolution – 'to go on and on', as she frequently said, and 'to get rid of socialism as a second force in British politics,' as she put it in her annual *Financial Times* interview in November 1986.

Indeed, for all the setbacks and improvisations of the early 1980s, Thatcherism has become more coherent as the decade has advanced. After her second election victory in 1983, and more particularly after 1987, Mrs Thatcher and her allies have deliberately attempted to defeat socialism and to challenge the traditional bases of Labour and the trade union movement in big city local authorities, council housing estates and nationalized industries. This has been aided by the divisions in the opposition parties. The success of privatization and the trebling of individual share ownership have leant an evange-lical tone to talk of popular capitalism. There has been a growth in the number, and activity, of free-market and anti-collectivist think tanks with a network of advisers linked to Downing Street and ministerial offices. These bodies have put forward a more consciously ideological agenda which has been accepted to a varying extent by the Government. Moreover, programmes like privatization, however accidental and ad hoc their origins, developed their own momentum. Selling off state assets became a virtue in itself – a yardstick of ministerial success.

However, the role of any particular government should not be exaggerated. Thatcherism has been working with the grain not only of domestic developments but also of international trends. The shift in economic policy towards tighter financial and public spending restraint began in the mid-1970s not only in Britain but also in the US, under the Democratic presidency of Jimmy Carter, and on the Continent of Europe. There have been similar problems and solutions in social provision and industrial policy based on the spread of privatization. These trends have been common under both left- and right-wing leaderships. Almost all the finance ministers in the west have been talking since the first oil price crisis in 1974 about the need to fight inflation and to rein back the public sector. One of Sir Geoffrey Howe's party tricks as Chancellor of the Exchequer was to quote a speech from his Chinese opposite number about monetary control.

The distinctive flavour of Thatcherism has mainly been because of Mrs Thatcher herself with her highly individual political style. But it has also reflected the particular British conditions of the late 1970s. The breakdown of the social-democratic consensus during the decade – dramatized by the events of the 'winter of discontent' – created the opportunity for a new lead and a new direction. If the origins of the shift in macro-economic policy lay in the mid-1970s and many of the problems were international rather than domestic, the way that Britain has developed during the 1980s has still owed a lot to Mrs Thatcher. Her special contribution has been to maintain the momentum of change and to develop new policies in response to problems as they have arisen. It has been the application of her middle-class values that has been characteristic of Thatcherism rather than any clear ideological blueprint. This book will explore what this approach has meant for Britain and how its economy and society have changed during the 1980s.

2

Economic Policy

It is the conquest of inflation, and not the pursuit of growth and employment, which is or should be the objective of macro-economic policy. And it is the creation of conditions conducive to growth and employment, and not the suppression of price rises, which is or should be the objective of micro-economic policy.

Nigel Lawson, Chancellor of the Exchequer,
Mais Lecture, 18 June 1984

The strength of the recovery in output owes little to the success of the macro-economic strategy as originally conceived. It owes more to its failures and subsequent modification. It was helped by the retreat from monetarism and it was helped by the failure of employers and unions to heed the exhortations in favour of a 'low wage' and 'low technology' solution.

National Institute of Economic and Social Research,
Economic Review, November 1987

There was a short-lived period of ministerial triumph following Nigel Lawson's tax cutting and reforming Budget of March 1988, when both he and Mrs Thatcher talked of Britain enjoying an economic miracle comparable in significance to that of West Germany in the 1950s, and Japan in the 1980s. Their words would have seemed absurd in the 1970s, fanciful in the early 1980s, and far-fetched even when the Tories began their second term in 1983. And they were swiftly challenged in the summer and autumn of 1988 when the current account of the balance of payments deteriorated substantially and worries over inflation reappeared. The language was more restrained in Mr Lawson's inflation-fighting 1989 Budget.

Yet it is a measure of the record of the Thatcher Government that such claims about an economic miracle could have been seriously made, and seriously debated, even if they were not uniformly accepted. The combination of sustained economic growth, low inflation, sharply falling unemployment and tax cuts had confounded the pessimists – at least in the short term. Several studies in the late 1980s, including some by non-Conservatives, acknowledged that the Government had a number of economic achievements to its credit. Even the strongly anti-monetarist National Institute had to concede in November 1987 that it had been:

unduly pessimistic about the effect of the strategy on output. The private sector, with no substantial fiscal stimulus to demand, proved more resilient than we expected. The profound shock to the economy of the 1979–80 recession may have served to awaken dormant entrepreneurship. This was probably helped by the Government's efforts to encourage enterprise and reduce reliance on state intervention. Many of the less efficient firms went out of business altogether. Others, in order to survive and in co-operation with the labour force they did retain, adopted new technologies or working methods which previously they had neglected, or been unable, to introduce. In return, they paid high real wages which strengthened consumer demand. Whether such innovations and such co-operation could have been better fostered by a less hostile macro-economic environment in the early days of the strategy remains an open question.

Similarly, the Organisation for Economic Co-operation and Development, the secretariat for industrialized countries, commented in its 1988 survey of the UK economy:

Decades of sluggish growth of output and productivity were gradually eroding her position as a world industrial leader, and this steady regression appeared to be irreversible. Recent economic performance has, however, raised the prospect that the 'British disease' may have been overcome. Years of steady growth have replaced the 'stop–go' of the past, with productivity growth accelerating markedly.

These conclusions have generally been heavily qualified, as they were by the National Institute itself in the passage quoted at the beginning of this chapter. Even strong supporters of the Government have accepted that its policy changed substantially, in execution if not intent, during the 1980s. The critics argued that monetarism had been buried at various dates from 1982 onwards. There was certainly

little evidence after then of theoretical, or technical, monetarism –
relating the growth of the money supply to the future rate of inflation
– which disappeared from view via the application of automatic,
pilot-type rules influencing business and union expectations and behaviour. But there remained a continuity of objectives and of
priorities which distinguished the Thatcher Government from both
its predecessors and from the alternatives on offer.

This chapter will discuss the Thatcher Government's economic
goals and the development of macro-economic policy, then it will set
out in detail the Government's economic record, and, finally, discuss
the feasibility of other approaches and whether, and how far,
Britain's long-term economic decline has been halted and reversed.
Later chapters will discuss the changes in the labour market,
the extent to which an enterprise culture has been created, the
privatization programme and moves to broaden the ownership of
capital.

From the perspective of the late 1980s, it is even clearer than it was
at the time that the British economy had been in crisis during the
1970s. This is not to dismiss, or to underestimate, Denis Healey's
long period as Chancellor. His record was much better than is
currently credited either by the Tories or by many in his own party.
From 1974 to 1979, Mr Healey began the process of adjustment
which Mrs Thatcher's administration carried through. Under the
Wilson and Callaghan Governments, and the Healey Chancellorship,
the steady, and at times sharp, rise in public spending of the 1960s
and 1970s was first checked, and financial discipline was imposed
throughout the public sector, while from 1976 onwards published
targets were set for the growth of the money supply. The public
sector borrowing requirement, the gap between what is spent by
Government and what is raised in taxes, first became a major
budgetary constraint in this period. The need to bring in the
International Monetary Fund in the autumn of 1976 may have
firmed up some of these developments but did not create them.
Moreover, the painful process of reducing inflation after the wage
explosion and the first oil price shock produced only a short-lived
reduction in living standards before growth resumed, and at the same
time there was a redistribution in favour of the less well-off. The
turning-point in macro-economic policy, if not politically, was as
much in 1976, as in 1979 or 1981.

However, the financial disciplines were never accepted by his party or by the Labour and trade union movement as a whole, and the resulting tensions finally exploded in the public and private sector disruption and strikes over wages in the winter of discontent, in 1978. This symbolized the breakdown of the 17-year-old series of Labour and Conservative attempts to do deals with the trade union leadership in order to hold down inflation. The price of deals which, at best, only delivered lower levels of pay increases for a short time was seen in concessions to the unions over subsidies, in price controls, and in legislation which gave them a favoured legal status in pursuing negotiations. The quasi-corporatist period ran into the sand in the winter of 1978–9.

So, for all the important, and often unappreciated, continuities with the period before May 1979, the election of the Tories both offered and represented a new approach. This involved a change of both macro- and miro-economic policy. In macro-economic policy, what John Fforde, then an executive director of the Bank of England, described as monetarily constrained 'Keynesianism' was replaced by monetarism. While under Denis Healey the goal of full employment was in practice abandoned, policy was still guided by attempts to reduce unemployment and to constrain inflation through incomes policy, with monetary targets as one of a number of economic influences and partly intended to appease the financial markets. However, after May 1979, monetary controls came to the forefront and a formal incomes policy was dropped. Any pretence of a full employment target was abandoned as the Government rejected the traditional post-war approach of trying to adjust the level of demand in the economy. Instead, the reduction of inflation became the prime, and for a time the sole, objective of macro-economic policy, to be achieved by limiting public expenditure and by strictly controlling the rate of monetary growth. The argument was that cutting back public spending would both reduce the public sector's claims on savings and permit cuts in personal taxes which would promote enterprise. The constant refrain of Sir Geoffrey Howe as Chancellor was that finance must determine expenditure, rather than expenditure determine finance, as in the past. This also involved a rejection of the late 1960s and 1970s approach of seeking improved international competitiveness by reducing the value of the pound, which had resulted in higher inflation. On the micro-economic side, there were measures intended to encourage the supply, rather than the demand, side by reducing regulations – by, for example, abolishing all restrictions on private-sector wage level and prices, rents, dividends, and exchange controls – but also by attempting to remove monopoly elements in the labour market. Both income and capital taxes were to be cut to promote incentives to enterprise.

Fiscal and monetary policy went through a number of stages. The first, enthusiastic, phase lasted from May 1979 until late 1980 or early 1981. During this period, the predominant target indicator, affecting interest rate decisions, was sterling M3, which is a definition of the money supply, including cash, and bank current and deposit accounts. Forward targets for lowering the rate of monetary growth, and for a steady reduction in both public expenditure and in public sector borrowing, were set out in the medium-term financial strategy in March 1980 to underline the Government's counter-inflation commitment. However, from mid-1980 pressures from the strong pound and a deepening recession increased. These eventually forced a departure from strict monetary guidelines as interest rates were reduced, despite an above-target growth of the money supply.

This policy change had two parallel, though related, aspects, as reflected in an impassioned debate during the summer and autumn of 1980 about how to achieve monetary control. The twin triggers were the continued appreciation of the pound and the sharp rise in sterling M3 in July and August of that year. The latter was largely, though not entirely, a result of the movement back of financial flows into categories covered by official monetary definitions following the end of the so-called 'corset' controls which restricted the growth of banking operations. The usefulness of sterling M3 as a guide was questioned by some of Mrs Thatcher's closest allies. Professor Alan Walters was appointed as the Prime Minister's personal economic adviser, and was to figure throughout the 1980s as a persistent critic of the Treasury. Even before he formally took up his post in January 1981, Professor Walters had been involved in the commissioning, via the Centre for Policy Studies, of a report from Professor Jurg Niehans of Berne University. This concluded that monetary policy had been too tight and contributed to the sharp rise in sterling. Monetary policy, Professor Niehans said, 'appears to have been more abrupt than even the most ardent monetarists advocated. This was a policy shift with few historic precedents.' In related discussions, other strict monetarists, such as Professors Milton Friedman and Brian Griffiths, argued for what was known as monetary base control, a more direct form of seeking to influence monetary growth by acting directly on the base of the banking system. This approach was discussed by the Treasury and the Bank of England, and was rejected, not least because some politicians disliked the probable consequence of more volatile interest rates.

The more flexible monetary approach was coupled with a greater emphasis on fiscal restraint, notably in the March 1981 Budget. Contrary to all post-war conventional economic wisdom, fiscal policy was tightened substantially in face of sharply rising unemployment. This was to permit lower interest rates, which were intended to check, and, it was hoped, reverse, the rise in the pound, and thus ease the pressures on industry. The tightening of fiscal policy prompted a letter of protest from 364 leading university economists, including four former chief economic advisers to the Government, which warned that present policies would deepen the depression. Yet, in the event, the spring and summer of 1981 saw the beginning of recovery and the March 1981 Budget is now widely seen as the turning point of the Thatcher administration. Indeed, only in the run-up to the 1983 general election was there any, short-lived, move towards fiscal expansion on more traditional Keynesian – and electoral – lines. Arguably, however, attempts to manipulate interest and exchange rates have replaced fiscal expansion as the Government's preferred means of fine-tuning the economy ahead of elections.

In this second phase, lasting from early 1981 until 1985, monetary targets were retained, but repeatedly readjusted upwards, notably in March 1982, to take account of past overshooting. At the same time, the exchange rate and the public sector borrowing requirement became the key policy guidelines, prompting criticism from strict monetarists. But John Fforde, never an enthusiast for oversimplified monetarism, referred in a speech in May 1982 to 'a relatively pragmatic approach,' representing 'a rather greater emphasis on empiricism in the monetary policy field'. In short, the 1981 shift represented the abandonment of a strict reliance on monetary targets, and its replacement by what the Bank of England has always liked, the exercise of its judgement. Mr Fforde noted, with clear satisfaction, 'except in some grave emergency, or in the initial phase of a novel strategy, the abandonment of judgment in favour of some simple, rigid, quantitative rule about the money supply does not reliably deliver acceptable results.'

Throughout this phase, the main objectives of the medium-term financial strategy in terms of monetary targets were retained, but were modified substantially in practice. In large part this reflected the intuitive approach of Nigel Lawson after he became Chancellor of the Exchequer in June 1983. Mr Lawson, though one of the architects of the medium-term financial strategy in 1980 as a junior minister, has the temperament of a financial operator, even perhaps a gambler, in contrast with the more literal, lawyer-like approach of his predecessor Sir Geoffrey Howe. The goal of fighting inflation as the pre-requisite for sustained economic growth remained the same, but the implementation changed. What evolved instead was a mixed approach – focusing on the containment of inflation at around 4 to 5 per cent ('maintaining downward pressure' in the commonly used Treasury phrase), rather than seeking to eliminate it altogether. This allowed more regard for the growth of output. Formal monetary targets were given less and less prominence, and more account was taken of the exchange rate, and of overall national income, or Gross Domestic Product. Some of the Government's Keynesian critics gloated that Mr Lawson had reverted to his pre-monetarist phase and was a closet Keynesian. This was wishful thinking on the part of the critics and was not reflected in the development of a tight fiscal policy.

Mr Lawson certainly departed from strict monetarism, with its emphasis on firm rules and targets, in favour of greater discretion and judgement. He believed that the uncertainties of economic life – and particularly of statistics and of financial markets – required continuing an active policy by the Government. In his Mansion House speech in October 1983, Mr Lawson noted this shift by stating that 'monetary targets have not been, nor have ever intended to be, a form of automatic pilot. Over the years we have adjusted the targets themselves; and we have always sought to take account of shifts in the demand for money, whether due to financial innovation or to institutional changes.' Whatever was in the small print of the medium-term financial strategy, this was not the emphasis of 1979–80.

During this second, more flexible, phase of monetary policy up to 1985, interest rates were several times adjusted in response to movements in the sterling exchange rate rather than to the growth of the monetary aggregates. Mr Lawson was also highly sensitive to traditional public spending and borrowing worries, as in July 1983, when an emergency £1 billion package of spending cuts and assets sales was announced to claw back some of the pre-election generosity. A year later a sharp fall in the pound on the foreign exchange markets led to a 2.75 point jump in interest rates, even though domestic monetary pressures were used as the immediate pretext. These interlinked problems of excessive monetary growth and sterling's weakness recurred in January 1985 and were compounded by confusion, the first of many, over apparent differences of tactics between the Prime Minister and the Chancellor. Interest rates again had to be raised, in response to the state of the foreign exchange market. As is often the case, sterling bounced back that summer, and interest rates were reduced to check the rise, even though the money supply was growing at well above its target rate.

The start of a distinctly different third phase was marked by Mr Lawson's Mansion House speech in October 1985 when he announced that the sterling M3 target was to be suspended for the rest of the financial year. He said the target set in the Budget that spring had been too low and bringing monetary growth back within the target range would result in an excessive tightening, that is, in a very sharp rise in interest rates. Indeed, the Chancellor redefined his approach − 'the acid test of monetary policy is its record in reducing inflation ... The inflation rate is judge and jury.' Monetary targets did not disappear altogether: in the March 1986 Budget, a target was set for sterling M3, but just for one year ahead, rather than the previous three- to four-year span. But the Treasury and Civil Service Select Committee of the House of Commons noted in its report on the Budget (1986) that, 'scepticism at the continued use of sterling M3 as a target aggregate stems in part from the fact that the authorities now seem to have virtually no control over it.' The Treasury's own Red Book (Financial Statement and Budget Report, 1986) acknowledged that a change in short-term interest rates was 'unlikely to alter the growth of sterling M3 significantly within the target period. But such action clearly affects the tightness of monetary conditions, which is what matters, and this would be likely to show up in the behaviour of MO and the exchange rate.' The latter was more directly affected by short-term interest rates. Again, this was very different from the early days of the medium-term financial strategy. The shift was underlined in October 1986 by Robin Leigh-Pemberton, the Governor of the Bank of England. In a major lecture at Loughborough University, he conceded that 'it cannot be said that our experience with our chosen framework for operating monetary policy has been satisfactory,' and he questioned whether it was at all worthwhile setting targets for broad monetary aggregates such as sterling M3. No target for sterling M3 was set for 1987–8. Targets were retained for M0, though the Treasury admitted that other indicators, such as sterling, house prices, the oil price and interest rates were taken into account in what amounted to an extremely broad church definition of monetarism.

The exchange rate became the crucial guideline as monetary targets became discredited. For instance, during the summer of 1986, monetary growth was rapid yet interest rates were reduced. During the second half of 1986 the halving in the oil price had helped to reduce the annual rate of increase in retail prices to around 2.5 per cent. But, instead of using the opportunity to try to hold the inflation rate down to West German levels, Mr Lawson acquiesced in a lower exchange rate so as to help the competitive position of industry. There was a clear choice between a firm pound with lower inflation, and a fall in the pound with faster economic growth and higher inflation. Mr Lawson opted for the growth option. One official later admitted that there had been a decision in favour of what was known as 'an oil-adjusted exchange rate.' Mr Lawson's view was that the shock of the steep drop in the oil price justified this temporary departure from the aim of a broadly stable pound. This led to higher inflation later.

Subsequently, during 1987 and up to the early months of 1988, Mr Lawson sought to impose the alternative financial discipline of a broadly stable exchange rate in place of sterling M3. The Treasury's aim was to shadow other European Community currencies in the European Monetary System, even though formally remaining outside the exchange rate mechanism. Mr Lawson, like his predecessor Sir Geoffrey Howe (now Foreign Secretary), had become persuaded of the merits of entering the exchange rate mechanism. This partly reflected a more general shift among finance ministers in favour of greater stability of exchange rates, as underlined by the Plaza Agreement of autumn 1985 and the Louvre Accord of spring 1987. But Mrs Thatcher and her strict monetarist advisers, notably Professor Alan Walters, were opposed to an EMS link for several reasons – they objected to surrendering sovereignty over domestic monetary policy, to linking to a potentially unstable system, which had been either excessively deflationary or, in contradiction, inflationary. So, the Treasury and Bank of England based interest rate policy on holding sterling within a close range of other EC currencies, principally the Deutschmark. But there was to be no published band of permissible exchange rate movements, or a target which could be tested by the financial markets, though they tried.

The result was a considerable degree of stability in the exchange rate during 1987, and this success reinforced the market's view that the pound was the key financial target. However, it was an informal one, about which the Prime Minister had doubts. Moreover, within the context of a broadly restrictive fiscal policy and in the absence of exchange and credit controls, the only policy instrument available to Government was short-term interest rates. So when strong upward pressure appeared on sterling in the early months of 1988 major strains appeared, both in decision-making and in execution. The barely disguised agreement to differ between Mrs Thatcher and Mr Lawson over the European Monetary System made this position more difficult to handle, particularly given the Prime Minister's tendency not to dissemble her basic instincts. She infuriated her Chancellor just before his March Budget when she took an apparently free market view of the level of sterling following a decision to let the pound rise against the Deutschemark. Mr Lawson agreed that there was no choice but to adjust upwards the previous informal trading range against the West German currency, but Mrs Thatcher's remarks appeared to rule out the kind of managed floating which the Treasury and the Bank of England had been undertaking for the previous year or so. However, Mr Lawson's political position was so strong that a further burst of prime ministerial frankness two months later led to a strong statement of support by her for the Chancellor, repeated in 1989 after further disagreements.

None of this put the genie back in the bottle. Mr Lawson's magician act with the currency had been exposed and it was difficult for him to regain either the mystery or mastery over the markets. A complicating factor had been the dramatic fall in share prices in October 1987 which had led to panicky talk, a repetition of the events of the 1930s when the Wall Street crash of October 1929 had been followed by the depression. The British authorities, in common with those in other countries, cut interest rates and injected liquidity, or money into the financial system to maintain confidence. But there was a price to pay for this monetary expansion. It quickly became clear that the stock market crash would have little effect on the economic boom in the main industrialized countries. But, as Mr Lawson later conceded, he was slow to tighten monetary policy again to check the upturn in inflation.

The Government's particular problem in the spring and summer of 1988 was that the domestic economy was overheating, requiring higher interest rates to produce a slowdown in activity, while the pound was strong, requiring lower interest rates if sterling was to be held down and industry was to remain competitive, as Mr Lawson wished. In the event, the sharp deterioration in the current account – to a 1988 deficit more than three times greater than that originally forecast – and a firmer dollar, took some of the pressure off sterling, allowing a series of increases in interest rates in the summer and autumn of 1988. Indeed, the trade figures were so bad as to force sharp increases, while the inflation rate also rose sharply. This was partly, in a somewhat circular manner, a reflection of the tightening of policy since the increase in interest and house mortgage rates quickly showed up in the retail prices index. This overstated the extent of the pick-up in the underlying rate of inflation, much to the annoyance of ministers. The priority of containing and reducing inflation was underlined by the March 1989 Budget with its tight fiscal stance and commitment by Mr Lawson that 'interest rates will stay as high as is needed for as long as is needed.' He reaffirmed that short-term interest rates would remain 'the essential instrument of monetary policy'. The absence of clear, and, equally important, credible, monetary targets, or the alternative of a formal exchange rate goal, meant that the Government was short of ways to influence the economy apart from frequent changes in interest rates. The problem was aggravated by the increasing ineffectiveness during 1988–9 of international efforts to achieve currency stability. This was far from the predictability which the strict monetarists had argued would result from adherence to money supply targets.

Macro-economic policy has undoubtedly travelled a long way since 1979. The earlier belief that there was some straightforward relationship between the growth of sterling M3 and future inflation has certainly been discredited, to the unconcealed joy of the Keynesians and the gloom of strict monetarists. Indeed, many of the latter, including Mrs Thatcher's economic *eminence grise* Sir Alan Walters, were highly suspicious of Mr Lawson for being insufficiently rigorous and too accommodating in fighting inflation though even he praised the stringent 1989 Budget. As evidence, they could point to his 1986 decisions which contributed to a lower exchange rate. A monetarist economist Nigel Healey argued (1987) that, while the downgrading of sterling M3 might be publicly presented in a way which maintained the illusion of continuity in 'the battle against inflation' through monetary restraint – to please the monetarist-orientated financial markets – it was 'equally possible to see this change as a major step back towards active government intervention in the economy.' Indeed, some strict monetarists felt vindicated in the first half of 1989 when an earlier acceleration in sterling M3 was followed by a sharp pick-up in inflation.

The Government's problem was that it tried to do something which was probably inherently impossible – to achieve control over the money supply at a time when the financial system was being turned upside down. Even a committed monetarist like Roy Batchelor has accepted (in Minford, 1987) that the behaviour of sterling M3 had been wayward and misleading. He has argued that this measure turned out to be a targeting disaster because of the distorting impact of changes in financial markets, such as the abolition of exchange controls, the corset controls on banks, and more competition between banks and building societies in providing similar types of service. (Bank deposits and loans counted within sterling M3, while similar ones by building societies did not.) Consequently, when the fallibilities of sterling M3 were exposed, and alternative broader measures including building society deposits had been rejected, the Government had no ready alternative financial discipline, given Mrs Thatcher's opposition to full participation in the EMS.

If by the late 1980s the Thatcher Government was no longer pursuing strict monetarism, it had not, as some commentators suggested, reverted to Keynesianism. Indeed, critics, like the National Institute, were torn between, on the one hand, welcoming the Government's conversion to expansionism in its exchange rate policy in 1986 and the pre-election increases in public spending in 1982–3 and 1986–7, and, on the other hand, criticizing a too restrictive fiscal stance as public sector borrowing was steadily reduced. The late 1980s policy might best be described as discretionary monetarism in the sense that while no particular target was crucial, policy was still guided by monetary indicators such as the price of assets, the exchange rate and interest rates. Money in the broadest sense still mattered. Moreover, the Government believed that it could not directly influence, or fine-tune, the level of demand and unemployment and macro-economic policy should be primarily concerned with fighting inflation. This aim was at times interpreted more broadly by Mr Lawson than by Sir Geoffrey Howe. Mr Lawson did not pursue the course of zero inflation in the mid-1980s. He was also proud of sustaining a steady, and at times rapid, rate of economic growth and was in practice willing to accommodate inflation at the 4 to 5 per cent range, though hoping it could be reduced. But when it showed signs of rising above that level the counter-inflation priority was reasserted firmly and unambiguously. It was perhaps less old-style demand management than inflation management, or rather inflation-constrained growth management, as in the US.

This account of macro-economic policy has focused on its development according to the Government's own objectives. Yet, in assessing its record and the impact on Britain, several other yardsticks must be introduced – the levels of output, unemployment, taxes, and so on. Mr Lawson may have referred to inflation as 'the judge and jury', but ministers have not been slow to introduce other measures when it has suited them. The main points in any balance sheet are as follows.

Output

Gross Domestic Product (GDP) fell by around 5 per cent between the first half of 1979 and the low point of the recession in the first half of 1981. Subsequently, output recovered steadily, so that in 1988 GDP was more than 21 per cent higher than in 1979 and nearly 27 per cent above the 1981 low. This marked considerable variations, with strong growth in North Sea output and in services offsetting a sharp initial fall in manufacturing. Output in manufacturing industries dropped by 15 per cent from peak to trough in the 1979–81 period, and it was only a very strong upswing in 1987 and 1988, when output rose by 6 and 7 per cent respectively, that took production in the former year to above the 1979 starting level. But manufacturing had declined from around a third to under a quarter of total output. Manufacturing investment also dropped sharply, by more than a third in real, inflation-adjusted, terms between 1979 and 1982, before recovering slowly in the mid-1980s. However, manufacturing investment rose sharply in the late 1980s, up 5 per cent in 1987 and 18 per cent in 1988, and there were also sharp increases in other areas of investment. This in large part reflected a major improvement in corporate profitability during the mid-to-late 1980s as price controls ended and industry made itself more efficient. Rates of return in both manufacturing and industry generally recovered from the low point of the early 1980s up to levels not seen since the late 1960s. But profits were vulnerable to rising unit labour costs and a strong pound.

Inflation

The 12-month rate of increase of retail prices accelerated from 10.3 per cent in May 1979 up to a peak of 21.9 per cent in August 1980, before falling back to single figures in April 1982, where it has remained. The rate touched 3.7 per cent in May and June 1983. However, there has been no further progress since 1983 in reducing the underlying rate which has fluctuated mainly in the 4 to 5.5 per cent range. But there have been regular variations – both upwards to 7 per cent in the spring of 1985 and again, up to more than 8 per cent in the middle of 1989, and downwards to a low of 2.4 per cent in July and August 1986. The average rate of increase of consumer prices, the main yardstick for international comparison, fluctuated in the 3.5 to 6 per cent range from 1983 to 1988, against 2 to 4.5 per cent for the other leading industrialized countries.

The annual rate of growth of average earnings for all industries and services accelerated from 13.4 to 22.2 per cent between the second quarters of 1979 and 1980, before falling back to 8.7 per cent by the beginning of 1983. Subsequently, it has remained in the 7.5 to 8.5 per cent range, picking up to well over 9 per cent in spring 1989 as the faster pace of economic growth pushed up bonus and overtime payments.

Living Standards

Real personal disposable incomes, which include gross earnings, taxes, and social security benefits adjusted for price changes, rose in the 1979–80 period, but then fell back under the impact of the recession and of rising unemployment. Most of those in work still enjoyed a rise in living standards. After 1983 real personal disposable income rose strongly, initially at rates of 2.25 per cent a year, rising to well over 3 per cent in 1986–7, and nearly 4 per cent in 1988, reflecting both the growth in real earnings and cuts in personal taxes.

As inflation came down to around 5 per cent and confidence about the economy improved, the savings ratio (measuring net savings as a percentage of disposable income) began to fall sharply in the mid-1980s, down from over 10 per cent in the early 1980s to 5.5 per cent in 1987, and to well under 3 per cent in 1988. A contributory factor was undoubtedly the deregulation of the retail financial services market, as banks and building societies competed vigorously with each other to lend, notably in mortgage loans, and as a result personal borrowing soared. This caused a strong consumer boom through the second half of the 1980s, increasing at around 5.5 per cent per year in the 1986–8 period in real inflation-adjusted terms – a period of unprecedented affluence for most of the population. For instance, the proportion of households with central heating rose from 55 per cent in 1979 to 71 per cent in 1986, the number with deep freezers from 40 to over 70 per cent, while those without cars fell from 43 to 37 per cent over the period.

Unemployment

Adult unemployment rose sharply during the first half of the 1980s. Under the definitions used at the end of the decade, the total rose from 1.09 million in May 1979 (4.1 per cent of the workforce) to 2.13 million two years later. The total peaked at 3.13 million in July 1986, before falling sharply thereafter down to well below 2 million by spring 1989. Although this is still well above the level at the start of the decade, the scale of the decline was much larger than most economists, let alone politicians, had predicted.

There was, however, considerable controversy over the nature of the figures in view of a number of revisions, some major, some minor, though totalling 28. In particular, there was a switch in definitions from counting people registered as unemployed to those claiming benefit, while there have been a series of changes in social security rules, virtually ruling out anyone under the age of 18 from being counted, and in the treatment of the over 60s. In addition, since 1986 those unemployed for more than one year have been called for interviews at Job Centres under the Restart Programme, while the availability of work test, to establish whether the unemployed are willing to take jobs, has been applied more stringently to new claimants. The result has been that a number of people, some presumably working in the black economy, have stopped claiming benefit, and therefore have ceased being counted as unemployed. These various statistical redefinitions may have reduced the recorded total by around 400,000, and possibly rather more previously, while the Government's various special training and work experience measures have cut the published total by 350,000. A complicating factor is that these influences have had varying effects at different times – the tightening of rules having a greater impact towards the end of the 1980s. This has affected not only the total, but also perceptions about the rate of decline. For instance, estimates in the annual Labour Force Survey using international OECD definitions of unemployment – someone who has been without work, but has looked for a job at some point during the previous four weeks – have pointed to a lower unemployment total than indicated by the usual figures, but also to a drop of less than half the official estimate. Some of the problems relate to changes in levels of participation in the labour market by people of working age. Professor Richard Layard of the London School of Economics, a leading academic and campaigner on employment issues, has argued that the true reduction in unemployment over, for example, the 1987–8 period was a quarter of the half million reduction claimed by ministers on the basis of the published figures.

These qualifications can be overdone so as to understate the undoubted change in labour market conditions in the second half of the 1980s, especially in southern England. Consequently, while the rate of decline in unemployment since 1986 may have been exaggerated by the Government, no one disputes that the total has fallen by a large amount, on a sustained basis, and that the demand for labour has picked up substantially, as indicated by a sharp rise in notified vacancies. This was reflected in a big growth in employment from March 1983 onwards. Employment proved to be more responsive than expected to a growth in economic activity. The total workforce in employment rose by over 2·5 million between the low point of March 1983 and early 1989. More than a third of this comprised the fast-growing group of the self-employed. The figures included as well a 330,000 increase in the numbers covered by work-related training programmes. Critics noted, however, that a large proportion of the new jobs were part-time, and for women, rather than for full-time male heads of households. Thus, as will be discussed in the following chapter, there were far-reaching changes in the balance of employment.

Monetary Policy

The general outlines of monetary policy have been discussed above. The record has, by any definition, been patchy, as table 2.1 indicates. The record is in some respects worse than this comparison implies since the targets are only those fixed in the Budget at the start of the relevant year. Not only were these frequently higher than previously set for the year, but the starting point was higher than previously projected because no attempt was made to claw back the previous overruns. When the sterling M3 target fell into discredit during the 1980s, greater emphasis was placed on the narrowly defined money supply M0 – which grew more in line with the official targets.

Increased attention was also devoted during the second half of the decade to money GDP, or national income in cash terms, as an indicator of overall monetary conditions. In 1986–7, its growth was below expectations, but it then rose sharply as both growth and inflation picked up. For instance, while the March 1987 Red Book (the Financial Statement and Budget Report, 1987–8) projected a rise in money GDP of 7.5 per cent in 1987–8, and 6.5 per cent in 1988–9, the outcomes were rises of 10 and over 11 per cent respectively underlying the strength of activity and of inflationary pressures.

Table 2.1   Monetary growth: per cent annual rate of increase

	Target	Result
1979–80	7–11	12.0
1980–81	7–11	19.0
1981–82	6–10	13.0
1982–83	8–12	11.0
1983–84	7–11	10.0
1984–85	6–10	13.5
1985–86	5– 9	15.3
1986–87	11–15[a]	20.0

[a] Targets for sterling M3 abandoned in 1986
Source: Treasury statistics

Public sector borrowing

The Government made the containment and reduction of the public sector borrowing requirements (PSBR) a cornerstone of its policies during its first term. The argument was that borrowing by the public sector was a major influence on the rate of growth of the money supply and on interest rates. This concern led, for example, to the increase in the tax burden in the 1981 Budget. Yet, because of the impact of the recession on holding down tax revenues and boosting expenditure, borrowing was regularly above target levels. For instance, the first version of the medium-term financial strategy in March 1980 laid out a declining path for public sector borrowing as a percentage of Gross Domestic Product from 3.75 per cent in 1980– 1 down to 1.5 per cent in 1983–4. In the event, borrowing in 1980–1 was 5.7 per cent of GDP and the decline was only to 3.2 per cent.

However, the finances of the public sector improved dramatically from the mid-1980s as a result of the combination of the levelling-off of unemployment (then the start of decline), the strong rate of economic growth, and the large-scale privatizations. Even ignoring the influence of these factors, the deficit declined steadily. Then in 1987– 8, the public sector was broadly in balance for the first time since it had been temporarily in 1970. Taking account of privatization proceeds the public sector repaid roughly £3.5 billion of debt in

Table 2.2 Public sector borrowing: per cent of Gross Domestic Product

1979–80	4.8
1980–81	5.7
1981–82	3.5
1982–83	3.2
1983–84	3.2
1984–85	3.1
1985–86	1.6
1986–87	0.9
1987–88	−0.8[a]
1988–89	−3.0[a]
1989–90	−2.8[a,b]

[a] Minus figures indicate net public sector debt repayment
[b] Treasury forecast
Source: Financial Statement and Budget Report from 1979–80 onwards

1987–8, and more than £14 billion the following year with a similar cash repayment forecast for 1989–90. Table 2.2 shows the change.

Taxation

Cutting taxes was one of the main Conservative pledges in the 1979 election. While the top marginal and basic rates were cut in the Budget of June 1979 Value Added Tax was also raised substantially. In later Budgets during the first term employee national insurance contributions were raised. Consequently, the overall tax burden increased – from just under 34 per cent of GDP in 1978–9, the last Labour year, to a peak of more than 39 per cent in the mid-1980s. It then declined to less than 38 per cent in 1988–9 and 1989–90, as the basic rate was reduced and income tax allowances were raised in real terms (the distributional impact is discussed in chapter 8. While revenue from North Sea oil made a substantial contribution in the mid-1980s its share shrank considerably in the late-1980s following the halving in the dollar oil price and declines in oil production after its peak in 1984. Government receipts from the North Sea, including royalties, petroleum revenue tax and corporation tax from North Sea oil and gas developments, reached a peak of £12 billion in 1984–5, but dropped to less than £5 billion in 1986–7, and to £3 billion a year in the late 1980s. It was tribute to the strength of the economy, and the resulting buoyancy of other tax revenue, that public sector borrowing still fell sharply over the period. The key was the sharp increase in corporation tax receipts as a result of the improvement in business profitability. These rose by more than three times to over £20 billion, fully offsetting the decline in North Sea tax revenues.

Public Spending

The Conservatives came into office, arguing, in the words of their first White Paper in November 1979, that 'public expenditure is at the heart of Britain's present difficulties.' Their initial policy was to reduce the volume of public expenditure. The March 1980 White Paper set the aim of cutting the total 'progressively in volume terms over the next four years to a level in 1983–84 about 4 per cent lower than in 1979–80'. In the event, the total rose substantially, by 6.3 per cent on the slightly different yardstick of real, inflation-adjusted, terms. This was partly because of the impact on spending of the recession and the associated sharp rise in unemployment. But this accounted for only about three-fifths of the gap between the original plans and the actual level of spending. The rest was explained by higher than expected spending on favoured programmes like defence and law and order, and regular sizeable overshoots by local authorities. Indeed, the striking feature was the Government's success in containing the extent of the rise in face of the deep recession and the long-term upward pressures on the core social security and health budgets resulting from demographic and other changes. Expenditure on education and housing was cut substantially below previously planned levels in the early 1980s. In the light of the long-term upward trend in public expenditure, in retrospect the Government did remarkably well in its own terms to limit the overall level of growth and overall spending as much as it did in the first half of the 1980s.

There was also a squeeze on central Government costs with a drive to increase managerial efficiency, via changes in training and the reviews of Government operations initiated by Lord Rayner of Marks and Spencer – which produced savings of £300 million a year. Civil service numbers were cut by about a fifth to 580,000 over the period up to 1988. The Government also accepted in 1988 that, where possible, the executive functions of government, as opposed to policy advice, should be carried out by separate accountable agencies, each headed by a chief executive accountable to a minister.

The Government was able to shift to a gradually more accommodating stance on public expenditure in the second half of the decade, as the recovery in the economy boosted tax revenue and helped cut public sector borrowing. This gave some room for manoeuvre over spending. The expansion of the privatization programme also helped since, under the British conventions for national accounts, proceeds from such flotations counted as negative expenditure. Hence, from 1986 onwards, the annual review of public spending each summer and autumn lead to sizeable upward revisions of the planning totals. (From the early 1980s these totals were stated in cash rather than volume terms to provide a tighter financial discipline.) But since the economy was growing so strongly, total public expenditure (excluding privatization proceeds) fell consistently as a share of national income from a peak of 46.8 per cent in the pre-election year of 1982–3, down to under 40 per cent by the late 1980s, the lowest level for 20 years. While the annually revised planning total was the operational guide for Whitehall decisions, reductions in the ratio of total spending to national income became the main medium-term objective. This had the advantage of giving flexibility for increases in the planning total while still pointing to a declining public sector share of national resources. In the 1988 annual review of expenditure, to general surprise, the Government confirmed its previous planning total for the following year. This reflected the strength of the property market, which had boosted sales of public housing, and the fall in unemployment, which had offset some of the usual upward pressures on the social security budget. Indeed, despite the earlier upward revisions, these and other favourable influences – together with tighter public sector management – ensured that expenditure for 1988–9 was slightly less than five years earlier, though 7.2 per cent higher than a decade before in the last year of Labour Government, 1978–9. If privatization proceeds are ignored, spending in 1988–9 was 1.8 per cent higher than five years earlier, and 12.8 per cent above the 1978–9 level. Table 2.3 shows the change in trend.

These figures show the impact of the brakes on public spending applied by Labour from 1975–6 onwards, the extent of the acceleration in the early 1980s, and the success the Tories have achieved in holding down expenditure in the second half of the 1980s, even if the impact of privatization is ignored. The rapid growth of the economy has explained much of the decline in the relative share of public spending in GDP.

Table 2.3   Public spending: (general government expenditure excluding privatization proceeds)

	Real terms (£ bn)	Per cent of GDP
1963–64 (last Tory year)	87.9	36.2
1969–70 (last Labour year)	115.6	40.2
1973–74 (last Tory year)	140.6	42.8
1975–76 (pre-IMF crisis)	157.5	48.5
1978–79 (last Labour year)	153.8	43.2
1982–83 (pre-election spending)	167.6	46.8
1988–89 (lowest ratio since 1967)	173.5	39.5

Note: the table shows real-term figures in constant 1987–8 prices
Source: *Autumn Statement 1988*

Table 2.4   Changes in spending programmes

	Per cent change in real terms 1978/9 to 1988/9	1989/90 cash plans
Defence	+18.2	(£20.2 billion)
Employment	−77.3	(£4.02 billion)
Trade/industry	−56.8	(£1.36 billion)
Transport	−16.6	(£5.36 billion)
Housing	−74.0	(£1.71 billion)
Home Office	+55.3	(£6.9 billion)
Education	+9.4	(£19.57 billion)
Health	+34.9	(£23.16 billion)
Social Security	+32.9	(£51 billion)
Planning total	+7.2	(£167.1 billion)

Source: *Autumn Statement 1988*

Over the decade, the combination of external pressures and specific Government decisions has resulted in major changes in the balance of spending between various programmes. The recession and demographic changes explain the sharp rises in spending on employment and social security, while the Government's priorities have been reflected in big increases in defence and the Home Office (see table 2.4).

External trade

The current account of the balance of payments moved from a deficit to a large surplus in the early years of the 1980s, reflecting both the impact of the recession on levels of imports, and, in particular, the build-up of a large surplus on the oil account in the period as North Sea oil production approached its peak. At its peak in 1984 oil accounted for about 16 per cent of total exports. The maximum current surplus was more than £6,700 million in 1981, and then it declined gradually, as the volume of imports rose substantially in line with the growing consumer boom, while the oil surplus was affected by the sharp drop in the dollar oil price in 1986, which fell from £8 billion to £4 billion between 1985 and 1986. It fell further over the following two years as the volume of oil production also declined.

The current account moved into deficit in 1986, and, with the consumer boom continuing and the pound rising, the deficit increased substantially in 1987 and 1988. The volume of imports rose by more than 7 per cent and 12 per cent respectively in those two years, while exports grew by only 5.5 per cent and 1.5 per cent. The share of UK exports in total world trade in manufactures declined sharply during the 1970s, but stabilized from the early 1980s onwards. However, the share of imports in total domestic demand rose sharply in volume terms during the decade from around 18 per cent to 23 per cent. Over the second half of the 1980s as a whole imports rose twice as fast as exports, producing a big deterioration in the external balance. The resulting rise in the deficit was much faster than expected. In March 1988, at the time of the Budget, a deficit of £4 billion was projected, but the outcome was more than three times higher at £14.7 billion. There was no problem financing this deficit since Britain had large official reserves of foreign currency, and investors had also built up large assets overseas during the years of surplus. The deficit was more significant as an indicator of the inflationary pressures within the UK and the extent to which key UK markets were dominated by imports, and so also the limits to any improvement in the country's competitiveness.

These figures represent a mixed record, which improved markedly in the second half of the 1980s as the rigours and shake up of British industry of the first half of the decade began to pay off in steadily rising output and living standards, and, at long last, in a fall in unemployment. The verdict after the first term was understandably harsh. In 1983 I wrote in *The Thatcher Government* that, 'on most counts of welfare and well-being, the Thatcher administration's record in its first term was worse than that of any previous post-war Government in Britain'. Five years later the verdict had changed. Even long-established critics like the National Institute had to acknowledge that their earlier pessimistic forecasts had been proved wrong, although they claimed this reflected changes in Government policy. While monetary policy has been modified significantly, fiscal policy has remained tight. With the exception of two years there has been a continuous tightening of fiscal policy.

The overall performance in the mid-to-late 1980s stands up well by comparison with the 1970s, though not with the late–1960s, as table 2.5 shows. So in historical terms, the performance, both during the whole 1980s and in the upturn since 1981 stressed by ministers, is

Table 2.5 Comparative performance of different economic indicators in terms of average annual per cent rate of growth

	Average over economic cycle			Trough-to-peak average		
	1968–73	1973–9	1979–87	1971–3	1975–9	1981–7
Output	3.2	1.4	1.9	5.1	2.9	3.1
Employment	0.2	0.2	−0.2	1.4	0.4	0.5
Inflation	7.9	16.0	7.7	7.7	13.6	5.3

Source: OECD, output as measured by real Gross Domestic Product, and inflation as shown by GDP deflator

a clear improvement only by comparison with what went immediately before. In some, though not all, respects, the 1980s principally represent a recovery from the horrors of the 1970s, and a return to the record of earlier days, notably the post-devaluation upturn in the late 1960s and early 1970s. However, that was the period when inflation first began to accelerate on a significant scale.

Two central questions have to be answered: first, whether the apparent gains in performance could have been achieved without the loss of jobs and severity of the initial squeeze; and, second, whether the gains can be sustained over the long-term.

It is possible to identify a whole series of mistakes made during the 1979–81 period which aggravated the already strong inflationary forces in the economy, intensified the financial squeeze, pushed up sterling, and therefore also increased the pressures on industry and boosted unemployment. An example was the decision virtually to double Value Added Tax, further raising high inflationary expectations, at a time when public sector pay was accelerating under the impact of the Clegg pay comparability awards. But there is no suggestion that the Government in any way deliberately planned an economic shock to produce the squeeze on industry and rise in unemployment of the scale which occurred. Its original approach was gradualist and it was wrongfooted by the mistakes listed above. Moreover, the Government's initial monetarism was too literal-minded – placing too much faith in one indicator, sterling M3, at a time when its reliability as a measure of financial conditions was under strain. The use of a broader guideline, such as 'money national income', would have permitted a more flexible implementation of

policy, responding more quickly to the unexpectedly sharp rise in the
pound and the steep industrial downturn of 1980. The counter-view
is that a shock was necessary – even if its scale had not been expected
– so as to force industry to end the previous over-manning and to
improve its efficiency. The strength of the subsequent economic
recovery and the improved productivity performance discussed below support the Government's view. Many mainstream economists –
and not just conventional Keynesians – urged fiscal relaxation in the
early-to-mid 1980s. For instance, even in 1985, when unemployment
was still rising, Gavyn Davies, a leading City commentator and
former economic adviser in Downing Street in the Labour years,
stressed the parallels with the 1930s, arguing that no less than in
1931–2, Britain needed a period of expansionary demand policy to
bring unemployment down. He and a number of other economists,
such as Professor Layard, were involved in the launch of the
Employment Institute which made a number of detailed proposals
for non-inflationary expansion and for targeted programmes aimed,
for example, at the long-term unemployed. Yet, as the economy
expanded strongly in the late 1980s, and public sector borrowing
was further reduced, and then eliminated, the alternatives of reflation
and incomes policy appeared increasingly implausible.

Yet, the price was a much larger rise in unemployment than in
other countries which were also affected by the second oil price crisis
and the recession. According to OECD figures, fiscal policy was
tightened by an amount equivalent to 6 per cent of GDP between
1979 and 1982, that is four times the average change for the other
leading industrialized countries. A variety of estimates have been
made of the 'Thatcher' effect on unemployment – perhaps somewhere between two-fifths and a half of the rise in unemployment in
the early 1980s could be attributed to Government policy. Yet,
equally, some of this excess could be linked to the extent of earlier
overmanning in British industry.

Even allowing for some of the macro-economic mistakes in failing
to anticipate the severity of the recession, the question remains of
whether the Government could have mitigated some of the effects.
The various work experience and training schemes which made such
an impact later in the 1980s were developed slowly and belatedly.
They could have offset some of the suffering of the earlier part of the
decade. Similarly, there was a lack of imagination and urgency in
dealing with the regional and inner city problems produced by the

Table 2.6 Output per head: annual average percentage changes

	1964–73	1973–9	1979–88
Manufacturing	3.8	0.8	4.5
Non-manufacturing[a]	3.0	0.5	1.8
Whole economy	2.8	1.0	2.3

[a] excluding public services and North Sea oil and gas extraction

Source: *Autumn Statement 1988*

decline of manufacturing – and preventing the alienation of the long-term unemployed.

The other key macro-economic question is whether all these upheavals have produced a lasting improvement in Britain's economic performance. There is no dispute that the productivity figures have improved, as can be seen in table 2.6.

These figures are clearcut, and indicate an improvement in manufacturing not only compared with the dismal 1970s, but also, unlike other economic indicators mentioned earlier, with the 1960s. However, perhaps a third to a half of the labour productivity growth may have reflected a substitution of capital for labour – which in turn is a reflection of continuing inflexibilities in the labour market which further boosted unemployment. Even when allowance is made for the wave of redundancies and the contraction of manufacturing industry of the early 1980s, an improvement is still apparent. Oxford economist John Muellbauer has argued (in articles in the *Financial Times* and the *Oxford Review of Economic Policy*) that a good measure of labour productivity is total factor productivity, which measures changes which cannot be explained by variations in the number of workers, by increases in the total capital stock or in the length of hours worked. Hence it shows changes in working practices, technology, and effort and efficiency by workers and managers. On his calculations total factor productivity in manufacturing rose by 3.5 per cent a year between 1980 and 1987, which was not only higher than in the 1970s, but also above the 2.6 per cent annual rate in the 1960s and early 1970s. The rate of growth of productivity in the services sector also appears to have been improving.

The unanswerable question is how far this change has been a largely once-and-for-all reaction caused by the shocks of the early

1980s, or whether it represents an acceleration in the underlying rate in response to improvements in management and industrial relations. The OECD warned in its comprehensive survey of the British economy in August 1988 that:

Stronger labour productivity growth has not been linked to capital investment, which, in fact, has remained lower relative to GDP than in earlier recovery periods. Rather it seems linked to changes in work organisation, with inflexible and outdated job demarcation giving way to more rational job allocation. This would indicate that a large part of the observed productivity growth rates in the 1980s are in fact successive level changes as opposed to underlying growth rates.

However, Geoffrey Meen (in *Oxford Review*, 1988) has suggested that there is evidence of some long-term improvement in UK productivity and the growth of productive potential may be permanently higher, primarily due to changes in the capital stock. In short, British industry has become more competitive.

Any optimism needs to be qualified. Britain may have improved its position, both by its own standards and internationally, but it still has a long way to go to catch-up with levels of productivity overseas, as is clear from tables 2.7 and 2.8.

Similarly, a survey by PA Consulting Group and the Confederation of British Industry of 800 companies shows that some 46 per cent acknowledged that in international terms their productivity was below average, while only 19 per cent claimed to be near the top of

Table 2.7 Comparative performance of labour productivity: average annual rates of growth

	1968–73	1973–9	1979–87
UK	3.0	1.2	2.1
US	0.7	0.0	0.6
Japan	7.3	2.9	2.9
West Germany	4.1	2.9	1.5
France	5.0	2.5	1.8
Italy	4.6	1.8	1.7
Canada	2.4	1.3	1.0
Total average	2.9	1.4	1.4

Source: OECD

Table 2.8 Comparative total output per worker

	1970	1980	1987
US	100.0	100.0	100.0
Canada	84.2	92.8	95.5
Japan	45.7	62.6	70.7
France	61.7	80.1	85.3
West Germany	61.8	77.4	81.1
Italy	66.4	80.9	85.5
UK	58.0	65.9	71.9

Source: US labour statistics quoted in *Brookings Review*, winter 1988–9

the international league. Nevertheless, the improved relative performance in the UK during the 1980s has meant that the international gap is not unbridgeable. For instance, the relative difference in productivity levels between Britain and West Germany has been narrowed to the levels of the 1960s, though as table 2.7 indicates there is still a much larger gap with Japan and the US. The OECD noted in its August 1988 review that:

The existing gap in productivity levels between Britain and her neighbours suggests that there is still significant scope for catching-up, and that productivity growth differentials in the past years might persist into the medium-term. However, if past productivity developments represent level changes, they will eventually taper off, although the process may continue for many years.

The other reservation concerns earnings. Throughout the second half of the 1980s the rapid growth in British productivity helped to offset the continued high rate of earnings growth and so hold down unit labour costs and maintain competitiveness. In manufacturing unit labour costs grew by only 4 per cent in 1986, and hardly at all in 1987, though they rose by 2.5 per cent in 1988. However, this was exceptional because of the size of the growth output – and to a large extent the benefits of a unusually large rise in productivity merely neutralized rising labour costs, preventing much real gain. So, with the rate of growth of manufacturing output likely to slow and the rate of earnings growth remaining high, unit labour costs may grow more rapidly, thus undermining competitiveness. This is all very familiar from the 1960s and 1970s, and relates less to macro-economic policy than to continuing weaknesses in the structure of the labour and housing markets, as will be shown in the following chapter. By the spring of 1989 prices in the UK were rising at nearly twice the average rate of the other leading industrial countries.

Looking at the overall record, Professor Nick Crafts has argued (in *Oxford Review* 1988) that the Thatcher Government has 'in some key respects improved supply-side policy and relative decline appears to have ceased.' However, he has warned that while

there have certainly been gains from the retreat from the post-war consensus, the accent on defusing the political legacy has caused important opportunities to be missed. Thus, for example, in privatisation policy, opportunities to promote efficiency through competition have been lost: in the housing market, regional mobility has been reduced and skill shortages probably exacerbated; in education, the power struggle seems in danger of jeopardising the effective provision of technical and vocational training which is of key significance.

These issues will be discussed in later chapters.

Any assessment has to balance the clear improvement in the productivity performance noted above and the strong growth in employment and living standards since 1983 with not only the persistence of high unemployment in certain regions but also, more particularly, with the failure to reduce inflation further since 1983. It is too early to say whether Britain is returning to the inflationary constraints of the 1960s, of which the current account deficit is a partial symptom. But the re-emergence of worries about these problems – and the uncertainties over exchange rate and monetary policy – makes the talk by ministers in early 1988 of an economic miracle sound both exaggerated and premature. The qualified verdict of 'two cheers' of many economists is nearer the mark.

3

The Labour Market

When we returned to office in 1979 one very major reason was that we were elected to curb excessive trade union power – of the trade unions over Government – and the abuse of trade union power vis-a-vis employees within trade unions. The background was that a good Government had been swept out of power in 1974 by a political miner's strike, and the Labour Government in the late 1970s had been firmly controlled by trade union bosses.

Kenneth Clarke, Paymaster General and Employment Minister,
11 October 1985

I have no doubt that, increasingly, members will be looking to their unions to provide progress without strikes and without pickets – quite simply, with the minimum of hassle, especially self-induced hassle.

Norman Willis, General Secretary of the Trade Union Congress,
25 October 1985

Many of the weaknesses of the British economy have been, and remain, in the labour market. Indeed, if, as the previous chapter showed, Britain's high rate of inflation by international standards – and areas of high unemployment – cannot be explained just, or even mainly, by differences in macro-economic policy, the causes must lie in structural failings in the labour market.

Yet the common diagnosis of these weaknesses has changed considerably during the 1980s. In the late 1970s and early 1980s the main topic of political debate was the power of the unions – whether any government could survive, let alone prosper, in face of union disruption. There were endless articles about whether the Thatcher administration could avoid the fate of its predecessors. But, gradually, during the first half of the 1980s, culminating in the defeat of the miners' strike in 1984–5, the dragon of union power was slain. Not only has the previously omnipotent National Union of Mineworkers become a defeated, divided and diminished force, but the unions generally have been much weakened. Membership of TUC affiliated unions has fallen substantially during the 1980s, in both absolute and relative terms, while their impact through industrial disputes and strikes has dropped dramatically.

The Thatcher administration may have solved the political problem of overmighty unions which had undermined previous governments for over a decade. But it is questionable how far it has solved the underlying economic problems of the labour market. These have helped to keep up the rate of earnings growth and have sustained inflexibilities in the movement of workers. The unions have only been one factor in these difficulties.

In any event, the trade union issue has largely disappeared from the centre of the political stage – with the annual exception of Congress week in early September when there is much despairing introspection on the theme of whither the unions. Trade union leaders are no longer leading figures setting the national agenda. The Government has brutally, even gleefully, brushed aside union leaders from their previous preeminence. Not only are there no more 'beer and sandwiches' chats in Downing Street to settle industrial disputes, but there are many fewer contacts of any kind. The role of the unions on tripartite bodies, along with employers and the Government, expanded considerably during the 1970s, but has subsequently been much reduced, with, for example, the winding-up of the previously semi-independent Training (formerly Manpower Services) Commission. Ministers could also scarcely disguise their boredom with having to spend a morning each month at meetings of the National Economic Development Council. These meetings are now quarterly, and the scope, and status, of the National Economic Development Office has been much reduced. The change has been vividly illustrated by the reduced standing of the general secretary of the TGWU (the transport and general workers' union), Britain's largest union. The power of Jack Jones in having a crucial say over the shape of the late 1970s incomes policies was replaced by the weak leadership of Moss Evans and the spluttering ineffectiveness of Ron Todd.

Not only have union leaders been battered by the experience, but some of the architects of the changes have been surprised. Lord

(James) Prior, the Conservative employment spokesman in opposition and Employment Secretary up to September 1981, was mainly responsible for the initial gradualist step-by-step approach. This was a deliberate contrast to the big bang sweeping reforms of the Heath administration introduced in one package in the early 1970s and which so spectacularly failed. In an interview for the Channel Four series *The Writing on the Wall* (later published by Philip Whitehead, 1985), Prior described the pace of union reform as 'almost inconceivable to someone who did actually see the passage of the (Heath) Industrial Relations Act and all that happened subsequently'. He acknowledged that by the end of the 1970s 'the mood was right for rather more legislation and quite a lot more union bashing than I ever thought could be justified or politically acceptable'.

The explanation is perhaps that all involved, both ministers and union leaders, who were in the battles of the 1970s, underestimated the extent of the change in mood. The ugly disputes of the 1978–9 'winter of discontent' – which involved the highly publicized incidents at hospitals and at cemeteries with bodies unburied – undermined the moral standing of the unions. They became much more unpopular, both with the public and with many of their own members. The wave of large-scale redundancies of 1979–81 shook the workers' confidence in their unions' ability to deliver. The result was that when the union leaders called their members out on strike, or in protest at Government actions, there was only a half-hearted response. A TUC-led Day of Action in 1980 was a damp squib with only limited support compared with the effective mass demonstrations of the early 1970s against the Heath administration. The protests of the unions against Government legislation were largely ritualistic – initial vehement opposition, followed by tacit acquiescence, and, eventually, acceptance. Not surprisingly, therefore, the Government grew in confidence over implementing its approach.

Strong supporters of the changes, like Charles Hanson, an economics lecturer, and Graham Mather, the director of the Institute of Economic Affairs, have argued (1988) that:

The step-by-step process of trade union law reform initiated by the Thatcher Government has been in many ways its most important and successful programme of radical innovation. Today it is too easily forgotten that in 1979 commentators and critics in all parties were almost unanimous in regarding effective trade union law reform as politically impossible. The trade unions were too strong and the collectivist attitudes which had permeated the British economy throughout the 20th century were, it was confidently asserted, altogether too deep-rooted to permit the policy to succeed. Fortunately, the critics have been proved conclusively wrong; even those who opposed every aspect of the reforms have been obliged to admit that many of them are here to stay.

The series of legislative measures have only been one of the factors weakening the power of the unions, Other influences include: the impact of the rise in unemployment; the wave of redundancies produced by the manufacturing shake-out of 1979–81: the revival of a self-confident management approach to unions; and the Government's success in appearing the victor in a series of bruising public sector disputes. The balance between these influences is impossible to determine. They reinforced each other – in turn weakening both the resolve and the morale of trade unions. The key change came with the recession of 1980–1 and the long steel strike of 1980 which, while resulting in a much higher settlement than originally offered, left the steelworkers too exhausted to resist the cutbacks and re-dundancies which immediately followed. This was later dramatically underlined by the defeat of the miners' strike in 1984–5 and the collapse of other public sector disputes. The pace of change in union power, especially in methods of bargaining, also accelerated after the mid-1980s as both union leaders and company managements accepted that there was unlikely to be a quick return to the conditions of the 1970s, since the Tories were in a strong electoral position.

The main initial impact of the legislation was symbolic, in showing the Government's intentions. Then, as it became clear that the unions had neither the will nor the popular backing to repeat their earlier successes, when they had defied the Heath administration, the next stages of the legislation were brought forward which reinforced the shift in the balance of industrial relations power. The four acts (1980, 1982, 1984 and 1988) were not sufficient in themselves to alter the position of trade unions, but without them the changes could not have happened.

The legislation had two aims – to make the unions more responsible and to limit their power. Initially, during James Prior's era (1979–81), the main themes were responsibility and accountabil-ity, creating what the Tories regarded as good democratic unions.

Later, particularly after Norman Tebbit became Employment Secretary in September 1981, the balance shifted more towards weakening the role of unions, regardless of whether they were perceived as good or bad. The measures included these main proposals:

1　In the 1980 act: restricting lawful picketing to exclude secondary action; providing compensation for people unreasonably excluded from a union in a closed shop and requiring that new closed shops must be approved by four-fifths of workers covered; and restricting immunity for secondary action, making available public funds for union ballots.

2　In the 1982 act: substantially increasing compensation awarded to individuals unfairly dismissed for not being trade union members in a closed shop; requiring regular reviews of closed shops by secret ballots and making it unfair to dismiss an employee for not being a union member in a closed shop unless this had been approved by 80 per cent of employees concerned or 85 per cent of those voting in a secret ballot; bringing the legal immunities from civil action for trade unions into line with those for individual officials, thus making unions liable to injunctions and damages if held responsible for unlawful industrial action; and restricting lawful trade disputes to those between workers and their own employers about pay, conditions of work and jobs, thus excluding disputes involving third-party employers.

3　In the 1984 act: requiring that every member of a union's principal executive committee must be elected directly by secret ballot of its members at least once every five years; making the legal immunity of unions in organizing industrial action conditional on the holding of a secret ballot in which all those due to participate in the action are entitled to vote; requiring that ballots must be held before a trade union authorizes or endorses industrial action; tightening up on records and complaints procedures; requiring that all unions with political funds seek new approval from members by a secret postal ballot or workplace ballot, and then at intervals of not more than ten years, together with a tighter definition of political objectives.

4　In the 1988 act: giving trade union members the right to take court action to stop their union calling them out on strike without a proper ballot; giving union members a right not to be unjustifiably disciplined by their union for failure to join a strike or other industrial action (even when a majority have voted for it) and for making complaints about the running of a union; making non-membership of a trade union an automatically unfair ground for dismissal; extending the requirement for regular elections by union members to the general secretary, president and non-voting members of a union's principal executive as well as voting members (under the 1984 act); improving internal union accountability and election procedures; establishing a Commissioner for the Rights of Trade Union Members.

These changes increasingly limited the unions' room for manoeuvre, and therefore their effectiveness in industrial disputes. The restrictions on secondary action and the closed shop, and the opening up of union funds to possible legal action in the courts severely restricted the options open to union leaders. It became more difficult for the unions to apply pressure on workers to join strike action. The legislation contributed to the defeat of the NUM in the miners' strike, by stopping secondary supportive action, though more important was the Government's careful contingency planning. The initiative in most of these actions was taken not by the Government but by private sector employers, notably Eddie Shah in a bitter dispute at the Warrington plant of his Messenger group. He took advantage of the new laws in combating secondary action by the printing unions which faced the imposition of heavy fines and the sequestration of assets. This opened the way for Rupert Murdoch's News International to beat the printing unions in the year-long dispute at the Wapping plant. In the 1984–7 period 77 injunctions were sought by employers under the 1980 and 1984 acts, of which 73 were granted.

The unions have, in varying ways, acquiesced in and accepted a number of the post-1979 changes. This has partly reflected the widespread support for the changes not only of the public but also of union members. Several unions changed their election procedures in accordance with the terms of the 1984 act. This may have contributed to a less left-wing stance in the leadership of some unions. Even before the proposals in the 1988 act further undermined the closed shop, the number of people working in post-entry closed shops fell from a peak of around 5 million in 1978 to well under 3 million by 1988. This reflected the contraction of the workforce in a number of industries where the closed shop had been strong, such as coal, steel and the railways, as much as the legislation itself. But no major new closed shops were created, and their effectiveness was undermined by the 1984 and 1988 acts.

However, around 400,000 workers were still in pre-entry closed shops, where new entrants already had to be members of specified unions, a figure which was only slightly down on the late 1970s level. Such pre-entry closed shops applied in shipping, printing, broadcasting, acting and to textile workers. While earlier legislation had made it unlawful for unions to use industrial action to enforce a closed shop and for a worker to be dismissed for not belonging to a union, it remained lawful for an employer to refuse to recruit someone who did not belong to a specified union. The unions argued that this ensured that properly trained people were recruited, but the Government had plans to remove what it regarded as an anomaly as part of a broader package of proposals, also including making unions more responsible for unofficial actions by their members.

The only substantial setback which the Government suffered in its union legislation was over the ballots on political funds in 1985–6. They were intended to weaken the links between the unions and the Labour Party, to make union members even more willing to vote Tory, or at least anti-Labour, and also further to undermine Labour's finances. However, following some unusually skilful campaigning, in which the Labour leadership took a back seat, all existing political funds were confirmed by large majorities, and there were even some small additions. The unions argued that the existence of such funds enabled them to defend their members, so the issue was turned into one of union loyalty, through careful wording of the ballot forms which ministers had not anticipated. Voting for a fund did not automatically mean affiliation to the Labour Party, though it usually led to such a commitment.

Naturally, ministers have focused on the reduction in the number of working days lost during disputes, as set out in table 3.1. However, there were still a regular series of large-scale disputes in the public sector – steel in 1980, civil servants in 1981, health workers in 1982, water workers in 1983, miners in 1984–5, and teachers in 1985–6. If these disputes are excluded, the fall in the number and duration of strikes was less spectacular, but the trend was clear. In the private sector the fall in strike activity was initially attributed to the impact of the recession. But, significantly, as the economy picked up in the mid-1980s and the number of disputes fell further, it

Table 3.1   Strike activity

	Number of stoppages	Working days lost (thousands)
1950–9 (average)	2,116	3,252
1960–9 (average)	2,448	2,555
1970–9 (average)	2,601	12,870
1974	2,946	14,750
1975	2,332	6,012
1976	2,034	3,284
1977	2,737	10,142
1978	2,498	9,405
1979	2,125	29,474
1980	1,348	11,964
1981	1,344	4,266
1982	1,538	5,313
1983	1,364	3,754
1984	1,221	27,135
1985	903	6,402
1986	1,074	1,920
1987	1,016	3,546
1988	725	3,752

Source: Department of Employment

became clear that a significant shift had occurred. Equally important, the widespread perception of Britain as a strike-ridden country disappeared as part of the Conservative Party's new claims about the rebirth of Britain under Mrs Thatcher. No longer was a strike regarded as a national crisis. Indeed, by the late 1980s, strikes had largely disappeared in the private sector, with many of the remaining disputes associated with the restructuring of bargaining in the public sector, as in the Post Office, British Rail and the London Underground, as well as British Coal. Disruption also followed the Government's plan to abolish the National Dock Labour Scheme which has protected jobs in 40 ports.

The Government's insistence on pre-strike ballots under the 1984 act may have played a part in certain well-publicized disputes. For instance, members of the National Union of Railwaymen on three occasions in 1985–6 rejected the call of their leaders to take action.

But in general, as my former *Financial Times* colleague Philip Bassett has pointed out (1986 and 1987), close observers of the industrial relations scene like Incomes Data Services doubted whether ballots were the cause of the drop in strike activity. It was more a matter of the general change in the employment climate.

As significant in influencing the attitudes of unions and their members was the impact of the collapse of the miners' strike in March 1985. The NUM, and in particular Mr Arthur Scargill, its president, had been the feared bogey of the Conservatives ever since the traumatic defeats inflicted by that union on the Heath administration in 1972 and 1974. In the eyes of Mrs Thatcher and her advisers any challenge by the NUM had to be defeated when the time was right, and there had been considerable discussion of contingency planning for this, going back to the opposition days in the late 1970s. When action was threatened in February 1981 over an acceleration of the pit closure programme the Government backed down because some ministers, particularly those previously associated with Mr Heath, believed they could not win since coal stocks were not high enough. While this was inevitably seen as a rebuff for the Government, ministers believed it was merely a breathing space to prepare for the expected confrontation, particularly after the landslide election of Mr Scargill to the union presidency in 1982. The prospect of a fight became more likely after the appointment of Ian MacGregor, who had earned a reputation as a tough, confrontational manager, especially as chairman of British Steel in the early 1980s.

In retrospect, a confrontation was probably inevitable. But as opposition leader Neil Kinnock pointed out in a biting post-mortem at the Labour conference in October 1985, after the end of the strike, the NUM leadership's tactics had been flawed from the start when there was no national strike ballot and areas were brought out on strike one by one. As quoted in the comprehensive analysis of the dispute by Martin Adeney and John Lloyd (1986), Mr Kinnock noted that:

the fact that the strike was called without a ballot denied to the miners the solidarity of the rest of the trade union movement. On top of that were given continued, repeated promises that coal stocks were on the verge of exhaustion, and it was never true. The strike wore on. The violence built up because the single tactic chosen was that of mass picketing and so we saw policing on a scale and with a system that has never been seen in Britain before. The court actions came, and by their attitude to the court actions, the NUM leadership ensured that they would face crippling damages as a consequence.

As a result the miners were divided, with substantial production still coming from the working miners who later formed the Union of Democratic Mineworkers based in Nottinghamshire. While leaders of other unions such as the transport workers and railwaymen expressed public support for the NUM, their members carried on working normally – thus allowing coal to be moved to power stations and to steel works. The Government's preparations – both in building up coal stocks at power stations and in organizing police resources and training to defeat mass picketing – further undermined the NUM. While Mr Scargill and his allies could claim solidarity in striking areas with the enthusiastic backing of young miners and the politicization of women in support groups, their resistance was isolated from the rest of the union movement and the rest of the country. So with the eventual defeat of the strike Mr Scargill's confrontational approach, vanguardism, was discredited, both within his own union and more generally. The result had both practical symbolic importance in dramatically underlining the shift of trade union power. Other union leaders, and their members, took note and the end of the dispute was followed by the lowest level of strike activity for 50 years.

The changed position of the unions has been reflected in the sharp decline in membership of those affiliated to the TUC, down from a peak of 12.2 million at the end of 1979 to 9.1 million by the end of 1987 (even before the departure in September 1988 of the 330,000 members of the expelled electricians' union). Ministers repeatedly pointed out that this total was less than the number of private shareholders. The decline has mainly reflected the sharp contraction of manufacturing, and other manual employment. The biggest drops in membership have been in industrial and general unions, such as the TGWU, the transport workers, (losing a million members in a decade), the AUEW (engineers) and the NUM. There have been similar declines before, notably in the 1930s in the aftermath of the recession. So there is no inherent reason why there should not be an upturn again. Moreover, the drop has principally been a response to changes in industrial structure, rather than a deunionization seen on a large scale at established operations in the US. So far decisions to abandon existing recognition of unions have been limited in the UK, though they gathered momentum towards the end of the 1980s.

However, new operations and expanding areas of British industry, such as small new technology companies, and particularly foreign-owned concerns and groups operating in southern England, tend either to have low union membership or to be non-union. The US computer giant IBM has consistently refused to recognize trade unions as negotiators and has had the support of the majority of its workforce. According to an analysis of data from the Government-funded Workplace Industrial Relations Surveys non-unionism among British manual workers almost doubled between 1980 and 1984 with the number of these manual workers in unionized establishments falling from 84 to 70 per cent of the total over the period. There was also a sharp drop in unionization among white-collar workers, as the unions have found it hard going in the growing private services sector. So TUC affiliated unions have not been making up the losses in heavy manufacturing and elsewhere with gains in the growing parts of the economy. The proportion of the total workforce in TUC unions has dropped from around 50 per cent to under 40 per cent in a decade. There have been far-reaching changes in the structure of the labour market; for instance, according to Labour Force survey estimates the number of self-employed people rose from 1.9 million in 1979 to 3 million in 1988, and similarly there was a sharp growth in the number of part-time workers, to over a fifth of the labour force. This has further weakened the unions' collective appeal.

Moreover, it is arguable that even where workers have continued to belong to unions, these have become less relevant to their members. They have no longer been able to fulfil the basic function of providing jobs. Opinion polls have pointed to considerable public scepticism about the value of joining a union and a low level of active participation among those who do. A Market and Opinion Research International (Mori) survey in 1985 suggested that even among union members only 30 per cent thought that belonging to a strong union was important for job security. There has been a greater emphasis on company and local rather than national deals and on individual rather than collective bargaining over pay. Norman Fowler, the Employment Secretary, talked in June 1988 of a revolution in industrial relations:

Increasingly the individual will want to negotiate his own terms and conditions of employment including his own pension arrangements. He will want his pay to reflect his own skills, efforts and capacities, not the outcome of some distant negotiation between employers and trade unions.

These trends should not be exaggerated, as will be discussed later in this chapter, but trade unions have become a more passive force in industrial relations than in the past.

Consequently, an agonized debate has appeared within the unions about their role. This occurred principally after the 1983 general election when Labour not only suffered a crushing electoral defeat but the party created by the trade union movement attracted the votes of less than 40 per cent of union members, down from more than 70 per cent in the 1960s. Together with the fall in union membership, the drop in Labour support from union members forced their leaders to come to terms with a triumphant Conservative administration. Initially, at the annual Trades Union Congress in September 1983, there was talk among right-wing and centre-right leaders of a 'New Realism' – a need to change attitudes and talk to the Government. This mood proved short-lived and was shattered the following January by the Government's unexpected decision to ban trade union membership at its large intelligence and signals monitoring headquarters at GCHQ, Cheltenham. The decision infuriated union leaders of all viewpoints – uniting them in a campaign around the fundamental right of anyone to belong to a union if they wished. This was soon followed by the retirement of TUC general secretary Len Murray, who had sought to re-open contacts with the Government. The 'New Realism' was further undermined within a few months by the start of the miners' strike which forced most unions, with some notable exceptions like the electricians, into at least nominal support for the miners.

However, while the 'New Realism' was on ice – with the Government also reluctant to make conciliatory gestures – the change in circumstances which prompted the reassessment had not disappeared and ultimately led to a split in the TUC in 1988. There were three broad strands. First, there was what has been called the new or business unionism of the electricians. They have sought single union agreements and no strike deals with employers, emphasizing a joint interest in improving efficiency and profits, while maximizing fringe benefits for union members. Secondly, there has been the remnant of the class-based confrontational approach, typified by the NUM, seeking to challenge management at all times as part of a socialist objection to capitalism, and, ultimately in the public sector, seeking to defeat the Government itself. Thirdly, and most significant in terms of numbers, there has been the attempt to revive traditional trade unionism by reaching out and organizing among groups who traditionally do not belong to unions or with low levels of unionization, such as women, the low paid and service workers (especially the growing numbers of part-timers). This parallels the example of what AFL/CIO unions have been seeking to achieve in the US when also faced with problems of falling union membership.

The modernization of the long-standing approach has been most forcefully expressed, and urged, by John Edmonds of the GMB, the general and municipal workers' union. In an interview in *Marxism Today* in September 1986 he set out his union's aims:

The nature of the union's membership is going to change quite rapidly. We are going to have to recruit a lot more women, because the industries we are talking about are predominantly staffed by women employees. That is going to change the nature of the union. We are going to have fewer members in manufacturing industry and be representing many more disadvantaged people. We are therefore going to be arguing for a national minimum wage, a list of legal rights and income redistribution. We are going to want a substantial social wage, because there is no point in ensuring people are lifted a little bit out of poverty if they have to pay for their health service or their education or whatever.

Not all unions have fallen neatly into one category or another. The engineers have sought to straddle the new or business unionism of the electricians and the traditional approach, while the transport workers have been divided and at times pulled towards a confrontational approach. The electricians have been the most vigorous proponents of the single union/no strike approach, and have generally agreed deals with employers before a plant is opened. For a long time they appeared to court confrontation with the TUC before their final expulsion in 1988. However, the electricians made limited progress in terms of new members with their single union/no strike agreements. Up to the late 1980s they covered only a small fraction of the workforce and these were mostly at new greenfield undeveloped sites, rather than at existing plants. The Government publicly supported such deals, but in practice most of its actions were aimed at weakening the position of unions of whatever kind.

The conflict between the new unionism and the traditional approach was most starkly illustrated by a proposed single union agreement between the engineers and Ford of the US at a new component plant at Dundee in Scotland initially employing 400 people. Defending the proposal, Gavin Laird of the engineering union pointed to single union agreements which his union had already agreed with Sony in Wales, Dunlop in Newcastle, Nissan in Washington New Town, Komatsu in Birtley and Timex in Dundee. He argued: 'What unions must do is reach deals with firms that contribute to their profitability and efficiency, which in turn underpin employment prospects by making the company more competitive. We were able and willing to negotiate with Ford on that basis.' However, the opposition to the deal from other motor industry unions, notably the transport workers, led to the withdrawal from the project by Ford in spring 1988 – to the fury of many in the Labour and trade union movement. The events at Dundee showed the limits of the unions' reappraisal, though it was not all a matter of principle and also reflected more traditional inter-union rivalry and competition for members.

The market-based trade unionism of the electricians and engineers with its identification of the interests of employers and employees was regarded as a betrayal by left-wing unions. The divisions within the union movement were to a large extent between those operating in the competitive market sector and those with members mainly in the public sector who favoured more traditional approaches. Yet increasingly union leaders like John Edmonds recognized that their members and potential members needed to be offered something new and wanted to avoid going on strike. But by the late 1980s there was little sign that trade unions generally had taken the necessary actions to reverse the declines in their membership and influence of the previous decade – especially since developments in the labour market were so unfavourable to them.

Yet the question remained: why, if the trade unions were so much weaker than before, should the rate of earnings growth in the UK have remained well above the international average? Indeed, as table 3.2 shows, the relative position worsened during the late 1980s.

Table 3.2   Earnings growth: percentage increase in yearly average

	UK	France	West Germany	Italy	Japan	US
1977	10	13	7	28	9	9
1978	14	13	5	16	6	8
1979	16	13	6	19	7	9
1980	18	15	6	22	7	9
1981	13	12	5	24	6	9
1982	11	17	5	17	5	7
1983	9	11	3	20	4	4
1984	9	8	3	11	4	4
1985	9	7	4	11	4	4
1986	8	4	3	5	1	2
1987	8	3	5	6	2	1
1988	9	3	4	6	4	3

Source: Department of Employment Gazette

Admittedly, these figures for earning include bonus and overtime payments as well as basic wage settlements – and these undoubtedly boosted the record earnings figure during the upswing in activity in the mid- and late-1980s. Moreover, for much of the period the rate of productivity growth was sufficiently rapid to limit the rate of increase in unit labour costs. Many individual employers were willing to pay high awards because their own efficiency was improving. In the 1982 to 1988 period, which was one of recovery, unit labour costs rose by between 3.2 and 5.5 per cent a year. For a time this helped to reduce the gap with other countries but did not eliminate it. The rate of growth of British unit labour costs was above the average of the seven major industrialized countries in the 1986–8 period, and was top of the range in 1988. So competitiveness was deteriorating. Employment Secretary Norman Fowler warned in 1988 that earnings growth was 'excessively high. We cannot rely indefinitely on improvements in productivity to keep our unit labour costs under control. We need to achieve the same moderation in earnings growth as our competitors.'

The key question has been why the continued high, though falling, level of unemployment has not worked through to affect behaviour in the labour market and reduce the level of pay awards and earnings growth. In economists' language has there been an increase in the

Nairu, the non-accelerating inflation rate? This is the level of unemployment at which inflation should be stable. It seemed that this had changed with a higher level of unemployment not having the expected effect, at least in full, on earnings. This unemployment/earnings relationship appeared odd given the reduced power of trade unions.

At the beginning of the 1980s some free-market economists focused on the impact of the social security system and the alleged unemployment trap whereby there was insufficient incentive for some people to seek work because of the small and even non-existent, gap between what they would receive from benefits and in work. This would have the effect of reducing the supply of labour relative to demand, thus boosting both earnings and unemployment. That group was probably small, though there were undoubtedly a number of people claiming benefit and earning money in various ways in the black and working economy. However, this was more to do with administration of benefits than any unemployment trap in terms of the level of payments and wages. Any incentive to remain unemployed was reduced by Government actions such as taxing unemployment benefits, increased stringency in applying the availability of work tests for those claiming unemployment benefit (including interviews for the long-term unemployed under the Restart Programme), together with cuts in tax for the low paid and the April 1988 social security changes which were intended to reduce both the unemployment and poverty traps. By most, though not all measures, there was a fall in the ratio of unemployment and associated benefits to average earnings during the 1980s, suggesting that this was not a big influence on earnings and unemployment.

After examining such evidence, Professor Geoffrey Maynard has suggested (1988) that an answer may lie in the distinction between insiders, who have secure jobs and can exert wage pressures, and outsiders, the long-term unemployed who are not in unions and whose interests are ignored since they have no say in bargaining. On this view as the proportion of long-term unemployed in total unemployment rises, as it did for much of the 1980s, the influence of the level of overall unemployment on inflation declines and the Nairu rises.

A number of complementary explanations have been offered – the continuation of traditional methods of pay bargaining, inflexibilities in the labour market and shortages of particular groups of workers.

It is arguable that the Government's legislation and the changed industrial relations climate has reduced the power of the unions to maintain restrictive practices, as classically shown in the Fleet Street revolution in newspapers, but this has only partially affected the structure of pay bargaining. For instance, the official Workplace Industrial Relations Surveys pointed to a drop from only 84 to 79 per cent in the percentage of manual employees in private manufacturing covered by collective bargaining procedures between 1980 and 1984, and there was a slight increase for other groups such as white-collar workers. John MacInnes has concluded from these and similar figures (1987) that 'the basic institutions of workplace trade union-ism survived the economic and legal assault of Thatcherism.'

However, such conclusions may be premature. Most of the available statistics only go up to the mid-1980s, and there is substantial anecdotal evidence of changes in practice in the late 1980s. In the second half of the decade managements became more assertive, and successful, in changing working practices, in spite of the persistence of collective bargaining procedures at various levels. A report produced in September 1988 for the Confederation of British Industry by Professor William Brown of Cambridge University noted that, while trade union recognition had survived the upheavals of the 1980s to a remarkable degree, individual employers were exercising greater control as the influence of joint national deals diminished. 'If employers continue to acquiesce in managing their labour with the assistance of trade union, there can be little doubt that they are doing so in a tighter, more controlled way.' Single-employer bargaining had become dominant rather than industry-wide deals. While this did not rule out the continued influence of going rate/pay round ideas, in which there is a common range of settlements, during one year's negotiations there was more evidence of performance-related payments, especially in the service sector, and increased use of profit-sharing. Companies like GEC, which had withdrawn from the Engineering Employers' Federation bargaining structure after the 1979 strikes in the industry, have decentralized their own negotiations. Similar moves were taken by some of the privatized concerns such as British Telecom and National Freight, as well as a number of large financial institutions which had previously been wedded to national agreements.

In so far as traditional collective bargaining procedures have still applied, the effect has been to push up levels of earnings by perpetuating ideas of the annual pay round, comparability studies, and the going rate linked to what other employers have been paying. The continuation of these ingrained attitudes has been instead of a primarily market-based system related to local labour market conditions and individual performance. Research by Professor David Metcalf of the London School of Economics has shown that the presence of unions in a workplace or company has been associated with lower labour productivity, higher relative pay, lower financial performance and a greater tendency to suffer job losses. His work pointed to an average wage premium of 10 per cent for union members compared with non-union employees – though 14 per cent for those in a pre-entry closed shop. Professor Metcalf argued that, on the basis of figures from the 1980–4 period, non-union establishments were twice as likely to boost employment by a fifth or more as they were to reduce employment. By contrast, unionized workers were twice as likely to cut a fifth or more of their jobs as they were to increase employment by that amount. Closed shop workplaces were four times as likely to suffer job losses as gains. Consequently, 'unionisation apparently reduced employment growth in Great Britain in the 1980s.' Professor Metcalf's conclusions were explicitly taken up by the Government to justify further reform of trade union law, particularly aimed at the closed shop, in its December 1988 White Paper, 'Employment in the 1990s'. But the Professor's work has been challenged by other industrial relations academics, notably from Warwick University. They have instead argued that there is no straightforward link between unionization and productivity. Some of the apparent contrasts can be explained by differences in industrial structure.

The Government has been concerned enough about the persistence of a high level of earnings growth not only to seek further action against the closed shop but also to urge increased local rather than national bargaining. A campaign to break up national negotiations was launched by Kenneth Clarke when he was Employment Minister. In a lecture in February 1987, at the City University Business School, he argued that, 'If we can move to a system where pay increases are based primarily on performance, merit, company profitability and demand and supply in the local labour market, we will dethrone once-and-for-all the annual pay round and the belief that pay increases do not have to be earned.' In the public sector the campaign was backed by calls on local councils to opt out of national pay negotiations. The Government sought to increase geographic pay variations to reflect more closely patterns of recruitment and retention for civil servants.

The Government also sought to increase flexibility at the lower end of the pay scale by reducing the role of Wages Councils. These have fixed minimum rates for more than 2.5 million workers in traditional low paying industries such as hotel, catering and textiles. Ministers argued that such pay-fixing discouraged employment, especially at the margin, since it raised wage rates above the levels which employers could afford to pay. In 1986 legislation removed people under the age of 21 from the scope of these councils, and their remit was limited to fixing a single minimum basic and overtime rate, rather than a range of rates, as had been done previously. In December 1988 the Government produced proposals including the abolition of the 26 councils on the grounds that they were still preventing pay flexibility and therefore impeding job creation. A consultative paper argued that since about a third of workers were paid on minimum rates, this showed that minimums set by Wages Councils remained above market rates needed to fill jobs. The unions argued that abolition of the councils would increase poverty.

During the second half of the 1980s there was an increased shift away from national deals, with moves towards linking pay to performance and offering wholly individual contracts, as has been happening in the newspaper industry. The Government has tried to encourage profit-sharing, as Nigel Lawson argued in his March 1986 Budget speech:

The problem we face in this country is not just the level of pay in relation to productivity, but also the rigidity of the pay system. If the only element of flexibility is the numbers of people employed, then redundancies are inevitably more likely to occur. One way out of this might be to move to a system in which a significant proportion of an employee's remuneration depends directly on the company's profitability per person employed.

A sizeable number of profit-sharing schemes were already in operation, though benefiting only about one million or so people. Mr Lawson's innovation, introduced in the 1987 Budget, involved the creation by companies of a profit-related pay fund covering at least 80 per cent of employees (other than new recruits), dependent on movements in profits. The tax relief allows half of the profit-related pay received by each employee to be tax free up to a maximum of 20 per cent of total pay, or £4,000, whichever is the lowest. For a married man on average earnings with 20 per cent pay taken in this profit-related form, the relief was worth almost 4p in the pound off the basic rate of income tax in 1988–9. However, the initial take-up was slow, rising to only 830 schemes by early 1989.

Individualism in place of collectivism has become a favourite theme of industrial relations discussion with previous patterns of collective bargaining being supplemented and replaced. There was, however, the dilemma for the Government that, if it encouraged employers to negotiate individually or locally in response to performance and market conditions, this would weaken any attempt to talk down the level of settlements by exhortation, let alone by any formal incomes policy of the 1960s and 1970s variety. The key influence would be an employer's particular priorities, rather than the Government's general worries over inflation. This could mean high awards if a company was doing well, as many were in the second half of the 1980s. A further twist was that many company managements felt they ought to pay their workers above the rate of price inflation since the rewards of senior executives were rising by 25 to 30 per cent a year in 1988–9. The Government's attitude to high pay awards was ambiguous – since many of the biggest rises to executives were to its own natural supporters, in line with its philosophy of rewarding efforts and talent as defined by the market. This inhibited general appeals to restraint – neatly illustrating the conflict in Thatcherism between individual and collective interests.

Some of the upward pressure on the rate of earnings growth, especially in 1987–9, resulted from shortages of particular groups of workers. The proportion of companies expecting skill shortages of skilled labour to constrain their output rose from 2.5 per cent in the early 1980s to well over 20 per cent by the late 1980s, according to the regular Confederation of British Industry surveys. This was still below the levels of the 1970s. The Association of British Chambers of Commerce reported in autumn 1988 that 49 per cent of manufacturing companies had been hampered by difficulties in recruiting skilled staff – and 84 per cent had been in the Thames Valley. Shortages of staff with expertise in microelectronics were the most quoted reason inhibiting companies using new technology. Philip Bassett reported in the *Financial Times* in November 1988:

there have been some exceptional pay increases in the south-east and the spread of local allowances to areas and town which were never before considered as part of the region... The £100 a day bricklayer has already arrived on London construction sites; at the Chelsea harbour on the Thames employers are offering £125 a day for skim-finish plasterers. To attract female workers who are returning to the labour market, Midland Bank recently brought in a pilot creche scheme and Natwest is extending its system of offering career breaks to women at all staff and management levels. Little, if any, of this seems to be the result of union pressure.

These pressures in the labour market, coupled with the greater decentralization of collective bargaining, have produced a much wider range of settlements than in the past. However, Professor Brown has argued that the going rate has not disappeared entirely since companies are having to match pay rises granted by their competitors to ensure that they can recruit and keep staff. He has pointed to the paradox that, 'if firms' pay rises are tending to chase those of other firms in their industry, at a time when the industrial employer organisations which might have imposed discipline are in continuing decline, it is hard to see what might contain Britain's endemic inflationary problems'.

Shortages of labour have co-existed with national levels of un-employment which, though falling from 1986 onwards, were high by all post-war standards except those of the first half of the 1980s. In spite of a near trebling in notified vacancies in the second half of the 1980s, the unions remained weak. In particular, there appears to be a mismatch in the labour market in regions of persistently high un-employment in northern England, Scotland and Wales. An analysis by the Bank of England in its quarterly bulletin of August 1988 noted that the problem of regional differences in unemployment has been concentrated among manual workers. Their earnings have been similar nationwide, showing a near 11 percentage point variation from top to bottom, because they have still primarily been affected by the national pay levels in each industry. By contrast, non-manual workers' unemployment differs much less, though their pay has varied more and they have moved more between regions. There are considerable difficulties about establishing causes and effect, but the Bank cautiously suggested that, where manual earnings were relatively high, employment had been hard hit in the first half of the 1980s. By contrast, earnings in East Anglia had traditionally been below the national average, partly reflecting the influence of relatively low agricultural earnings, and this region experienced the fastest growth in population and employment during the 1980s. In other words, the relative inflexibility of wages between regions has meant that changes in demand initially affect levels of employment rather than earnings. But in certain regions, such as the south-east, a smaller rate of employment growth can be seen more as a reflection of problems in attracting labour rather than a discouragement to the growth of employment.

By the late 1980s, employers were being forced to depart from national pay rates with bonuses of various kinds in the south-east, though mainly to non-manual workers – contributing further to changes in bargaining practices. However, in the other direction, high house prices and commuting costs have led to an outflow of manual workers from the south-east. By contrast, there was overall no net outflow of manual workers from the most depressed regions, so labour mobility between the regions made no contribution to reducing unemployment. This is unlike, say, the US where emigration is well-established and 15 to 20 times greater than such movements in the UK.

While the persistence of nationally negotiated pay deals may have been a partial explanation for some of the regional variations in unemployment, other blockages have existed to the smooth functioning of the labour market. An important explanation for the relative immobility of labour has lain in the housing market, one of the main failures of the Thatcher Government for most of its term in office. Oxford economist John Muellbauer has argued: 'The housing market is as important as the deficiencies of UK labour market institutions and its system of training and education in explaining the county's relatively poor post-war economic performance. We now appear again to have embarked on a spiral of domestic inflation in which house prices feed wages and wages feed house prices.' He has suggested that rising house prices relative to earnings and widening regional differentials were responsible for a 4 per cent plus rise in real manual wages in the 1984–8 period. Apart from the general impact on inflation, John Muellbauer has maintained that 'when house prices rise those in the more prosperous areas lead. This makes it more expensive for those in less prosperous areas to move and increases the mismatch between unemployed people and unfilled job vacancies.' However, the Bank of England in its analysis disputed the view that variations in house prices, by discouraging migration between regions, affected hourly earnings in different areas.

Government policy has not yet eased the problem significantly. While many council tenants have been freed from being permanently tied to their local authorities as a result of buying their houses, the impact has largely been offset by the continued decline of the private rented sector. Renting provides an essential link in assisting labour mobility in the first stages of people moving. The Government's 1988 Housing Act was intended to aid labour mobility by providing incentives for the revival of the private, or more significantly socially owned housing associations, rented sector. Under this act council tenants were also encouraged to opt out of local authority control, and there were general pressures to raise council rents nearer to market levels, thus removing artificial barriers to mobility. But the impact of these changes would be gradual. Buying a home has given many people greater financial independence, but that has not helped them bridge the regional gap in house prices, which by 1988 were 2.5 times higher in south-east England than in the north. However, the freezing of the upper limit for mortgage tax relief at loans of £30,000 has meant that increases in interest rates have a larger relative effect on housebuyers in the south-east where there is both more borrowing and a higher proportion of mortgages above that level than in the north. This should help narrow regional differences. But the replacement of domestic rates by the community charge, or poll tax, in 1990 was expected to make the problem worse. As a uniform per head tax unrelated to property values the charge would have the effect of making housing even more attractive, raising prices on average by up to 20 per cent over five years, according to the estimates of some economists.

Major changes are, however, likely in the labour market during the 1990s. After a 2 million rise in the population of working age between 1976 and 1986, a slowdown then started with a rise of 500,000 expected in the 1986–90 period and a stabilization in the mid-1990s. After estimating changes in the proportion of people seeking jobs – in turn heavily dependent on the level of unemployment – the Department of Employment projected a rise in the labour force of 900,000 between 1987 and 1995. Most significant of all, the 16 to 19 year age group, the main source of new recruits for employers, was projected to decline by nearly one million to 2.6 million between 1988 and 1995. The largest declines are expected in the areas of currently highest unemployment, a rare but encouraging sign for those currently out of work in such areas. As Employment

Secretary Norman Fowler commented, 'in future employers will need to train and retrain existing adult employees on a scale they have never done before.'

These prospective changes have focused attention on the broader deficiencies of training and education in Britain which received increasing attention during the second half of the 1980s, especially as skill shortages grew. Indeed, one of the most frequent complaints of industrialists was the low level of skills in Britain compared with its main competitors. The evidence was stark, as Charles Leadbeater pointed out in the *Financial Times* in December 1988:

1 In West Germany, 30 per cent of school-leavers at 16 had an intermediate certificate based on an assessment of 10 subjects including compulsory German, mathematics and a foreign language. Only 12 per cent of British school-leavers reached a comparable level. The average West German standard for the lower half of the ability range is the same as the range for all English pupils. The average Japanese 13½-year-old knows more mathematics than the average British 15-year-old.

2 In Japan more than 95 per cent of young people are in full-time education to the age of 18, compared with 32 per cent in Britain. About 38 per cent of Japanese 18-year-olds enter higher education, against only 15 per cent in Britain.

3 In West Germany about 600,000 young people a year start a three-year training course in industry and commerce leading to a vocational qualification. Between two and three times as many people qualify as fitters, electricians, and building craftsmen as in Britain.

4 A report by Professor Charles Handy for the National Economic Development Office found that 63 per cent of West German managers had a degree, 51 per cent of senior managers in the US had a second degree, while only 21 per cent of British managers had a degree.

Moreover, research by the National Institute of Economic and Social Research showed that France had made considerable advances in the 1980s towards creating a vocationally qualified workforce, as had Japan and West Germany. France trained two to three times as many electricians and mechanics as Britain by a system of vocational schools. In the UK there has been a two-year Youth

Training Scheme from which the majority emerge without a vocational qualification.

The Government responded slowly to these problems. The employment assistance schemes were originally devised in the mid-1970s as a response to the sharp increase in unemployment, rather than as training initiatives. The initial emphasis was on temporary subsidies to avoid, or at any rate postpone, redundancies and to help particular groups such as school-leavers. As unemployment soared in the early 1980s the special schemes were substantially expanded particularly under the leadership of Lord Young, first as chairman of the Manpower Services Commission and then as Employment Secretary, and through the innovatory work of a civil servant Geoffrey Holland. The measures were intended to prevent the unemployed losing touch with the world of work and becoming less employable. Among the main schemes were the community programme, which involved nearly 300,000 people doing work of benefit to the local community, and enterprise allowances to encourage the unemployed to set up their own businesses. There were also a whole series of other smaller-scale initiatives to encourage job opportunities.

The training content of such schemes was initially small. Indeed, the Government reduced its involvement in training in 1981 when the statutory system operated by levies on employers through the Industrial Training Boards was substantially scaled down. The replacement of voluntary training bodies run by employers was much criticized for being ineffective. However, the Government became more involved in 1983 with the belated launch of the Youth Training Scheme, providing help initially for one year, expanded to two years in 1986, offering a guaranteed place of training to every 16- or 17-year-old. The Department of Education and Science also became more involved with a series of initiatives to improve preparation for employment in schools. Closer links between schools and industry were encouraged, and a technical and vocational education initiative was launched to see that the curriculum was related more to the needs of employers. After Kenneth Baker became Education Secretary in 1986 other broader plans were launched, including the experimental City Technology Colleges and a national core curriculum; these developments will be discussed in detail in chapter 7. A job training scheme was launched for 18- to 25-year-olds to provide on-and-off training and work experience.

This piecemeal and often confusing list of initiatives were pulled together in 1988 into a unified budget of £1.5 billion offering 600,000 places for job training. The aim was that people un-employed for more than six months would be given a year's work and training. An additional premium above benefit levels was introduced to attract older heads of families. The scheme provoked fierce initial opposition from the trade unions, notably at the annual Congress in September 1988. This provided an opportunity for the Government to wind up the tripartite Training (formerly Manpower Services) Commission. In December 1988 the Government brought forward plans for a radical overhaul of industrial training. Instead of tripartism, private sector employers were to be given a central role on local training councils, where they would occupy two-thirds of the places on governing bodies. These councils were modelled on West Germany's Chambers of Commerce, and on the private industry councils in the US. The 100 local training and enterprise councils were intended to handle most of the £3 billion a year training budget. They would assess local training needs, draw up plans and arrange contracts with local training providers such as colleges of further education.

These belated changes in Britain's training system and the large gap behind achievements in competitor countries – for example, in standards of training and vocational qualifications – were symptomatic of the continuing weaknesses in the labour market. Many changes have been overdue, notably in reining back the power of the trade unions and removing obstacles to industrial innovation. If the bogeys of the 1970s have now been not only slain but buried, there are still plenty of problems to be tackled in the 1990s – not least the persistence of a large core of long-term unemployed. Moreover, shifting bargaining procedures away from national norms and the going rate will take time. So, despite a strong productivity perform-ance, there remains an inflationary bias in the wage-fixing structure with the rate of earnings growth well above the rate of price increases for all the 1980s. The Government has also only begun to tackle the barriers to labour mobility in the housing market.

Nevertheless, there has been a movement away from collectivism, underlined by the growth of the flexible labour force of the self-employed, part-time and temporary workers to well over a third of the total, and possibly nearer two-fifths. Together with the sharp decline in the number of young people entering the workforce in the 1990s, this trend will further alter the labour market, creating new problems of training and retraining.

4

Enterprise Culture

Very few sincerely want to be rich. Most people in Britain neither want nor expect a great deal of money. Even if they could get it, the vast majority do not seem prepared to work harder for it: most of our respondents thought we should work only as much as one needs to live a pleasant life. It seems clear that the British today prefer economic stability to rapid economic growth.

New Society, survey of British attitudes to money and work, April 1977

When we look around the world we can only see that those nations that have achieved the best standard of living have been those who have relied on the enterprise of their citizens. We can see it in the success of American entrepreneurs that has been reflected in the standard of living of Americans generally. We can see it here, in the alacrity with which people have adopted Government policies, with the result that our income per head has improved relative to our major European competitors, reversing a decline that has been evident for more years than we like to recall.

Lord Young of Graffham, Employment Secretary, Conservative Political Centre Lecture, Blackpool, 9 October 1985

The key to the Thatcher Government's claim to have reversed Britain's decline lies with the assessment whether or not British business has moved onto a new self-sustaining path of wealth creation. In short, has an enterprise culture come into existence?

People working in business certainly talk of a new freedom to manage, and of a new self-confidence. Lord Young, the super-salesman of the enterprise culture, entitled his October 1985 lecture quoted above 'Enterprise Regained'. He argued that the common factor behind the revival of self-employment and the large-scale creation of new businesses was the sense of enterprise. In his view what has been created − or rather re-created − has been some of the spirit shown by entrepreneurs in Victorian Britain or contemporary America.

Both Lord Young and his mentor Lord (previously Sir Keith) Joseph base their view of what went wrong before 1979 on a mixture of the historical, the sociological and the economic. In particular, they rely heavily, and explicitly, on the explanations for decline offered by historians Correlli Barnett and Martin Wiener. Barnett has argued that the English disease is not a novelty of the past 10 or even 20 years but a phenomenon dating back more than a century and related to social, educational and cultural values. He concluded (1985) that 'Britain came out of the Second World War as an obsolescent industrial economy with grievous weaknesses. Instead of first devoting possible resources and efforts to remedying this she chose to load this economy with the vast and potentially limitless cost of the welfare state, placed current expenditure before capital investment, and thus set the pattern of the next 30 years.' Wiener went back further to the mid-nineteenth century to argue that a pervasive middle and upper class frame of mind hostile to industrialization and economic growth developed. Contrasting different middle class traditions for innovation and enterprise and opposition to it, he concluded:

At the end of the day, it may be that Margaret Thatcher will find her most fundamental challenge not in holding down the money supply or inhibiting Government spending, or even in fighting the shop stewards, but in changing this frame of mind. English history in the eighties may turn less on traditional political struggles than on a cultural contest between the two faces of the middle class.

Both these theses are highly controversial, and they are discussed in, for example, the summer and autumn 1987 issues of the *Contemporary Record*. What has mattered more is that Mrs Thatcher's close allies have accepted the analysis. Lord Joseph in the spring 1987 issue of *Contemporary Record* said, 'I'm a Correlli Barnett supporter. I believe that managements, helped by trade unions and helped by government, were not nearly effective enough.'

The other central strand in the Thatcherite analysis has been that the problems of the British economy lie on the supply, rather than the demand, side – in rigidities in various markets. This view was put succinctly by Sir Geoffrey Howe in June 1979 in his first Budget speech as Chancellor of the Exchequer:

The poor performance of the British economy in recent years has not been due to a shortage of demand. We are suffering from a growing sense of failures on the supply side of the economy. Many of these failures are themselves the result of actions and interventions by Governments themselves – laws that stand in the way of change and stifle enterprise and, as important as anything, a structure of taxation that might have been designed to discourage innovation and punish success.

On this view, which has tended to be mixed with the cultural/historical analysis of a century-old decline, the British economy had become increasingly arthritic and hostile to enterprise during the 1960s and 1970s. High taxes and over-regulation by the state had discouraged effort, and, together with the growth of trade union power, had circumscribed and demoralized management. On the Joseph/Howe/Young view, the combination of longer-term historical changes and increased market rigidities produced a crisis in the late 1970s. However, the same analysis was put forward in the early 1960s and led to the attempts at modernizing British society by the Wilson and Heath administrations which ended in failure. The difference after 1979 lay not only in timing – and there was a much greater acceptance of the need for change then – but also in the extent of the shift of policy.

The post-1979 approach attempted to revive enterprise and the entrepreneurial spirit by a variety of measures. A common theme of the actions initiated by Sir Geoffrey Howe as Chancellor and taken on by Lord Young and others has been the belief that by removing restrictions and promoting competition, enterprise would be encouraged. This has involved both short-term moves to remove market rigidities as well as longer-term measures to encourage a revival of an enterprise culture.

Much of the drive during the mid-to-late 1980s came from Lord Young, who worked first as a special adviser in the Department of Industry, and then, successively, as chairman of the Manpower Services Commission, as a minister without portfolio for a year, as Employment Secretary for nearly two years, and as Trade and Industry Secretary from June 1987 onwards. Like many businessmen commenting on politics he has a tendency to over-simplify – 'a bit broadbrush' as even Mrs Thatcher has been heard to say – but that approach has highlighted his main goals. In a White Paper 'Building Business – Not Barriers' (May 1986), issued by him as Employment Secretary, it was argued that the US experience showed that the key to creating more jobs lay in a more entrepreneurial society and this in part turned on 'a freedom from regulations foreign to most Europeans'. Among the initiatives launched as a result of this deregulation drive have been simplification of planning regulations and of procedures for Value Added Tax and for PAYE income tax, changes in employment law to make it easier to dismiss employees, and an easing of rules affecting companies in setting up and conducting businesses.

On moving to the Department of Trade and Industry, Lord Young called for a similar rethink which resulted in a White Paper in January 1988 ('DTI – the department for Enterprise') and a high profile advertising campaign for the related enterprise initiative. This involved a rejection of the previous sponsoring role and automatic grants for certain groups investing in particular regions and a shift to a more discretionary and advisory approach. The responsibility of government was specifically defined as 'creating the right climate so that markets work better and to encourage enterprise'. The DTI would therefore act as 'a facilitator of open markets and of enterprise'. This approach was intended to provide 'the most comprehensive self-help package offered to business by Government ... The emphasis of the enterprise initiative is on transferring best practice and providing information.'

The very number and variety of measures in the following list show how wide-ranging the implications of a belief in the supply side and enterprise culture are:

Moves to Encourage Enterprise

1 Tax cuts – top marginal rate of income tax reduced from 83 to 40 per cent, and basic rate from 33 to 25 per cent, with reduction to 20 per cent promised when prudent. Tax allowances raised by 25 per cent in real terms. Investment income surcharge of 15 per cent abolished. Corporation tax rate cut from 52 to 35 per cent, though some allowances abolished. Capital transfer tax simplified and top rate reduced from 75 to 40 per cent on inheritance. Capital gains tax restructured to eliminate taxation of inflationary gains.
2 Deregulation – price, dividend, pay and foreign exchange controls all entirely removed. Restrictions on bank lending and hire purchase abolished. More than 180 'bureaucratic' burdens reduced

between 1979 and 1987 to cut costs and extent of compliance. Office Development Permits and Industrial Development Certificates abolished. A total of 25 enterprise zones set up to provide small areas where business benefits from exemption from non-domestic rates, generous capital allowances, and relaxation and speeding up of some planning and administrative controls.

3 Promotion of competition – mergers policy primarily guided by competition yardstick with faster procedures and legally binding undertakings to remove anti-competitive practices. Changes to restrictive trade practice laws to deal with anti-competitive effects in professions and business, and to provide stronger powers for investigation of illegal cartels.

4 Liberalization – freeing of controls over, first, long-distance, and, then, short-haul bus routes (outside London) to promote competition; breaking of British Telecom's monopoly and opening-up to competition the supply of a wide range of equipment, and licensing of Mercury as an alternative carrier; increased competition in domestic air routes, and in supply of spectacles; advertising restrictions on solicitors, accountants, stockbrokers, opticians and vets relaxed.

5 Small business initiatives – business expansion scheme to encourage investment in smaller growing companies through tax incentives for investors; loan guarantee scheme to assist expansion by bank borrowing; enterprise allowance scheme to assist unemployed to set up on their own; local enterprise agencies to provide advice and stimulate the setting-up of businesses; business development initiatives covering design, marketing, business planning, finance and information systems, management of computer aided manufacture, and encouraging development of management skills through the use of management consultants.

6 Industrial aid – switch of direction of programmes (with DTI budget being cut by a quarter in cash terms since 1979) from blanket support in assisted areas (with ending of regional development grants) and from subsidies to nationalized industries (reduced privatization and elimination of losses). Instead, increased emphasis on backing for innovation and research and development and technology transfer, especially through advisory services. Support concentrated on collaborative research programmes, such as LINK bringing together academic and industrial researchers, and the Eureka initiative for collaborative research in Europe.

7   Education – technical and vocational initiative for 14-to-18-year-olds, and two-year youth training scheme. Encouragement of links between industry and schools, with work experience by teachers and young people, and the use of computers in all schools.

The very breadth of these initiatives makes it difficult to assess their contribution to the revival of enterprise. As important may have been the general change in the macro-economic and industrial relations climate discussed in other chapters. There has, for example, been much debate about the impact of the cuts in direct taxation. In a pamphlet published in June 1988, Nigel Lawson claimed that the economics of lower tax rates were simple: 'if you reward enterprise, you get more of it.' He argued that tax reform had helped to produce a better performing economy by shifting taxation on companies from employment to profits, and on individuals from income to spending – imposing much less of 'a drag on work and effort and enterprise.' The Chancellor backed this claim by pointing to sharply increased tax revenues. In particular, in spite of the reductions in tax on the higher paid, the top 5 per cent of taxpayers were in 1988–9 expected to account for 28 per cent of overall income tax receipts, up from 24 per cent of the total when rates were much higher in the last Labour year in office of 1978–9. Similarly, the single higher rate was expected to make as large a relative contribution in 1988–9 as the nine higher rates and the investment income surcharge did in 1978–9.

Economists disagree as to how far this reflects specific incentive effects as opposed to other factors such as the rapid growth in earnings for the higher paid and senior managers during the 1980s – in turn a reflection both of the end of incomes policy controls and the growth of the economy in the period. An officially commissioned study of the behaviour patterns of several thousand households suggested that there was no evidence that, on average, tax cuts encouraged people in employment to work harder or longer. The research, co-ordinated by Professor C. V. Brown of Stirling University, found that the incentive and wealth effects broadly cancelled each other out. In particular, lower taxes tended to encourage women, especially those in the growing group of the part-time employed, to work longer hours because they would keep more of their earnings. For men on average earnings, the boost to existing income provided by lower taxes took precedence over the incentive effect. More than three-quarters of employees covered by the survey claimed they had little opportunity to work extra hours.

However, these findings have to be qualified. The tax cuts may have had a larger effect for those at the top end of the income scale, given the size of the reduction in rates, and at the bottom end, in view of the large number of people taken out of tax altogether. An analysis for the Institute for Fiscal Studies of the 1979 cuts in higher rates of income tax found that these reductions may have encouraged people to work harder, but the case was unproven. Andrew Dilnot and Michael Kell argued (1988) on the basis of Inland Revenue data that it was possible to explain all of the changes in the aggregate level of tax paid between 1978 and 1986 by factors such as alterations in investment incomes, employment and earnings. However, changes in the distribution of payments between income groups cannot be explained completely by such factors. This finding, the authors maintained, was 'consistent with, though not proof of, moderate behavioural changes in response to the reductions in higher rates of income tax in the 1979 budget'. Incentive effects may also have been reflected in the rapid growth of part-time and other forms of flexible work during the 1980s, as well as of self-employment. These are patterns of employment which can be varied and are therefore more responsive to changes in take-home pay produced by tax cuts. Moreover, lower taxes may encourage people to set up small companies and take risks.

More generally, it is possible to identify a number of indicators of new enterprise as well as of changes in the behaviour of existing companies. There has undoubtedly been a revival of self-employment and many more new businesses:

1 An average net increase of 500 new firms every week since 1979 (after deducting closures), according to VAT statistics which exclude the very smallest concerns. In 1987 there was a rise of 45,000, or nearly 900 a week, to a total of 1.51 million, compared with 1.29 million at the end of 1979. Company registrations were also at record levels in the 1986–7 period.

2 A rise of around 1 million in the number of self-employed people during the 1980s to more than 3 million by late 1988, over six times the increase in the previous 30 years. This total was equivalent to more than 11 per cent of the employed labour force.

3   Over 3,000 companies raised £750 million between 1983 and 1988 from the business expansion scheme (offering tax relief to investors in unquoted trading companies).
4   Venture capital industry grew from virtually nothing to invest more than £1 billion in 1987.
5   Unlisted securities market grew from £12.5 million investment in new issues in its first year of operation in 1980 to £191 million in 1987.
6   A sharp rise in the number and scale of management buy-outs. In 1987–8, for example, 3i, the investment capital group, spent £191 million backing 109 management buy-outs, up from £101 million the year before.
7   Government backed loan guarantee scheme launched in 1981 to assist expansion of smaller companies had made available over £635 million up to 1987, helping over 19,000 businesses.

These figures provide impressive evidence of a revival of entrepreneurial activity. The sharp rise in self-employment and in the number of small businesses has undoubtedly been helped by Government initiatives such as specific schemes to aid smaller firms as well as by tax cuts. The revival has been stimulated by changes in the industrial structure favouring the growth of small-scale operations in the newer technologies and services.

These developments have been borne out by anecdotal evidence of, for example, new concerns in retailing and small-scale manufacturing in any town in southern England and the Midlands. It was not just in the City of London in the pre-October 1987 stock market crash period that signs of a changed attitude to money-making could be found. It was also a matter of one's age. Those who had become adults during the Thatcher era – up to the age of 30 by the late 1980s – appeared to have a more materialist attitude, exemplified by the high-living yuppie culture of the affluent young. The jibe 'Thatcher's children' used by Labour politicians (discussed in chapter 9) to attack selfish money-grabbing hooligans could be turned on its head as evidence of a more entrepreneurial generation prepared to work and earn money. The paradoxes of this shift were reflected in the slogan 'Loadsamoney' which became popular in 1987–8. Originally invented by self-styled left-wing comic Henry Enfield to attack the attitudes of some of the new affluent young, it was taken up almost as a badge of pride – such is the fate of many such insults, like Tory and Whig.

Survey evidence has, however, been ambiguous on the extent of any underlying change in attitudes. A detailed poll carried out by Mori for the *Sunday Times* and *Weekend World* in June 1988 showed that voters believed that Britain had become more Thatcherite than they wished. For instance, some 75 per cent of the sample thought that Britain had become a society in which the creation of wealth was more highly rewarded, compared with just 16 per cent who wanted to see greater rewards. There was greater support for a society which allows people to make and keep as much as they can – 73 per cent believed that Britain was like that, against 53 per cent who wanted to see such a result. Similarly, the annual British Social Attitudes Survey taken in 1988, which has a large sample of 3,000 people, showed that, if Mrs Thatcher had succeeded in transforming British cultural attitudes towards enterprise, the public would regard the fruits of business investment and entrepreneurship as a legitimate reward for shareholders and top managers. Yet, the authors of the survey argued that such views were embraced by only a minority of the public. Since the start of the surveys in 1983 public opinion has become more alienated from many of the goals of the enterprise culture. 'To the extent that attitudes have moved, they have become less sympathetic to these central tenets of the Thatcher revolution.' However, only a minority need to embrace the values of an enterprise culture to produce an improvement in economic performance.

There is ambiguous evidence about a change in attitudes from the figures for applications to university courses and about the employment of graduates. Between 1983 and 1987 demand for places in accountancy rose by over a half, with applications for economics and management studies courses up by more than a third. By contrast, demand for places in mechanical engineering and computer studies fell. There was a sharp increase in the number of graduates going into financial work, particularly with accountants but also with brokers and banks before the 1987 market crash. But there was little change in the number going into engineering and science support work. This suggests that whilst the events of the 1980s may have made young people more inclined to accept the money-making aspect of the enterprise culture – and work in the City rather than in the public sector – it has not produced any great enthusiasm for going into manufacturing industry.

The picture of unqualified success in the creation of an enterprise culture offered by ministers has not been universally accepted. The business expansion scheme has been described by Labour Party critics as an inefficient way of raising capital for business, though an efficient way of organizing tax shelters for the wealthy. A study by the Small Business Research Trust (1988) argued that the scheme had largely failed in its main aim of providing capital for small businesses, particularly those in high-risk ventures and manufacturing. Most of the money raised went to service sector businesses, mainly with wholesale, retail, property and leisure interests. The proportion of total finance invested in manufacturing declined from about a third in the first year of 1983–4 to less than a quarter in 1985–6. The popularity of issues following the publication of prospectuses meant that companies seeking smaller amounts of money via the scheme had been squeezed out, leaving an equity gap of between £100,000 and £500,000. But the Government has pointed to a study by consultants Peat Marwick McLintock in 1985 which found that only a third of the finance raised under the scheme would have been raised as equity otherwise. The expansion of other forms of venture capital after 1983 was used to justify the introduction of a restriction in the 1988 Budget limiting to £500,000 the total investment in any scheme in a single year.

Similarly, doubts were expressed about the Department of Employment's programmes to help small businesses by the National Audit Office, which examines Government accounts and activities on behalf of Parliament. Its report (August 1988) concluded that the programmes have given funds to many people who would have become self-employed anyway, while a large proportion of the companies created put existing concerns out of business, with a significant minority of the new operations failing quickly. The NAO acknowledged that the programmes had been relatively successful in supporting a large number of individuals and businesses at low administrative cost, but value-for-money could have been improved if support was focused more carefully on those concerns most likely to succeed. For instance, the enterprise allowance scheme, providing £40 a week for a year to unemployed people wanting to start their own businesses, had succeeded in helping more than 325,000 people over five years. However, roughly one-in-six have dropped out within the year, and of those businesses that completed the initial 12 months of help, a quarter failed within the next six months, mostly within four weeks of the allowance being withdrawn. After three years about three-fifths of the concerns were still in business. About two-thirds of these entrepreneurs did not employ anyone else and after three years the rate of job creation was 114 jobs per 100 surviving concerns. The NAO estimated that 44 per cent of the entrants would have gone into self-employment without the subsidy, while about half of the businesses set up with the help of the allowance displaced existing companies. The NAO pointed out that the Government scheme guaranteeing 70 per cent of a loan made by a bank to someone starting up a business had resulted in the writing-off of bad debts equivalent to a quarter of the total sums guaranteed up to 1987. Moreover, more than half of the businesses would have got bank loans without the scheme, with about three additional jobs being created per loan.

An alternative analysis is that such a failure rate is satisfactory. On this view the essence of an entrepreneurial society is to create opportunities and this inevitably leads to failures as well as successes. What matters is that there are clear and sizeable gains. For instance, Employment Secretary Norman Fowler described the results of the enterprise allowance scheme, in particular this success/failure rate, as 'very encouraging', and said that it provided further evidence of 'a growing enterprise culture.' Indeed, the small business and self-employed sector has been one of the main engines of the recovery in employment during the mid-to-late 1980s.

But as important for overall industrial performance and prospects has been the change in attitudes affecting established companies. Reports by the Confederation of British Industry, the Institute of Directors and other industry-wide bodies have been full of claims about a new climate for managers and for business. Like ministers, senior corporate executives have accepted that a fundamental change occurred in the 1979–81 period, both as a result of the shock effect of the recession and of the change in the industrial relations climate. Sir Christopher Hogg, the thinking-man's industrialist with a taste for literature, and chairman of Courtaulds, has talked of a decisive shift for the better in the British approach to business since 1979, while John Gardiner of the Laird Group has said that Mrs Thatcher's big contribution has been 'to burn up the controls and release us all. The thing she has changed is the view that the state has to solve all our problems' (both quoted in *The Thatcher Years*, 1987). In an adulatory survey in *Fortune* magazine in May 1988, entitled 'Britain is back', John Banham of the Confederation of British Industry was quoted as saying, 'there's a new generation over here. They're hungry, and they like winning.' Sir John Harvey-Jones, former chairman of ICI, claimed that, 'today's managers understand their jobs are about change – change and continuous improvement.' Professor John Stopford of the London Business School, and an industrial consultant, said, 'what's really changed in this country is that in the past business executives were never willing to put on the hair shirt of competition and take the pain. Now they are.'

The shake-out of the early 1980s improved profitability following the cutback and closure of inefficient plants and operations, with the associated large-scale redundancies. As evidence of lasting change industrialists cited improvements in the quality of financial management and sharper responses to marketing changes. Managers have also reported that, with the change in the industrial relations climate, they are having to spend less time dealing with trade union matters and officials, and more on marketing and new developments. The 3i investment and venture capital group, formerly known as Investors in Industry, has claimed that managers of smaller companies have become more willing to take risks and to expand. Sir John Cuckney, the company's chairman, attributed a sharp improvement in its 1987–8 results to a radical change in managerial attitudes to business enterprise. 'The changes taking place are both profound and positive. They constitute a social revolution that is generating significant improvements in corporate profitability', he argued.

There seems to have been a multi-stage process. First came the upheavals of the early-1980s; secondly, the consolidation of the mid-1980s as companies reorganized; and, thirdly, in the late-1980s, an aggressive phase as strengthened British groups, benefiting from a substantial recovery in profits and liquidity, began to expand and to emerge as major forces in world markets. The last phase was associated both with the stock market boom which reached its peak in the early autumn of 1987 – producing a wave of takeover activity reaching £13.5 billion in 1986, with a series of large-scale acquisitions overseas. Leading British groups expanded both in the US on a large-scale and in Europe where possible. Among the British companies with sizeable acquisitions in the US in the late 1980s were BP (the minority of Standard Oil not already owned), BAT (Farmers

Insurance), Grand Metropolitan (the Pillsbury food group), Maxwell Communications (Macmillan), Beazer (Koppers), Hanson (Kidde on top of its existing large interests), ICI (Stauffer Chemicals, also on top of large existing investments), Marks and Spencer (Brooks Brothers), Tate and Lyle (Staley), Blue Arrow (Manpower), WPP (buying advertising agency J. Walter Thompson), Saatchi and Saatchi, while Imperial Group, and Unilever, for example, also had very large assets. Such expansion meant that overseas operations of various kinds, especially in the US and the rest of the European community, have become proportionately much more important for virtually all leading British companies. In many cases domestic sales and profits constitute well under half the total – a change of profound, and still under-appreciated, importance for the conduct of industrial policy, reducing the impact of the actions of any interventionist government.

This activity has been matched by a high level of foreign investment into the UK. The annual report of the DTI's Invest in Britain Bureau showed that 303 direct investment projects in Britain were announced by foreign companies during 1987. This ensured the safeguarding, or creation, of nearly 37,000 jobs, a 42 per cent increase on 1986. US groups remained the largest investors: their spending in the UK was equivalent to the total US investment in West Germany, France and Italy combined. Nevertheless, the scale of overseas mergers and acquisitions, as opposed to direct investment in factories, by British companies, especially in the US, was much higher than the takeovers of UK concerns. Overseas acquisitions and mergers by UK companies totalled £8.9 billion in 1986, £11.5 billion in 1987, and £8.4 billion in 1988, of which over three-quarters was in the US where Britain is the largest purchaser of investments. By contrast, acquisitions in the UK by overseas groups totalled £2.9 billion in 1986, £2.3 billion in 1987 and £45.0 billion in 1988 (the last total was boosted by the Nestle takeover of Rowntree).

Yet if Britain has become a much more attractive place in which to invest, and British managers have become more assertive, many questions remain about the extent to which an enterprise culture has been created. It is uncertain how far the gains have represented underlying changes, as opposed to a short-lived response to the macro-economic upheavals of the early 1980s. It has been argued that the revival of the entrepreneurial spirit has occurred primarily in the service and distribution sectors. These advances should not be underrated, and the London stock market, for instance, made long-overdue changes in the mid-1980s to be able to compete for international securities business. At the prompting largely of the Bank of England, a deal was agreed between the Government and the Stock Exchange in 1983 which led to the scrapping of the previous restrictive rules, including the distinction between jobbers and brokers. This led rapidly to a new framework whereby most of the leading firms became part of larger concerns with much bigger capital resources and able to transact business on a bigger scale. The counterpart was a new regulatory system supervised by the Securities and Investments Board. The changes, though controversial, were regarded as essential if London was to retain its place as a world financial centre. However, the number of participants in the market shrunk following the sharp drop in share prices in October 1987 and the consequent drop in business. Within the financial services sector, evidence of a more entrepreneurial attitude was also seen in the greater competition for customers between the banks and the building societies, with a broader range of services offered.

By contrast, such a revival of entrepreneurial activity has been seen only in a few expanding areas of manufacturing where the most intense international competition has to be faced. These have included pharmaceuticals, aerospace and related defence equipment where Britain has world leaders. For instance, Glaxo's Zantac anti-ulcer treatment has overtaken its US competitor as the world's best-seller. Britain has brand leaders in some other consumer markets while British Aerospace and Racal have won overseas orders against US competition. And British Steel has transformed its productivity performance by international standards.

But in the late 1980s there were no internationally competitive UK volume car makers or consumer electronics and telecommunications business companies comparable with Philips or Ericsson. Moreover, the biggest British manufacturers have dropped out of several markets where imports have risen sharply, such as production machinery and small screen televisions. Many companies, especially in engineering, have brought in more components from cheaper production areas like the Far East. A survey in November 1988 by *The Financial Times* of 30 of the largest manufacturing companies suggested that as a result of the changes in the 1980s producers had become 'exceedingly risk-averse. They are now more cautious about expansion, more focused on specific markets, and interested more in the value of their products than in volume.' After the big contraction of manufacturing in the second half of the 1980s, the question remains whether British industry had been left at a lasting competitive disadvantage, unable to regain lost markets and showing only isolated signs of winning a large share of expanding areas.

For example, the problems of the electronics sector were underlined by a report published in the summer of 1988 by the National Economic Development Office. This warned that, on recent trends, British companies' share of the home electronics market would have halved by 1991 compared with 15 years earlier, with little compensating success overseas. Growth had come from foreign competitors located both inside and outside the UK. According to management consultants McKinsey, who prepared the report, there has been an outdated management style with a lack of vision and strategic direction in companies such as GEC, Plessey and Ferranti – despite, or in part because of, a heavy dependence on highly successful defence subsidiaries. While the report was seen as a corrective to the over-optimistic belief that all of British industry was in the middle of a great rebirth, reservations were expressed. It was argued that the rest of Europe has few companies to rival the Japanese in the electronics field. Many of the criticisms made about the UK electronics sector – that it concentrated too much on short-term financial results and on domestic sales – have also been made about US companies in the micro-electronics, consumer electronics and personal computer areas. Moreover, the UK could boast a successful international challenger in the personal computer market in the shape of Amstrad, run by Alan Sugar, an East Ender who epitomizes the enterprise culture.

A pointer to the future of UK and other European companies came in late 1988 when GEC and Siemens of West Germany sought to take over Plessey in a major restructuring of the telecommunications and defence electronics sector. GEC also decided to merge its power generation and other heavy engineering activities in a joint company with Compagnie Generale d'Electricité of France. These operations were equivalent to a quarter of GEC's total turnover. The moves were seen as a recognition of the need for large-scale reorganization if British and other European groups were to compete in world markets.

The qualified nature of the British revival has been further underlined by a meticulous study of the manufacture of kitchen cabinets in West Germany and the UK published by the National

Institute of Economic and Social Research in its November 1987 review. The kitchen furniture industry, accounting for 19 per cent of furniture production in the UK and nearly 2 per cent of total manufacturing employment, does not involve a high degree of technical complexity which, in theory, should mean that the West German advantage in engineering does not count for much. However, the study found that in the production of cabinet panels output per employee in 1986 was twice as high in West Germany as in Britain. For the whole furniture industry West German productivity was 66 per cent higher than in Britain. The authors listed a number of explanations, including greater investment in machinery and training, differences in production organization with greater use of computers in West Germany to match customers' orders, and shortages of qualifications and skills on production lines in Britain. Yet this did not mean the British furniture industry was about to die. Far from it – many British furniture companies have been highly profitable. The comparison highlighted the differences in international competitiveness with the British companies exporting only 4 per cent of their output, while the West German businesses sold a third of their production overseas.

Yet if the record of domestic business has been patchy, the very scale of the inward investment by overseas groups could be a mixed blessing. It has raised the question whether large integrated foreign companies have been using the UK as a manufacturing satellite and the UK is in danger of becoming a branch economy. Although such companies, notably the Japanese ones, may, and often do, raise the general quality of middle management, technology and shopfloor relations through their own practices and as an example to others, the entrepreneurial drive comes from abroad. So, while these companies may indirectly influence attitudes towards enterprise, encouraging the provision and training of graduates for industry, they produce more of a managerial than an enterprise culture.

Parallel questions have arisen over the moves to create a common internal market in the European community after 1992. This will involve the removal of barriers of regulation, product specification and standards between member countries, and hence requires the establishing of common rules. The British Government has sought to ensure that the single market in goods and services is achieved.

Critics were concerned that the DTI's approach would make Britain vulnerable to overseas predators, through both exports and takeover bids. A particular worry of British industry was that the Government's merger rules might operate unfairly and discriminate against domestic companies. Thus, while a foreign company could acquire a major British concern, a merger between the two leading domestic groups in a sector to create a large force in the wider European market might be ruled out. This would be because such a deal would create a monopoly in the domestic market, even though the enlarged group would not have such a dominance in the community as a whole. British industrialists argued that this interpretation of merger policy gave foreign groups an advantageous opportunity to acquire leading British companies, and their brand names, while domestic companies have one hand tied behind their backs. On this view, merger policy should be amended to take into account Europe-wide considerations. Ministers, and Sir Gordon Borrie, the director-general of fair trading, argued that existing policy was based on the relevant market where competition applied, whether domestic or international. And this depended on how far goods were traded across national borders. Some products, which might theoretically be internationally tradeable, remained largely domestic. Following the highly controversial takeover battle for the Rowntree chocolate group in the spring of 1988 there was concern among British industrialists about the potential vulnerability of their companies to overseas takeovers.

There were also questions about the level of investment and innovation. The Government's critics argued that the recovery of manufacturing industry in the second half of the 1980s was essentially a short-term phenomenon, and that the necessary measures and developments to support a continued revival had not been taken. For instance, a report by the House of Lords select committee on science and technology in early 1987 argued: 'ultimately the goal is the UK's survival as a leading industrial nation in world competition. The UK must therefore spend sufficient to improve (or at least to maintain) its industrial and cultural base relative to those countries which are judged to be its natural competitors, making allowance for differences in size and resources. Neither Government nor industry is spending enough at present levels to restore our industrial position in world markets.' The committee, which included both chairmen of leading companies and prominent scientists, argued for a renewed Government drive and for greater action by industry to increase research efforts and associated development of new products. In its response (July 1987) the Government accepted a number of detailed recommendations for improving Government co-ordination and funding, but put the onus for raising the level of research and development firmly on industry itself. It noted that 'the prime need is for industry to increase the level of research and development it funds'.

Yet the worries continued with complaints about inadequate Government support. There was, for instance, a running debate about a decline in the world standing of Bristol scientists, which was threatening Britain's international competitiveness. A study by the Science Policy Research Unit at Sussex University found a decline in research output and impact during the 1980s, particularly in metallurgy and chemical engineering, with Japan, in particular, making large strides. The report concluded that 'the longer-term implications for the chemical and pharmaceutical sectors, one of the few science-based industrial areas where technological performance indicators show Britain still has a world-class presence, are especially worrying.'

The overall picture has, therefore, been mixed. There has undoubtedly been evidence of a revival of entrepreneurial activity, especially in the service sectors and in small business, and of a recovery of managerial self-confidence in much of manufacturing industry. These changes in attitudes, significant though they have been, do not mean that all Britain's industrial problems have been solved. The evidence has been that in many internationally competitive sectors, especially with a high technological content, British companies are not among the world leaders. Indeed, there has been a growing trade deficit in high-technology products, such as telecommunications and some consumer electronics. The familiar difficulties of managerial weakness and inadequate employee training are only being dealt with slowly.

Nonetheless, the early 1980s appear to have marked an important turning point for British industry – and for those working in business and enterprise. Sir Ian MacGregor, who led the counter-revolution at British Steel and then at British Coal (formerly called the National Coal Board), may have been exaggerating when he told a *Sunday Times* seminar in June 1988 that 'there is absolutely no question that for the first time in this century we are seeing in Britain a positive leadership role (in industry) being developed by a broad range of people. The generation of leaders lost in the First World War is now being replaced.' Yet he caught a common mood among industrialists – expressed more realistically at the same seminar by Denys Henderson of ICI 'we have got on our bikes, and we have to pedal like mad to keep up.'

5

Privatization

Privatisation is bringing about a fundamental change in the operation and efficiency of key sections of the UK economy. Its success is self-evident.

John Moore, Financial Secretary to the Treasury, Speech to Hoare Govett,
17 July 1985

First of all the Georgian silver goes, and then all the nice furniture that used to be in the saloon. Then the Canalettos go.

Harold Macmillan, first Earl of Stockton, Speech to the Tory Reform Group, 8 November 1985

Privatization has been the most striking policy innovation since 1979. The frontiers between the public and the private sectors created by the Attlee Government's nationalization programme of the late 1940s – and extended in the late 1960s and 1970s – have changed substantially.

Between 1979 and early 1989 about two-fifths of the previously state-owned industries were sold to the private sector. Major flotations before the next general election in 1991 or 1992 will raise that to two-thirds, including the electricity industry and the water authorities, and probably the rest of the Government's shareholding in British Telecom. The presumption now is that everything that can be sold should be – with British Rail and British Coal planned to follow after the next election – while the existing sales have created millions of first time shareholders.

Main privatization sales

British Aerospace: 1981 (and 1985 for remaining shares)
Cable and Wireless: 1981, 1983 and 1985
Amersham: 1982

Britoil: 1982 and 1985
Associated British Ports: 1983 and 1985
Enterprise Oil: 1984
Jaguar: 1984
British Telecom: 1984
British Gas: 1986
British Airways: 1987
Rolls Royce: 1987
British Airports Authority: 1987
British Steel: 1988

The above list excludes offers in existing quoted companies (notably British Petroleum) and sales not initially involving public flotations, such as National Freight, International Aeradio, BR Hotels, British Gas Onshore Oil, Sealink, ICL, Fairey, Inmos, Royal Ordnance and Rover Group (mostly disposals to existing quoted companies).

Privatization has been as significant a change in ownership as between 1945 and 1951, and it also represents the jewel in the crown of the Government's legislation programme, around which all shades of Tories can unite. The idea has been taken up, and copied, with explicit acknowledgement of the British influence, not only by other industrialized countries, but also by Third World governments.

But what has been achieved? Has there been an improvement in the performance of the companies and industries concerned – in their efficiency, productivity and profits? Have managers taken advantage of their increased freedom from civil service and ministerial interference? Has the consumer benefited? Has the taxpayer? What difference has having a multitude of shareholders made to the running of companies? Has independence imposed limitations on the Government's ability to pursue social objectives such as regional policy?

John Moore, then Financial Secretary to the Treasury, claimed in 1985 that the success of privatization was self-evident. But there is a difference between impact and achievement. The evidence so far is that the results have been less spectacular than claimed by ministers. Many economists have doubts about its success, particularly about the implications for the industrial efficiency of the industries concerned.

That is, however, a problem of analysis. The privatization programme has been not simply a matter of shifting assets from the public to the private sectors. It has had several goals, as Mr Moore admitted in his 1985 speech:

Our policies have been specifically designed to further a number of objectives. They are designed to lead to greater efficiency and this is demonstrated by the subsequent achievements of the companies which we have already sold. They reduce the role of the public sector and provide substantial sale receipts. They allow employees to take a direct stake in the companies in which they work and this leads to major changes of attitude. And, importantly, they provide a major stimulus to wider share ownership.

The snag is that these objectives have not necessarily, or even frequently, been compatible. The pressures to secure a rapid, uncomplicated flotation have conflicted with the desirability of increasing competition by, for example, breaking up an existing monopoly supplier, such as gas or electricity. Such reorganization takes a long time to implement.

At the heart of these criticisms is the question of whether ownership really matters in promoting economic efficiency, or whether market structure and regulation are more important. The initial debate over privatization focused mainly on ownership with both Conservative and Labour politicians arguing the advantages and disadvantages principally in terms of Whitehall versus the private sector. Nationalization was originally seen in the 1940s as a way of making public utilities like coal, the railways and power more efficient. The ethos of what became known as Morrisonian nationalization was managerialist. During the 1950s and 1960s state-owned industries were judged to have a good record of productivity, investment and management. They were added to in the late 1960s and 1970s, with British Steel, Rolls Royce, British Leyland (later Rover Group), the British National Oil Corporation and the aerospace and shipbuilding industries. But in the 1970s these industries were increasingly criticized for inefficiency. This reflected greater ministerial intervention via price controls, which led to a loss of market discipline, coupled with a stronger assertion of trade union power. This led to a demoralized and frustrated management – as well as sharply rising financial deficits.

Hence, in the early 1980s, much of the argument over privatization was about the problems of the 1970s – Whitehall interference and trade union power. Over time, however, the debate shifted, partly in response to the complaints of consumers, and as a result the worries of economists over the regulation of monopoly utilities have been given greater attention. Professor John Kay has noted (1988) how privatization was at first seen primarily as a means of reducing the power of public sector trade unions, as an instrument of labour market reform, but has since become politically central of itself, with a momentum of its own.

Privatization has only been given coherence in retrospective analysis. David Heald (1987) identified several of its elements – the substitution of (and increase in) user charges for public sector services in place of taxpayer finance; the contracting-out of local authority and public sector services to private sector companies rather than directly employed staff; denationalization whereby public sector enterprises are sold to the private sector; and liberalization whereby statutory restrictions on market entry are relaxed or removed so that previously protected public enterprises are subject to greater competitive pressures. One aspect, denationalization, has tended to be regarded as synonymous with privatization, yet others such as contracting out and liberalization have been important and may have brought greater efficiency gains, as, for example, in opening up local and long-distance bus services to competition.

Before 1979 the thinking of the Conservatives in opposition on this matter had mainly been negative – how to deal with the problem of the nationalized industries. There was considerable discussion about what to do, and Nicholas Ridley, one of the first to turn against Heathite intervention in the early 1970s, chaired a study group which produced a number of proposals for denationalization (as it was then still generally called) which appeared in *The Economist* in 1978. However, even Mr Ridley saw the main scope for action in industries which had competitors and he was sceptical about disposing of the main utilities since this would merely involve the transference of a monopoly from the public to the private sector. The Tories' public document, 'The Right Approach to the Economy', published in 1977, had noted: 'The long-term aim must be to reduce the preponderance of state ownership and to widen the base of ownership in our community.' But little specific was said.

The Conservative leadership was cautious in practice. Its 1979 election manifesto solely promised the sale back to the private sector of the recently nationalized aerospace and shipbuilding concerns, together with the aims of selling shares in the National Freight Corporation and of disposing of the National Enterprise Board's shareholdings in the private sector. The suggestion that the British National Oil Corporation (BNOC) might be sold was toned down, at the insistence of some Shadow Cabinet members, by the reference to a 'complete review of all activities of BNOC'.

As with so many other policies since 1979 it was the experience, and the frustrations, of office which produced a more radical approach. Initially, the disposals were mainly of businesses operating in a competitive environment, such as Amersham International, British Aerospace, Cable and Wireless, the National Freight Corporation and Britoil (the production side of BNOC), rather than the core public utilities.

These sales were seen as a means of holding down the public sector borrowing requirement. This became the central target for the Treasury within the medium-term financial strategy from 1980–1 onwards, especially because of the problems of controlling the money supply. But the total proceeds from sales of public sector industries were small by later standards (totalling £1.76 billion in the first 1979–83 term).

The Government's initial approach to the core nationalized industries was to establish a better relationship between Whitehall and the corporations. Tight limits were set on external finance (borrowing) with clear financial targets for rates of return over the medium term. But there were immediate problems. Borrowing needs, which count as part of public spending, were pushed up by a rapid growth in the earnings of the industries' workers and by the impact of the recession on demand for the corporations' products, and hence their finances. There were also conflicts over Whitehall pressures to reduce existing subsidies (thus pushing up prices) and over the levels of investment which affected overall public expenditure totals. The chairmen of the industries also sought greater freedom to raise capital.

A series of inquiries in the 1979–81 period examined ways of trying to improve the relationship and introduce more flexibility into the corporation's investment plans. There were, for instance, proposals to take some defined projects or financing methods outside the normal public sector borrowing limits. The snag was that it would be cheaper to raise money within the normal PSBR definitions and, anyway, the markets would believe that loans raised by bodies like British Telecom had implicit Treasury backing since the company could never be allowed to go under. Problems over the suggested Buzby Bonds for British Telecom led to acceptance of the idea that the utility should be privatized, largely as a way of overcoming these constraints on its capital investment. That idea was put forward by Patrick Jenkin, who became Industry Secretary in September 1981 in a wide-ranging ministerial reshuffle which also brought Nigel Lawson to the Department of Energy, giving a new impetus to the whole programme.

By then the frustrations had led both ministers and nationalized industry chairmen to see privatization as an attractive solution. Mr Lawson summed up the new mood in a speech in September 1982, when he argued that 'no industry should remain under state ownership unless there is a positive and overwhelming case for it so doing'. That led to an increase in the sales of parts of the public sector, such as Associated British Ports, and, in particular, to the proposed disposal of British Telecom.

The programme only developed coherence and prominence after the 1983 election when Nigel Lawson became Chancellor. Under his direction John Moore became responsible for privatization and produced a detailed forward programme involving all departments, together with a campaign of speeches to explain and justify the policy. The target for proceeds from sales of state industries was increased, first to over £2 billion, and then to £5 billion annually from 1986–7 onwards, as shown in table 5.1.

Table 5.1   Privatization receipts

Financial year	£ million
1979–80	377
1980–81	405
1981–82	493
1982–83	488
1983–84	1,142
1984–85	2,132
1985–86	2,702
1986–87	4,403
1987–88	5,161
1988–89 (estimated)	6,000
1989–90 (planned)	5,000
1990–91 (planned)	5,000

Source: Treasury statements

The change of pace, and mood, has been vividly explained by Gerry Grimstone who was the Treasury assistant secretary responsible for privatisation from 1982 to 1986 before moving to the merchant bank Schroders. He noted (1987) that 'in the early days of the privatisation programme, sales were generally regarded within the Government as a series of individual market transactions best conducted within traditional parameters that had served the City well over the years'. But following the early successes there was a change of pace: 'a privatisation programme rather than a series of ad hoc sales began to emerge'.

In the Government's second term, 1983–7, sales included half the Government's holding in British Telecom (involving a number of innovative marketing techniques and incentives), followed by the whole of British Gas, the Trustee Savings Bank (though this produced no financial gain for the Treasury), British Airways, Enterprise Oil, Sealink, Jaguar, and Rolls Royce, together with the residual holdings in British Aerospace and Cable Wireless. British Airports Authority followed just after the 1987 election.

At first glance, the record of the privatized companies looks good. Ministers can, and do, point to significant increases in the profits of both Cable and Wireless and British Aerospace since privatization in 1981, and a three-fold improvement in National Freight's profits up to 1987, and a trebling in Amersham's profits in the six years from its flotation in 1982.

Yet, impressive though these figures are, they have to be seen in the context of a sharp improvement in the profitability of British industry generally since the late 1970s – and, in particular, a dramatic turnround in the results of those industries remaining in the public sector. Professor John Kay of the London Business School has pointed out (in Kay, Mayer and Thompson, 1986) that 'the most marked improvement has occurred, not in the privatised industries, but in those which have remained in public ownership'. For instance, British Steel achieved rises in output per person of 10 per cent a year between 1979 and 1987, well ahead of privatization. Similarly, British Rail's efficiency gains have exceeded those of British Telecom and British Gas.

The Treasury's own figures (1987) show that among these industries still in the public sector in late 1987 there was a 45 per cent increase in productivity (as measured by output per person employed) in the eight years up to 1986–7. This compares with a rise of

Table 5.2 Productivity in public and privatized sectors: total factor productivity, annual percentage rate of increase

	1979–88	1979–83	1983–8
British Airports	1.6	0.0	2.8
British Coal[a]	2.9	0.6	4.6
British Gas	3.3	−0.2	6.2
British Rail	1.3	−0.4	2.7
British Steel	12.9	8.4	12.4
British Telecom	2.4	2.0	2.5
Electricity supply	1.4	−1.6	4.0
Post Office	3.7	3.6	3.3
Average	3.7	1.6	4.8

[a] adjusted for effects of the 1984–5 coal strike.
Source: Kay and Bishop, 1985

less than 40 per cent for the more efficient manufacturing sector, and of just over 20 per cent for the whole economy, excluding North Sea Oil. There are similar comparisons for other measures of cost control – the Post Office reducing unit costs by 11 per cent in real terms in the five years to 1986–7 – and in profitability, mainly since 1983. The starting point in the late 1970s was, of course, very low after what the Treasury has called 'years of financial problems and subsidisation.' Overall, as table 5.2 shows, there does not appear to be anything uniquely good in the performance of companies which have been privatized compared with those which have remained in the public sector.

Professor Kay (in Kay and Bishop, 1988) has suggested that the answer may lie in a more assertive management style, matching what was happening in the economy as a whole, though more marked because of the extent of earlier problems. The frustrations of the 1979–81 period led to the imposition of tight financial controls and the appointment of dynamic chairmen – such as Lord King at British Airways and Sir Ian MacGregor at British Coal (formerly the National Coal Board). There have been confrontations between management and trade unions at British Steel, British Rail and British Coal, with far-reaching reorganizations and labour cutbacks also at British Airways. The steel and coal battles with the unions during the long and expensive strikes in 1979–80 and 1984–5, respectively, were only won by their managements because they were in the public sector. The coal and electricity industries' losses of £3 billion resulting from the miners' strike were funded by the Government. Yet the industries might never have got in the position leading up to such strikes if they had been in the private sector. But, like elsewhere in industry, there has been a drop in days lost through strikes in both privatized and nationalized concerns.

The clearcut picture of the advantages of privatization as often presented by ministers is naive and over-simplified. There have been gains, both before and after flotations. This has worked in various ways. The prospect of privatization has meant that groups have reorganized and put themselves on a more commercial footing – bringing in new senior management and moving away from a bureaucratic mentality. There is also greater freedom to take decisions when matters do not have to be referred to Whitehall for approval. Top managements have wanted to secure the greater rewards of the private sector. This has been reflected not only in the higher salaries of senior executives in privatized, as opposed to nationalized, concerns, but also in the opportunity to build up wealth by owning shares in these companies. Even after the sharp fall in the stock market in October 1987 the share prices of most privatized concerns were still above their flotation levels.

Widely recognized examples of a more commercially aggressive approach after privatization include National Freight, Jaguar (though its profits were rising sharply anyway before its flotation), and Cable and Wireless. The list attracted a highly respected new chairman in Sir Eric Sharp who has proved to be an innovator in the private sector, helping to set up Mercury and expanding its involvement in the Far East. Associated British Ports has also been developing 2,000 acres of land which had been ruled out when it was state-owned. In some cases it may have been as much the preparations for privatization as the disciplines of the market which led to a sharpening-up of management and an improvement in performance. For instance, the very large advances by British Steel were given an added impetus by the desire of top management under chairman Sir Robert Scholey to see the corporation privatized as quickly as possible. By contrast, companies like Amersham had already been operating since 1965 on a commercial basis and argued that much of what it had done since being sold would have been undertaken anyway.

The internal impact of privatization was summed up by Sir George

Jefferson, the then chairman of British Telecom, in the Quilter Goodison lecture in 1985. He maintained that before privatization British Telecom had only been an administration, not a business. It had only one profit centre and its accounts were regularly qualified. Promotion owed more to hierarchy than to risk-taking and the commercial development of the business was centred on engineering concepts rather than market and commercial needs. But all this, he said, had changed with privatization. There were new attitudes as methods of appointment were changed and initiative by managers was encouraged. Yet outsiders wondered how much had really changed at British Telecom given its mixed performance after privatization.

The main qualification applies to the public utilities – British Telecom, British Gas, the electricity and water industries – which have traditionally been monopoly suppliers. There has been a lengthy, and growing, debate about how those industries should be privatized. As discussed earlier, the Tories were initially reluctant to transfer a monopoly from the public to the private sector given the apparent limitations on increasing competition. In the case of British Telecom a measure of liberalization was introduced before the privatization decision was taken. Legislation in 1981 removed British Telecom's monopoly on the provision of attachments to the tele-phone network and allowed greater competition in the market for equipment. At the same time, the Government said it would licence Mercury as a competitor to British Telecom in long-distance tele-phone services (initially it had been a consortium involving Cable and Wireless, British Petroleum and Barclays Bank, but now is wholly owned by the privatized Cable and Wireless). However, Mercury took some time to get into its stride, in part because of trade union opposition and hurdles erected by British Telecom. The latter still had the vast majority of the business market and, apart from Hull, virtually all domestic consumers.

The decision in principle to privatize British Telecom was largely a response to its desire for greater freedom to raise capital. But there was a lengthy internal debate in Whitehall about the method. Suggestions were made that the 1981 liberalization should be extended and the corporation should be broken up into regional operating groups – on the precedent of the partial break-up of ATT&T in the US, to ensure more competition.

However, in a crucial decision which set the later pattern, the

Government decided to privatize British Telecom as one entity. It was argued that a break-up would result in a delay of anything from two to five years as separate companies were established with distinct commercial structures. But there was pressure from the Treasury to go ahead more rapidly to raise money to hold down public sector borrowing. The merchant banks advised that a single unit would be most attractive to investors, particularly given the desirability, and need, to gain support of the public. Reflecting a continuing conflict of objectives, speed of sale and market considerations were all valued more highly than competition.

Consequently, emphasis was put on the regulation of what would remain a monopoly supplier to most of its customers. The decision was taken to set up the Office of Telecommunications (Oftel) to protect the interests of users and to oversee the rules to ensure competition. A similar body, the Office of Gas Supplies (Ofgas) was then set up to regulate British Gas and others were established for later industries. Ground rules for British Telecom were laid down following a report by Professor Stephen Littlechild. He recommended that the increase in British Telecom's prices should be tied to the retail prices index minus an arbitrary figure designed to reflect cost-reducing changes in the technology of the industry. A figure of minus 3 per cent below the rate of increase in retail prices was chosen.

A number of economists – plus a handful of MPs – had doubts about whether this regulatory regime would be tough enough in the absence of greater competition. Two Oxford economists, John Vickers and George Yarrow (1985) made the general point:

If liberalisation and regulatory reform offer clear advantages, and if the net benefits from a change in ownership are at best ambiguous, then the primary focus of policy should be on liberalisation and regulation reform, rather than on changing ownership. Above all, policies to transfer ownership should not be allowed to stand in the way of proper and adequate measures to reduce entry barriers, increase competition and generally improve incentive structures.

In particular, Vickers and Yarrow questioned the method of privatizing British Telecom which, they said, seemed to be based on selling the company rapidly. On their view, the Government did not go far enough in regard to competition: 'for the most part an illiberal regime of competition has been created.' Instead, they favoured changes to remove restrictions on the resale of transmission capacity and they argued that regulation of British Telecom's tariffs should not necessarily be seen as temporary, but should be continued and toughened, depending on whether effective competition emerged.

However, the doubts of many economists were overshadowed by the remarkable marketing success of British Telecom, attracting 2 million shareholders, more than a half new investors. According to Gerry Grimstone (1987), this sale set the precedent for the future: 'it showed what could be done and thus put into play even the largest of the nationalised industries.'

Mr Grimstone noted: 'there had always been a reluctance within the Government to privatise British Gas as a monopoly despite, or perhaps because of, (chairman) Sir Denis Rooke's preference for this course of action.' In the post-British Telecom euphoria, 'a pragmatic shift of opinion occurred within the Government in favour of wider share ownership and it suddenly became attractive to privatise British Gas in its present form rather than to break it up. British Gas might not be the most exciting of investments but because of its market position it was certainly safe, at least for the foreseeable future. A well thought-out regulatory regime could limit any economic damage.'

Similarly, an exuberant John Moore argued in April 1985 that privatization had proved to be of 'such major benefit' that the Government had decided it was right to extend it progressively to natural monopolies – where economies of scale and barriers to entry are such that it would be artificial, wasteful or impractical to break them up. 'I firmly believe that where competition is impractical privatisation policies have now been developed to such an extent that regulated private ownership of natural monopolies is preferable to nationalisation.'

So the programme continued with British Gas in 1986, British Airports Authority in 1987, and electricity and water in 1989. Yet the language of Mr Grimstone and Mr Moore is revealing. Mr Grimstone referred to the need for limiting any economic damage. Mr Moore almost brushed aside worries about competition by arguing that privatization increased productive efficiency, whether or not a monopoly is involved, because of the pressure from outside shareholders and capital markets.

The Government was in alliance with the managements of the

industries in working to retain monopoly structures and to limit competition. Ministers were enthusiastic about wider share owner-ship and rapid flotations, and executives wanted to preserve the status quo. Professor Kay (in Kay and Bishop, 1988) has pointed to the paradox that privatization can be speedy and harmonious only if it is supported by the senior managers of the industries. But this support and co-operation has reflected the absence of any incentive for managers to impose new competitive disciplines upon themselves. This was reinforced in the case of British Gas when the sponsoring department was headed by a minister, Peter Walker, who was a supporter of Sir Denis Rooke (having appointed him in the first place) and was highly sceptical about the scope for introducing competition. Treasury ministers were heard to complain about Mr Walker being in Sir Denis's pocket.

The post-flotation strength of the share prices of British Telecom and British Gas, and their profit records, continued to quell public doubts for some time. Moreover, Professor Sir Bryan Carsberg proved to be an effective first director-general of Oftel. He was not afraid to stand up to British Telecom. For instance, in October 1984 a joint venture between British Telecom and IBM to run a manage-ment data transmission and processing network was blocked on the grounds that the scale of the project would deter new entrants and thus limit competition. A year later, in October 1985, Oftel made a ruling on the terms and conditions by which British Telecom should connect Mercury's system at exchanges. In spite of British Telecom's lobbying, Oftel's decision was seen as helping Mercury and was important in establishing Professor Carsberg's credibility as an independent regulator.

Cento Veljanovski describes Oftel's record as a good one in his broadly sympathetic study of privatization (1986). He points out in response to criticism that 'it is a strange lapdog that threatens its master with the Restrictive Trade Practices Court.' However, he adds that without detracting from the effect of Professor Carsberg of Oftel, 'the telecommunications sector is perhaps unique among the utility industries because in it competition is possible. Gas, water and the other utilities pose much more serious problems and it is disturbing that Ofgas has much narrower powers and is a much smaller agency.' Moreover, Vickers and Yarrow have argued (1988) in a more sceptical study that, while Oftel has been energetic in price regulation, nothing required the regulator to adopt the active pro-competition stance it has taken. They have concluded: 'the effectiveness of regulation in the future will depend heavily upon the attitudes that regulatory bodies, the Monopolies and Mergers Commission and government ministers choose to adopt.'

Apart from Professor Carsberg's warnings, an underswell of public annoyance developed about the quality of British Telecom's services to its customers. Curiously, and fortunately for the Conservatives, these complaints only reached the front pages after the June 1987 General Election. Afterwards, there was an upsurge of public discontent, as previously ignored complaints and two breakdowns in central London were given maximum publicity.

Behind the dramatic headlines which followed there was evidence of public concern. In July 1987 the National Consumer Council published a Mori report showing that 52 per cent of the 1,900 people interviewed thought that British Telecom's prices were unreasonable. This compared with 40 per cent who had held the same view in 1980. British Telecom has consistently argued that it had been improving its standard of services with its replacement programme for out-of-date equipment and exchanges. The liberalization of the early 1980s had reduced waiting lists for subscriber equipment, and also led to a flourishing of the independent installation industry which was given a further boost in 1988 with the removal by Oftel of British Telecom's monopoly of the approval of telecommunications equipment put in by private contractors on business premises. Indeed, the greatest benefits to the consumer appear to have come in areas where there has been liberalization and greater competition, rather than in the core businesses.

Professor Carsberg quickly made clear his sympathy with consumer complaints. Under pressure from him British Telecom announced a series of service targets, which led to a sharp improvement in the number of working call-boxes during the first half of 1988, the more rapid clearing of faults, and the quicker completion of orders. British Telecom went further in offering to compensate customers for delays beyond its control in repairing faults and installing lines from April 1989 – at a rate of £5 a day for every day's delay in installing a line after an agreed date and if it failed to repair a fault within two days of a report. British Telecom set itself the target of clearing business faults in five hours and residential faults in a day. Similarly, Mercury also offered compensation for late installation.

More fundamentally, British Telecom was under threat from

reviews of its pricing system and of its competitive position. There was general agreement that price regulation of British Telecom's services should continue where there is no effective competition. Further ahead, the Government faced a decision on whether to break the British Telecom/Mercury duopoly of basic services such as two-way telephone lines, international calls and business data transmission. It looked unlikely that they would because additional mainstream competitors might damage Mercury more than British Telecom. Mercury has begun to consider moving from its initial concentration on large corporate customers to attracting small business and residential consumers as well – with, for example, Mercury phone boxes.

New competition in the 1990s is likely to come away from the core businesses in, for example, mobile communications and telecommunications services over cable television networks. In February 1988 the Government had already proposed a liberalization of satellite communications services involving transmission from a single source to a number of subscribers. A possible example was the transmission of television signals of horse races by large bookmakers to hundreds of High Street betting shops, so far handled by British Telecom. Moreover, the Government is likely to inject competition by allowing companies to lease circuits from British Telecom and to resell them for simple direct communications known as single voice traffic.

There has been less public controversy over the services provided by the other major utility, British Gas. However, there have been arguments between James McKinnon, director of Ofgas, and British Gas over the provision of adequate information about the formula which determines the corporation's prices. This has allowed British Gas to raise prices by two percentage points less than the annual rate of retail price increases – plus an amount to compensate for increases in the cost of gas supplies from the North Sea – in order to guard against the corporation making excess profits from its domestic consumers. Mr McKinnon eventually won a year-long battle with British Gas, which included the threat of legal action, so that figures would be prepared separating its profits in the monopoly business serving domestic customers from profits in the unregulated industrial market.

Nevertheless, the controversy over British Telecom's standards affected the privatization debate from summer 1987 onwards. Even leading advocates accepted that there was a danger of the whole concept of privatization being brought into disrepute. According to Mori surveys, public backing for the sale of the electricity industry fell. However, overall, there was a small net balance believing that privatization was a good, rather than bad, thing for the country as a whole. On a longer-term basis various Mori surveys have pointed to a steady decline in the number favouring denationalization since the start of the programme in the early 1980s.

Ministers concluded that the privatization of electricity had to be different from that of British Gas. Consumer interests had to be seen to be protected by the injection of competition. This produced a lively debate during the autumn and winter of 1987–8 between the free-market advocates supporting the injection of competition and the Central Electricity Generating Board (CEGB) run by Lord Marshall of Goring who defended an integrated generating and transmission system. There was the further twist of an Energy Secretary, Cecil Parkinson, who was eager to re-establish himself after four years in the wilderness.

The debate turned on the scope for extending competition. But this tended to obscure discussion of the CEGB's longstanding weaknesses – the inefficiency and high cost involved in the construction of new power stations, and its reliance, by Government instruction, on expensive domestically produced coal. In the debate it was accepted that distribution to consumers had to remain a monopoly, albeit a highly regulated one, since it would be impossible to have competing power lines in a street. Secondly, the transmission system through the national grid had to stay as a single entity. In has been owned by the CEGB, but its ownership could be transferred either to the distribution companies or to a separately controlled public utility. Finally, there was the core generating business which offered the main scope for competition.

The CEGB argued that the way to secure more competition was by the construction of new power stations – though this would leave it the dominant operator for decades. The board said that an integrated system was the best guarantee consumers could have that the lights would stay on since this offered flexibility and economies of sale. By contrast, the CEGB said fragmentation would threaten security of supply and reduce efficiency, while also raising questions over the development of nuclear power and the new generation of pressurized water reactors being started at Sizewell in Suffolk. This view was backed up by a research paper commissioned on behalf of the CEGB from George Yarrow, the Oxford economist who had earlier pressed for greater competition in British Telecom. Yarrow argued that the special characteristics of electricity put a high premium on the benefits of co-ordination and integration. He said the central question was whether such co-ordination could be achieved more effectively by contractual arrangements with several parties as within a single organization. Yarrow maintained that the experience of California and other US states indicated the feasibility of promoting competition via effective regulation of a dominant incumbent utility. By contrast, he argued that a break-up would not automatically ensure competition, but would have to be managed, involving a detailed regulation more complex than would be the case with one dominant firm.

In the end, the radical, or rather semi-radical option, won and the Government's White Paper (published in February 1988) outlined a scheme involving the break-up of the CEGB. Its monopoly of electricity generation would be ended by transferring 30 per cent of its existing capacity (including a range of coal, oil and gas, but not nuclear plants) to a competing company (Power-Gen). The rest of the CEGB, to be known as National Power, would own the remaining 70 per cent of capacity, including the nuclear stations. The CEGB would also lose control of the national grid to a company owned jointly by all the distribution companies and would thus no longer have a statutory obligation to provide bulk supplies of electricity. The 12 existing area boards would be privatized as distribution companies which would take on the statutory obligation to supply in their areas. These distributors would also have the right to generate electricity themselves where this would not create local monopolies in production and supply.

The Government argued that this would ensure greater competition since the distributors would have a choice of supply among the following: the two main generating companies created out of the CEGB, private generators, their own generating capacity, the two separate Scottish supplies, or from France. However, both the transmission system through the national grid and the local distribution framework would remain natural monopolies and, like British Gas, would be regulated by a structure of price control with the creation of an Office of Electricity Supply. Moreover, the proposals envisaged a guaranteed standard of service with a pre-determined level of financial compensation in the event of failure to meet these levels of provision.

Free-market critics who had been critical of the monopoly aspects of the British Telecom and British Gas privatizations gave a guarded welcome to the electricity proposals. However, some commentators wondered whether the Government might not have gone further and created four or five, rather than two generating companies, thus allowing scope for yardstick regulation whereby prices would be geared to the costs of the most efficient. Professor Colin Robinson argued in a paper for the Institute of Economic Affairs (1988) that the proposals gave only the appearance of competition since there was the risk of collusion between the two successor companies to the CEGB, over-dependence on the regulatory authority and difficulties for new market entrants faced with established companies with an ability to cross-subsidies and engage in predatory pricing. George Yarrow was also concerned that the generators would collude in an attempt to keep newcomers out. This might lead to underinvestment because of the increased uncertainties, and he saw a need to regulate wholesale, as well as retail, prices to ensure fair competition.

Critics also pointed to an apparent inconsistency between the Government's avowed free-market beliefs and the large subsidies for nuclear power built into the privatization plans. Distributors would be required to buy a minimum proportion of non-fossil fuelled generating capacity and there would be a specific nuclear levy identified in consumers' bills. This would be in addition to up to £2.5 billion in grants, loans and guarantees for other nuclear costs, including decommissioning atomic stations at the end of their life. This might in practice give artificial protection to the nuclear programme, in view of its very high development and construction costs which increased the price of the electricity it produced relative to coal and oil fired stations. (However, the distributors would be free to buy from France.) The Government argued that such support for nuclear power was necessary not only to ensure diversified sources of supply by, for example, helping to defeat the miners' strike, but would also ensure that Britain retained an involvement in this sort of power if the economics of nuclear generation should improve in time. Oxford economist Dieter Helm commented that, 'nuclear power is an example par excellence of the contradictions in Thatcherism – trust the market as long as it gives the "right" answers.'

The fear of Labour and the trade unions was that the more

competitive structure would undermine the traditional relationship between the CEGB and the British Coal – as ministers intended it to do – and would threaten jobs in the pits. The CEGB has traditionally bought coal at well above world prices; British Coal has cost between £500 million and £700 million more a year for the electricity industry than buying coal from overseas. The extent of changes in costs will depend both on British Coal's improvements in efficiency and on movements in the free-market price of coal, which would be affected by big purchases by the British electricity industry. Labour spokesmen also argued that electricity prices were being raised by an unnecessarily large amount to increase rates of return ahead of flotation – about 7 per cent in real terms in 1989–90.

The Tory-dominated Commons select committee on energy (1988) also expressed doubts about the privatization plans. The MPs said it was clear that the Government was 'daily discovering new problems which need to be solved'. Its doubts focused on the restructuring of the industry, the lack of precision over the regulatory arrangements (over which the Government will retain considerable powers), the place of nuclear power and the future of the coal industry.

In parallel, there has been considerable controversy about the proposed sale of the water authorities, with widely expressed environmental as well as commercial objections. The Government plans to sell the existing regional water authorities separately, though only their water and sewerage functions. Responsibility for environmental and regulatory matters such as reservoirs, rivers, and fishing rights, will stay in the public sector through a new National Rivers Authority. This privatization, while raising very different issues from the others, turned into one of the most bitterly fought and uncertainly handled by the Government, with arguments over standards of water purity and threatened large price rises. Public support for water privatization was much less than for other utility sales.

The other side of the privatization debate has been how far publicly quoted companies are subject to the disciplines of the capital market – to shareholder, as well as customer, pressure. This is separate from the debate about the inherent desirability, and impact, of spreading share ownership as part of popular capitalism, as will be discussed in chapter 6. The theory is that as a result of the transfer from Whitehall control to a quoted status, the boards of privatized companies are continuously subject to market pressures to improve their performance. The level of share prices affects the ability to raise new capital – and crucially its cost – while the ultimate market sanction for the managers of quoted companies is being taken over. For dominant public utilities like British Telecom and British Gas this can create a conflict between the ability and desire of managers to maximize returns for shareholders and the dangers of such exploitation of monopoly power for the interests of the consumer. That is why the initial decisions on the regulatory framework have been of such crucial importance in privatization.

Moreover, shareholdings have been widely spread, both because of the size and stock market capitalizations of the privatized utilities and the desire to boost wider share ownership. This is despite the fall in the number of private shareholders in the years after flotations and the concentration of most shares in the hands of the leading financial institutions. Consequently, no single holder, or group of holders, has been large enough to challenge the dominance of the management. In practice, most of the privatized utilities, as opposed to the smaller manufacturing concerns, have been seen as bid-proof and never likely to be taken over, for reasons either of size or political importance. Hence the management of British Telecom and British Gas have been free of the threat applying to all but the largest other publicly quoted groups. The disciplines of the market have been qualified.

A further constraint has been the existence of special or golden shares enabling the Government to outvote all other shareholders. The practical significance of such shares has come under question following the takeover bid by BP for Britoil. Initially, the Treasury said it would use its golden share to resist a change of control. But then after BP pressed ahead with its bid the Treasury said that it was mainly concerned about an 'unacceptable' takeover, and, in February 1988, it negotiated an arrangement with BP intended to safeguard Britoil's Scottish identity. In all other cases, except Enterprise Oil, the golden share was intended to prevent any single shareholder owning more than 15 per cent of a privatized company's equity, hence preventing unwelcome large foreign owners. While doubts have persisted about the practical effects of the golden share provisions, at least the privatized utilities can be regarded as bid-proof.

A different form of shareholder influences has existed through the deliberate policy to encourage employee investors in the privatized companies. For instance, over 95 per cent of employees participated in the original offer of shares in Cable and Wireless, Amersham and

British Telecom, while in several other concerns the involvement was well over 70 per cent, with only Jaguar below 20 per cent. In some cases, the advice of trade unions not to buy was totally ignored. Of course, this was a response to very generous terms, such as discounts and free shares. Moreover, most of these worker share-holdings were small in relation to the companies as a whole, amounting to less than 2 per cent of the total for British Telecom and to less than 4 per cent for both British Aerospace and Amersham. Only in the much trumpeted case of National Freight did the workers control the company, with over 80 per cent of the shares. This was because of the unusual circumstances of the management/employee buy-out. Otherwise, it is hard to find examples of the employees exerting any control over their companies. But the attitudes of these worker-shareholders may have changed. However small their share-holdings, both for themselves financially and relative to the com-panies' total equity, they may identify more with the company and its prospects, and profits, and this may affect industrial relations. This could be a contributory factor to the reduced number of strikes in these companies.

For the utilities, as the row in 1987 over British Telecom's services to consumers showed, the only real disciplines are applied by the regulatory bodies, not the stock market. Professor Sir Bryan Cars-berg of Oftel is more important than any shareholder. Admittedly, British Telecom's annual meeting in 1987 proved to be a very lively affair, but that was largely because small investors were using the opportunity to make protests as customers rather than as share-holders. In general, powerful chairmen like Sir Denis Rooke re-mained, before his retirement, as much barons as they were in the days before privatization. And, depending on the effectiveness of their regulators, they are even freer of external constraints.

In any overall assessment, privatization has had a positive impact on the efficiency and commercial success of the companies con-cerned. As Professor John Kay (in Kay and Bishop, 1988) has argued: 'it is very doubtful whether any of the changes in nationalised industry attitudes could have occurred if privatization had not been on the agenda.' Privatization is 'neither necessary nor sufficient for improving efficiency, but it has been a central part of the story'.

The industries are now in general operating on a more commercial basis than when they were under close Treasury control and subject to political pressures on pricing and investment. Some of this reflects the specific shake-up produced by the privatization drive, and some the more general shift in the balance of power within industry away from the trade unions towards management. The sharp rise in the profits and performance of the privatized concerns may therefore reflect once-and-for-all influences. There is no doubt that some industries are stronger and more efficient than before. But the criticism of the service of British Telecom's core business and its mixed success with new initiatives, like its Mitel acquisition, indicate caution. The main gains to the consumer have come in areas like the provision of equipment and new services where there has been liberalization and the opening-up of competition – together with the prod of the regulator.

There have been obvious defects. The cost of the sales, in fees to City institutions and in advertising, has been high, amounting to a total of £620 million, or roughly 6.5 per cent of the total proceeds, in the cases of British Telecom and British Gas. The pricing of some issues has been widely regarded as too generous to those fortunate enough to obtain shares. Premia at the end of the first day's trading for the main privatizations have varied from 12.5 per cent for British Gas up to 43 per cent for British Telecom (where on paper and in theory there was a £1.29 billion increase in capital values for share-holders in a single day) and 44 per cent for British Airways. First day premia are not in themselves unusual, but the scale has been two to three times higher than for other new issues. Several reports from the Public Accounts Committee of the Commons have recommended changes in the methods of sale, both to reduce underwriting fees and to cut the size of the first day premia – they suggest this might be done, for example, by variations of sale by tender, as was partly used with the British Airports Authority offer in July 1987. But as the flop (for investors) of the large BP sale in autumn 1987 showed, the underwriters can lose. As Professor Kay noted:

Whatever the wider economic consequences of privatization, it has proved a highly remunerative activity for three groups: the initial shareholders of privatized companies; the managers of these companies (whose salaries have risen sharply, in part to catch up with private sector levels); and the extensive group of professional advisers who have been involved in the privatization process.

Vickers and Yarrow (1988) have argued that a less hasty programme of share sales would have enabled the Government to sell a proportion of the shares, in smaller tranches (rather than an entire company), as the Japanese did with an initial offer of just 10 per cent of the NTT telecommunications group. This would have permitted the more accurate pricing of late tranches. The authors have also questioned the distributional consequences by arguing that in economic terms the transfers of wealth are arbitrary and undesirable since the gainers have borne little risk and many of the windfall profits have gone overseas. Overall taxation is also higher than it would have been if pricing were more accurate, and sale proceeds greater.

The rush to privatize has often resulted in inadequate industrial structures. Privatization has been regarded as a good in itself, with insufficient regard for broadening competition and consumer interests. Both British Telecom and British Gas have enjoyed a continuing monopoly position in their core domestic businesses, even though more competitive options were available. Effective regulation is no substitute for greater competition. Yet this does not of itself invalidate the case for removing these utilities from the control of Whitehall, while also reducing trade union influence. Indeed, one of the most intriguing, and little discussed, results of privatization may have been to reduce Whitehall's ability to influence industrial decisions, such as the location and construction of certain types of power station, or the prices charged by the industries through subsidies.

If privatization appears a more flawed programme than Conservative propaganda pretends, it is undoubtedly an idea whose time has arrived. Privatization is one of the few British economic developments which has been consciously copied overseas. The Treasury pointed out in 1986 that 'many governments and state enterprises have sent delegations here to study at first hand the practical techniques that have been employed. The UK's lead in these developments is also opening-up opportunities for City firms to market their expertise abroad.' France has been particularly active in selling state enterprises, though with some problems in 1987–8, as have Italy, Spain and West Germany. Canada and Japan have been the most prominent outside Europe in selling state assets, although the idea has also been taken up by Third World countries like Brazil and Mexico, to help reduce the size of their state sectors and their public deficits. As Oliver Letwin has pointed out (1988), there have been substantial cost savings from the privatization of US bus services and from the contracting-out of a wide range of services in Japan.

Within the UK, most of the privatizations since 1979 appear irreversible, at least in the sense that it is highly improbable that they would be renationalized in their previous form. However, such is their central importance to the economy that if any of the main privatized industries ran into serious trouble in, for example, a recession, the Government of the day would be forced to provide help, even if it fell short of a state rescue and takeover as with Rolls-Royce and British Leyland in the 1970s. However, this is unlikely since the monopoly public utilities are almost by definition able to protect their financial position.

The Labour Party modified its approach following its defeat in the 1983 election to one of 'social ownership' whereby control of public utilities would revert to the Government. Individual shareholders would remain, albeit on a restricted non-voting basis, with an alternative of selling at the original flotation price. A Labour government would take stakes in some strategic industries such as aerospace. However, following its further defeat in the 1987 election, Labour started to alter its approach even further. Alan Tuffin of the Union of Communications Workers has argued that the attempt in 1987 to square the circle of protecting individual shareholders' rights without rewarding speculators appeared both to trade unionists in the privatized sector and to the general public as a state 'grab-back'. He urged a broadening of share ownership to workers, through wage-earner funds and US-style employee share ownership plans. According to Mr Tuffin, 'whether an enterprise is under private or public ownership is secondary to the wider needs of the British economy'. Such talk was anathema to the party's vocal minority of fundamentalists. But Labour's revisionists argued that new forms of Government – industry partnerships – were necessary, based on the familiar Japanese and Swedish examples. Overall, it was necessary to go back to first principles when deciding how far market operations should be regulated and controlled, while accepting, in the words of trade and industry spokesman Bryan Gould, that 'nationally-directed public ownership is right for natural monopolies and other strategic industries'. This new emphasis was reflected in the party's May 1989 policy review statement. Yet, as its opposition to electricity privatization showed, Labour's attempt to be the party of consumers was affected by its links to the producer interest of the unions.

Cento Veljanovski, a strong supporter of privatization, has argued

(1987) that the political returns from privatization have been high for the Tories:

The party has shown it is radical and willing to take a committed approach to industrial problems. There has not been any serious political opposition and the evidence so far indicates that it has been well received by the electorate. The opposition parties are largely in disarray and very few, even within the Labour Party, regard renationalisation as a serious option.

However, even he concedes:

On the minus side there are justifiable criticisms of the way some of the shares were priced, the costs involved and the failure to break up British Telecom and British Gas to create a less monolithic structure for the utility industries. The tensions between competition, revenue maximisation and wider share ownership could have been largely removed by an even more radical approach to privatisation – simply giving the shares away.

This last point has also been advocated by my *Financial Times* colleague Samuel Brittan. Critics of these policies, like David Heald (1987), have rightly pointed to the problem of separating changes in the external environment in the 1980s, such as the general recovery in activity and profits, from the impact of the transfer to private ownership. Moreover, any even interim assessment must take account of the piecemeal way in which the programme emerged, resulting in a conflict of objectives. The interests of the Treasury in securing early flotations have been foremost – along with the aims of existing managements. Consumers, and the goal of increasing competition, have come second, particularly with the privatization of British Telecom and British Gas. But the energy and persistence of a regulator like Professor Sir Bryan Carsberg of Oftel have shown what can be achieved. British Telecom has been forced to be more responsive to consumers than it was before privatization.

In the most comprehensive study of the subject to date, Vickers and Yarrow (1988) have expressed strong reservations about the Government's approach to the privatization of the monopoly utilities, pointing to the obstacles to competition which have been left in its place. They have concluded:

Mrs Thatcher's Government has been guilty of just the sort of 'short-termism' that has coloured policy toward nationalised industries in the past.

The desires to privatise speedily, to widen share ownership quickly, and to raise short-term revenues have stood in the way of devising adequate measures of competition and regulation for the industries concerned. (In the event revenues have not been maximised either because of the underpricing of shares.) In the process, the Government has partly been captured by the managements of the firms being sold, since their co-operation is essential for rapid privatization. Short-term political advantage may have been won, but longer-lasting gains in economic efficiency have been lost.

The privatization programme deserves considerable attention, both because it has been a novel initiative and because it has fundamentally changed the boundaries of the public sector in Britain. Yet perhaps its real significance lies in its being the prime example of the broader economic trends of the 1980s, the assertion of managerial power, the weakening of trade union influence, and the spread of share ownership.

6

Popular Capitalism

The nation has been fundamentally changed by the spread of ownership to an extent hitherto undreamed of. It is the basic human – and essentially captialist – instinct of self-improvement which lies behind this phenomenon. And its moral worth is increasingly clear, as the visible enhancement of personal responsibility demonstrates for those who have eyes to see.

Nigel Lawson, Chancellor of the Exchequer, 19 January 1988

A centrepiece of the Thatcher Government's political strategy – indeed its moral vision – has been the creation of a property-owning democracy. Under the slogan of popular capitalism there has been an attempt to increase the number of people with a direct, and lasting, stake in the community – a source of not only wealth but also personal independence. This has not been seen as a way of shifting the balance of power in the economy or industry, but has been concerned with the individual and the family. It has chiefly focused on the spread of home and individual share ownership but has also included the encouragement of personal pensions.

A philosophical justification of the new morality has been offered by John Moore (1987). He spoke of knowing at first hand 'the feelings of responsibility that ownership creates, the sense of a personal interest in the stability and improvement of the community. I know that ownership teaches the finiteness of resources, the virtues of thrift and the risks and rewards of investment ... Widespread ownership diffuses power and prevents the concentration that is the prime ingredient of tyranny.'

The political, and social, implications of this view are profound. As Nigel Lawson has pointed out (1988), the spread of ownership will 'increasingly display another crucial dimension, as one generation of owners creates a second generation of inheritors, a fact which will serve most powerfully to entrench the changes which we, as a government, have sought to bring about. This entrenchment is a political fact of the first importance.'

But will the moves towards popular capitalism give people more control over their lives and their future? Or do they, in the language of the left, reassert the divisions between the insiders and the outsiders by offering short-term gains to those with the resources to participate? Is it all a glossy populist exercise as exemplified by the vacuous 'Tell Sid' campaign for the British Gas privatization?

The idea of a property-owning democracy is not new. Robert Rhodes James has recorded (1986) how Anthony Eden coined the phrase in his speech to the Conservative Party conference in Blackpool in 1948. He was thinking as much of industrial co-partnership as of home ownership. Eden said it was 'essential that the worker in industry should have the status of an individual and not of a mere cog in a soulless machine.' This meant encouraging schemes 'for the distribution of capital ownership over a wide area, and for giving men and women a closer interest and share in the purpose and operation of the industry that employs them.' Subsequent Conservative administrations of the 1950s, and 1960s and 1970s only lived up to these broad aspirations in the area of housing. In particular, there was the remarkable expansion in owner occupation, up from 29 per cent of all housing in 1951 to 53 per cent in 1975. However, the growth rate slowed in the 1970s. The long-term increase was the result of the encouragement of housebuilding by governments (notably by the abolition of the schedule A tax on owner occupiers and the continuation of mortgage tax relief), the sharp decline of the private rented sector and broader social changes such as greater affluence and the increased number of single households. But there were fewer achievements in terms of industrial co-partnership despite the encouragement of joint consultation in factories and, in the early-and-mid 1950s, the era of close co-operation between Government and trade unions notably during Walter Monckton's period as Minister of Labour.

The difference since 1979 has been the extent to which the Thatcher Government has sought to extend owner occupation, and, equally significantly, to encourage other forms of ownership. On the housing front the key has been the 'right to buy' legislation, allowing council tenants to buy their homes at a substantial discount. This was initially set at 33 per cent for tenants of three years' standing rising by stages to 50 per cent for those of 20 years' standing or more. Later changes made the terms more generous and sought to encourage the purchase of flats as well as houses. Various other measures were taken to encourage home ownership, such as the sale of land for low cost homes, and shared ownership (part rental and part mortgage schemes). The retention of tax relief on mortgage interest payments has also encouraged a substantial increase in owner occupation relative to renting. Mrs Thatcher successfully pressed in 1983 for an increase in the upper limit for mortgage tax relief from £25,000 to £30,000, a rare case when the Treasury was overruled.

By 1988 the number of people owning their own homes had risen by nearly 3 million compared with 1979, of which more than 1 million was the result of sales of public sector housing. Consequently, owner occupation had increased from 56–7 per cent of all housing in 1979 to around 63–4 per cent in 1988, one of the highest figures in the industrialized world. Hence the Government's actions accelerated the rate of increase. Moreover, house prices were also rising rapidly for most of the period, well above the general rate of inflation, particularly in London and the south-east.

These trends have been significant both in increasing the independence and freedom of the purchasers and in creating a generation of inheritors. In this context the Government's actions in further boosting owner occupation are relatively unimportant compared with earlier increases in ownership, and the length of time for which those houses have been owned. What has happened is that the post-war generation of first-time buyers have begun to leave homes (generally with mortgages paid-off) to their children who often already own a home. According to estimates by economists at Morgan Grenfell there has been a sharp increase in the number of heads of household over the age of 65 who are owner-occupiers – up from 12 per cent in 1949, to 25 per cent in 1970 and 50 per cent in 1984, with a forecast level of 60 per cent by the year 2,000. This had already produced an average inheritance per household of £35,000 in the mid-1980s. Property inheritance rose in real (inflation-adjusted) terms from £3.7 billion in 1970 to £7 billion in 1987.

These trends have little to do with the actions of any particular government, but they could have wide-ranging effects for property ownership generally. For example, the supply of houses coming onto the market could increase. Coming at a time of declining numbers in the 20–30 age group this could also have a dampening effect on house prices. Moreover, the inheritors, who would mainly already be houseowners, might sell their parents' houses and use the money to diversify their assets. The Morgan Grenfell analysis talked of an increased demand for discretionary savings such as equity shares, unit trusts, and single premium life policies in relation to non-discretionary savings such as housing and pension fund contributions. The transfer of assets from one generation to another produced by the big rise in owner occupation in the 1950s and 1960s could therefore help to stimulate wider share ownership. But all this has more to do with Father Time than Mrs Thatcher. Families could therefore begin to have sources of income separate from their jobs and sources of wealth separate from their home.

However, these figures need to be treated with some caution. The older generation may not pass on the full benefits of the increase in their capital assets to their children, but may themselves take some of their equity out for current consumption. A variety of ingenious schemes have been marketed to enable retired people to take advantage of the big increase in house prices in the mid-to-late 1980s. This has been reflected in the big rise in personal credit during the 1980s which is in part related to, and secured on, higher house prices. Similarly, possible Government initiatives to encourage greater private provision of health may lead to higher expenditure by the elderly on providing for themselves in old age.

Moreover, the benefits will only accrue to those who are the children of existing owner occupiers. The Morgan Grenfell analysis suggests that just under a half of households aged over 65 are not owner occupiers and the figure will still be 40 per cent in the year 2000. Hence a substantial minority of the population, even if they are themselves homeowners, will not inherit property – or if they are one of a large family they may be engaged in a squabble typical of a Galsworthy novel about dividing the inheritance. While the overall effects of these changes should be to increase the wealth of the majority of owner occupiers, the redistributive effects will be limited by the reductions in the impact of capital taxes and cuts in the higher rates of income tax which solely benefit the wealthy.

The other side of popular capitalism is the growth of share ownership. While this has always been one of the Conservatives' general objectives, it only assumed significance as a policy priority in the second term, after the 1983 General Election. As with other aspects of the Thatcher Government's policy development, this was in response to the problem of how to sell British Telecom, the largest flotation ever planned. John Moore, then Financial Secretary to the Treasury has recorded (1987) how

Necessity came to the aid of believers in wider share ownership. It was clear to anyone contemplating the approaching British Telecom sale that new markets would have to be tapped if it was to succeed. Grudgingly it was accepted that if such a massive offering was to be successful it would have to attract a new audience, ie the mass public, as well as the traditional institutions. Even so, there was little confidence the mass public would buy it, and here is where the lack of understanding of the passion for ownership that ordinary people have, showed most clearly.

The overwhelming marketing success of the British Telecom offer, partly through its underpricing, made wider share ownership a central part of the privatization programme, and made popular capitalism a central theme of Thatcherism.

Various other actions have also stimulated share ownership. Employee share schemes run by companies increased from 30 in 1979 to more than 3,000 in 1987. This was, however, largely the result of profit-sharing proposals in the 1978 Finance Act put forward by the Liberals during that party's pact with the then Labour Government. The scheme was extended with savings-related share options after 1980 and stock options for executives on an increased scale after 1984. In addition, in the 1989 Budget, an incentive was given, via the extension of corporation tax relief, to the growth of employee share ownership plans (Esops), a collective means for workers to hold shares which have grown rapidly in the US. The most radical idea, in inspiration if not execution, was the introduction from January 1987 of Personal Equity Plans (PEP), under which adults can invest up to £2,400 a year (£4,800 after the 1988 Budget) in these plans which in turn are put in UK equities, with up to half in unit trusts and investment trusts. Provided an investment is kept for between one and two years all reinvested dividends and capital gains are entirely free of tax. After the end of the qualifying period, investments can be realized without loss of tax relief. Share ownership has also been encouraged by the introduction in 1983 of the Business Expansion Scheme offering income tax relief to individuals investing up to £40,000 in an unquoted UK trading company – though it should be seen more perhaps as part of the attempt to revive the entrepreneurial spirit.

The results of these policies have been striking. The number of individual shareholders (excluding unit trusts) rose from 3 million to 9 million between 1979 and the beginning of 1989 (after the October 1987 stock market crash), according to a survey carried out by NOP Market Research for the Treasury and the Stock Exchange. This was equivalent to about 20 per cent of the adult population (against 7 per cent in 1979), which is not far short of the figure for the US and three times that of Japan. Norman Lamont, Financial Secretary to the Treasury, has claimed (in E. Butler, 1988) that 'if I had to choose a statistic that summed up the Thatcher years it is that. The number of people owning shares in British industry is not much less now than the number of people who belong to trade unions.'

The growth in share ownership appears to have halted from mid-1987 onwards, with only a small rise during 1987 and little change overall during 1988. There were the offsetting factors of the sharp fall in share prices of October 1987 and several privatization offers, such as British Airways, Rolls Royce, the British Airports Authority and British Steel. So there was presumably a reduction in the number of individual shareholders in previous privatization issues.

Nevertheless, there has still been a sharp increase in the number of first-time shareholders who have not sold. The early 1989 survey suggested that of the roughly 6 million people owning privatization shares, about a half were new shareholders. Around 2.25 million owned only privatized shares. Overall, some 1.5 million workers, including only those owning other shares, had a stake in the companies which employed them. This has been the result both of the high level of employee participation in privatization offers and of employee share schemes. The 1989 survey also pointed to a wide spread in share ownership since two-thirds of British shareholders have come from outside the ranks of managers and the professions, and two-thirds from outside the south-east.

Impressive though these figures are, they have to be treated with considerable caution. A sizeable proportion of the new shareowners turned out to be short-term holders. People have put money in at the time of the flotations, attracted by what has appeared to be a one-way option to make a profit, and then they have sold. For instance, an analysis of 14 privatization offers shows that the number of shareholders declined by roughly 40 per cent between the time of flotation and the end of 1987. The number of British Telecom shareholders dropped from 2.3 million initially to 1.3 million over nearly four years, with British Gas down from 4.4 million to under 3 million. Arguably, the decline would have been even steeper and faster but for the various loyalty bonus shares, vouchers and other incentives to keep initial applicants in for the first two or three years after a flotation. As the 1987 and 1988 experience showed, the overall total of shareholders has remained stable only because of the steady flow of new offers – though a big boost to the total number of shareholders might come from autumn 1989 onwards as the electricity generation and distribution companies and water authorities are sold, together with the conversion of the Abbey National Building Society into a public company.

Moreover, the expansion of shareholding has not been deep. Mr Michael Howard, the then corporate and consumer affairs minister, talked optimistically in February 1986 about flotations like British Telecom being 'not just a one-off event but a step on the road to a more lasting change in attitudes and habits: a significant number of the British Telecom first time buyers, around 40,000 to 50,000, went on to invest in other shares in the six months or so following the British Telecom offer.' But more significant is the finding, according to a Dewe Rogerson survey, that 56 per cent of the new shareholders, or 5.4 million, only invest in one company. Only 800,000 shareholders have between four and nine stakes, and a mere 300,000 have what can reasonably be described as a portfolio of over ten shares. An analysis by Professor Paul Grout of Bristol University (1987) has concluded that, 'the interesting feature of the recent growth in share ownership is that, although it involves a surprisingly large number of people, it is almost as thin as it could possibly be.'

Most shareholders therefore have small stakes. Excluding the wealthiest individuals, most holdings may have been worth no more than £2,500 per investor, even before the October 1987 stock market fall, with a large number amounting to hundreds of pounds. Survey evidence suggests that many of the new shareholders see their holdings as a hobby rather than as a long-term channel for savings. The average holding in shares probably represents only about 5 per cent of wealth per household and is dwarfed by the value to most of the new investors of their homes or pension rights. Even indirect investment via unit trusts is limited with only about 1.5 million holders with average stakes of perhaps about £20,000. The tax system is biased in favour of saving by buying a house through a mortgage and contributing (generally without any choice) to a pension scheme. In both cases there is tax relief, where buying shares is out of post-tax income.

Moreover, the specific tax incentive to buy shares offered through PEPs has only had a limited impact. This is partly because the existing tax free allowance for capital gains makes the relief from capital gains under PEP irrelevent for most ordinary investors, except those on higher rates of tax. Consequently, the evidence from the first two years of operation, 1987 and 1988, was that many of those taking out PEP plans were existing shareholders, making lump-sum payments, who were relatively well off and were in a position to benefit from the tax incentives. Despite ministerial talk of a successful start, only just over a quarter of a million people took out such plans in its first year, and this fell to little more than 50,000 in 1988. So, as noted earlier, further concessions were introduced in the 1989 Budget to stimulate demand for PEPs.

For all the ministerial talk about popular capitalism, the proportion of UK shares held by individuals has continued to decline. Between 1963 and 1981 (before the privatization flotations) the proportion fell from 54 to 28 per cent as financial institutions, such as insurance companies and pension funds, increased their holdings. Despite the heavy involvement of ordinary investors in the privatization offers the figure dropped to below 25 per cent in 1987, and could have been even lower according to some estimates. Individual investors remained net sellers of shares to the amount of around £1 billion annually in 1985 and 1986, both boom years for the stock market – and in 1987 the proportion of Stock Exchange transactions by value involving individual investors, rather than institutions, was only 21 per cent. The interest of the ordinary shareholder continued to be overshadowed by the heavy investment of financial institutions, and this was tacitly accepted by the Treasury in the 1989 Budget concessions to give unit and investment trusts a larger role in PEPs.

There have also been considerable doubts as to how keen the Stock Exchange is on attracting small investors, especially in its more competitive post-Big Bang era. Even John Moore (1987) has reported a comment in the mid-1980s during a City lunch, 'at which I was enthusiastically promoting the virtues of wider share ownership the chairman of a major brokerage house actually said to me, "But surely we don't want all those kind of people owning shares, do we?" It is always interesting to see how many people – intelligent, educated people – will pay lip service to an idea, for instance the idea of individual freedom: yet when it comes to implementing policies that will make the idea a reality – such as wider ownership – they resist them strenuously.'

More specifically, Nigel Lawson, as Chancellor, complained in 1987 about the impact of problems in the Stock Exchange settlement system and the resulting increase in minimum commission charges. He said, 'the City therefore needs to find ways not only of over-coming the present settlement problems but, with imagination, of cutting dealing costs and making it easier for the small investor to buy and sell shares; and in general to develop a far more vigorous retail business than at present exists.' He went on to argue that more public companies needed to recognize that the wider benefits of a large share register far outweighed the administrative burden. Labour's then City spokesman Tony Blair claimed that as a result of a survey he carried out in late 1987 the Stock Exchange was giving 'a third-class service at first-class rates to small investors'. He asked 151 Stock Exchange firms listed as helping the small investor to sell 200 British Telecom shares and found that one-third refused to deal at all, and a further third would only deal at rates of commission so high as to wipe out the entire annual capital gain in the shares. There was generally an absence of competition and a discrimination against the small investor. He concluded the small investor had no equal access to the market with the big players and was left with 'the unapproach-able face of capitalism'. Indeed, concern was so great that the Office of Fair Trading looked at the high degree of similarity in rates offered to small investors.

From within the City, doubts were expressed by even such a prominent figure as banker Stanislas Yassukovich. In a paper to a London School of Economics seminar in June 1987, he argued that the Government's hard sell might be dysfunctional by confirming the public's view of the stock market as an exclusive place and by giving the impression that share ownership was not a form of savings but rather an opportunity for short-term gain. He said the problem was that in Britain the main financial advisers to most individuals were the clearing banks and building societies, but they were excluded from distributing shares. He said reforms which would facilitate banks to sell and distribute shares, along French lines, were required before a more diffuse and lasting share ownership is achieved. This points to a conflict between all the talk by ministers about popular capitalism and the practice for aspiring shareholders.

There may in practice be four classes of individual investor. First, there has been the large number of people who have subscribed to the privatization issues in the hope, generally realized, of a short-term profit, but who have no real intention of becoming long-term shareholders. Secondly, there is the large group of first-time share-owners who have stayed in, are more interested than before in the stock market, but are still essentially dabbling, relative to their total wealth. Thirdly, there is a small, but not insignificant, group of well-off people whose real incomes have risen sharply during the Thatcher years and who have taken advantage of the tax changes, Personal Equity Plans and the Business Expansion Scheme. Fourthly, there is a small group of the wealthy, who have also been major beneficiaries from the tax changes and rising stock market of the 1980s, and who have big equity stakes in their own companies and widespread equity holdings.

Politicians understandably focus mainly on the first and second groups, because that is where the votes are, but the real deepening of share ownership has occurred amongst the third and fourth groups. Their activity is reflected in the growth of the Unlisted Securities Market and of the newer Third Market, as well as in the high level of involvement in the Business Expansion Scheme. The defenders of the latter argue that it is not a tax dodge for the rich since only 30 per cent of people investing in the scheme pay tax at the top rate and over 20 per cent only pay the basic rate of income tax. Nonetheless, this scheme is mainly for the better-off rather than the ordinary investor.

To a considerable extent the real beneficiaries from popular capitalism have been the minority of the existing well-off, while the majority have been given the illusion of participation, and some of the icing off the cake from privatization. The Government hopes that, despite the flop of the BP sale in autumn 1987, the success of the flotation of British Steel in November 1988 – to be followed by the remaining 49 per cent holding in British Telecom, the electricity industry and the water authorities – will deepen the public's holdings. However, Professor Grout (1987) has argued that it is difficult to assess the long-term trend of wider share ownership. While many small shareholders retain their stakes in privatized companies, it is uncertain whether they are likely to increase their holdings. One possibility, he has suggested, is that, given high transaction costs for entering and leaving the stock market, the individual holder is largely a passive investor. 'If this is the case then the widening of the share base may stop as abruptly as it started, once there are no more major assets to be privatised.' However, the privatization programme still has many more years to run, and employee share ownership has still been increasing – though this also tends to be passive.

The key test will be whether the new breed of shareholders diversify from privatization stocks and stakes in the companies for which they work into other holdings. It is arguable that the Government has been too cautious in encouraging such a broadening and deepening of holdings in existing quoted companies. Its tax incentives, notably PEP, have been limited and not on the scale seen in different ways in France and the US. In relation to the privatized concerns a really adventurous option, though not one compatible with the demands of providing money for the Treasury, would have been to distribute shares free to all adults, as advocated by Samuel Brittan. Similarly, employee involvement in the equity of an enterprise could be taken much further, as under the various suggestions for a capital/labour partnership to promote a share economy which have been put forward by Professor James Meade (1986) – though this would involve a much more radical shift in economic power than might be acceptable to the present Government and its supporters.

The obstacles to participation in the stock market for small investors also remain great, and have in some respects grown since the Big Bang deregulation. Some big companies are also reluctant to incur the expense of servicing a large number of shareholders, though the Government announced in March 1988 that it was proposing to give listed public companies the option of supplying shareholders with a short form of the annual report and accounts.

Yet what matters in broader political terms has been the change in attitudes, and here the propaganda associated with the privatization offers may have had some effect. People who own even one or two stocks, and occasionally look at the financial pages, may identify more with the capitalist system than before. For the many employee shareholders this may help to alter industrial relations in the firms concerned. A Mori survey in March 1986 of those who first bought shares in the British Telecom flotation showed that as a result of owning shares 21 per cent of those questioned were now more in favour of companies in general making it their top priority to increase profits – with 72 per cent saying it made no difference.

Certainly, these shareholders appear to have provided fertile ground for Conservative Party tilling. The Mori survey indicated that only 14 per cent intended to vote Labour, compared with 53 per cent supporting the Conservatives, and 31 per cent the SDP/Liberal Alliance – and this was a difficult time nationally for the Tories. The Labour Party then adopted ambiguous proposals on social ownership, offering investors in British Telecom and British Gas the choice of either non-voting shares of highly uncertain value or repurchase of their holdings at the original flotation price (well below the then market price).

All this gave the Conservatives an opportunity to gather, and increase, support among first-time and other shareholders which they seized with alacrity. In the six months before the 1987 General Election Conservative Central Office devoted considerable resources to obtaining lists of shareholders in privatized companies. Letters were sent out by the then party chairman Norman Tebbit warning shareholders of what they had at stake, and allegedly might lose, if Labour came to power. The direct mail exercise apparently paid for itself and resulted in a sizeable inflow of new party members. The theory was that someone who has obtained a stake in the community does not want to lose it.

This issue appears to have helped the Tories in the June 1987 General Election. According to a Harris Research exit poll for ITN, of those who said they voted Labour in 1983, one in twenty who had first purchased shares since then had switched their votes elsewhere. Some 29 per cent of the sample had acquired stocks at some stage in the previous four years – and in some cases clearly also sold. (Two-thirds of this group had made their first purchase.) Some 38 per cent of Conservative supporters had bought shares and 32 per cent of Alliance voters. Labour's problem was shown by the fact that, while only 14 per cent of its own supporters had bought shares, 33 per cent of trade unionists had.

Similarly, the Conservatives have benefited from the extension of owner occupation – though the 'right to buy' programme may be a declining political asset for them, especially as Labour has changed its attitude. The Harris Research survey suggested that the Conservative share of the vote among home owners has steadily declined since 1979, when it was 53 per cent, down to 47 per cent in 1987. But this was a lower share of a much higher total, so that, in absolute terms, the Conservatives received about the same support from home owners in 1987 as in 1979. The Harris/ITN survey also suggested that Tory votes by many of the former council tenants cushioned Conservative losses, mainly to the Alliance, among more traditional home owners in both 1983 and 1987. In short, some of the middle-class professionals in the suburbs may have defected, but the new skilled worker owner occupiers in the council estates moved over to the Tories and stayed loyal.

Perhaps the clearest testimony to the effectiveness of this strategy has come from the opposition parties. They have been forced to adapt to the Conservatives' initiatives – first accepting owner occupation, and then share ownership. Labour's trade and industry spokesman Bryan Gould has argued in favour of extending employee share schemes – what he has described as 'popular socialism'. He has said the Left could call Mrs Thatcher's bluff by using employee share ownership as a means of providing workers with a real stake in the enterprises for which they work.

Yet, the Conservatives have retained the advantage. Other parties may adapt and accept wider share ownership, as they have done over owner occupation. But popular capitalism is a programme associated with the Tories. By the time of a general election in 1991–2 more people will have had the opportunity to buy shares in privatization issues, and, equally significantly, to spread their portfolios. There will be a more broadly entrenched interest unwilling to risk its new found assets.

The Government has, however, been rather more cautious in its treatment of pensions. For most people the financial investment tied up in pensions is as important, if not more so, than the value of their house, and much more significant than any shareholdings. But either in an occupational or state pension scheme it appears remote and outside people's control. Since 1979 there have been a number of moves to give individuals greater control, through, for example, provisions to allow the transfer of pension rights for those changing jobs, thus aiding labour mobility. While ministers have talked of encouraging personal portable pensions for all offering direct control, the actions have been limited. After a considerable row the Cabinet decided in December 1985 not to scrap the state-earnings related pension scheme (SERPS), as originally intended, but to retain it in a considerably modified form, at reduced cost. Moreover, there has been no attempt to tackle the considerable tax privileges enjoyed by pension funds relative to individuals.

The new personal pension scheme introduced in July 1988 offered incentives to contract out of SERPS. But there was little incentive for those already in occupational schemes to convert completely into portable pensions because they would lose the benefit of payments based on final salary. These offer greater certainty than the money purchase schemes provided by financial institutions where payments are dependent on the level of money put in and how the resulting investment performs. But there would be scope for those in occupational schemes to top up with personal pension schemes. The latter's main appeal might be to younger employees expecting to be mobile between companies. After mid-1988 a wide range of financial institutions were marketing personal pension saving schemes for individual customers. While these were likely to be dwarfed for a considerable time by occupational schemes catering for 11 million people, personal pensions provided an additional source of wealth for individuals – comparable to the independence provided by owning shares. Yet proposals in the 1989 Budget to put a £60,000 limit on earnings qualifying for pension benefits from tax approved and exempt schemes worked in a contrary direction by making it harder to recruit senior staff and undermining the Government goal of greater labour mobility.

Popular capitalism has proved to be a powerful political slogan for the Conservatives. The reality of a property-owning democracy may have much more to do with the long-term post-war build-up of owner occupation, and inheritance, than the post-1979 initiatives of giving council tenants the right to buy their homes or attractively priced share offers. But the Tories have identified with, and taken considerably further, these successful and widely accepted developments. The result will not be a shift in economic powers – since managements may ensure that there is more independence for owners rather than less as a result of wider and less concentrated shareholdings. The true significance may be to give greater control to individuals over their own lives. This has already been provided by growing owner occupation, and maybe also by personal pensions. So far increased individual share ownership has had less effect on patterns of wealth, but has been an important symbol and indicator of a change in attitudes. Popular capitalism has become a central part of the individualist challenge to collective provision – while the extension of ownership has given people something to defend.

7

The Welfare State

There are powerful reasons why we must be ready to consider how far private provision and individual choice can supplement, or in some cases possibly replace, the role of the Government in health, social security and education. Many of these reasons are economic. The need to reform our system of social provision would be pressing on public spending grounds alone.... The way forward must embrace a constant readiness to consider market mechanisms as a means of promoting greater cost consciousness and of extending choice.

> Sir Geoffrey Howe, Chancellor of the Exchequer, Conservative Political Centre lecture, 3 July 1982

For more than a quarter century after the last war public opinion in Britain, encouraged by politicians, travelled down the aberrant path towards even more dependence on an even more powerful state. Under the guise of compassion people were encouraged to see themselves as 'victims of circumstance'.

> John Moore, Social Services Secretary, speech in London, 26 September 1987

The welfare state has proved to be the most intractable problem facing the Thatcher Government. While moves away from state control towards individualism and privatization have been largely endorsed, or at any rate tacitly accepted, in the economic and industrial areas, the same has not been true of social provision. A wide variety of evidence has shown strong public support for the principles of collective universal provision of health, education and social security, whatever the particular complaints about standards of services. As Professor Ivor Crewe memorably pointed out (1983) after the Tories' victory in the 1983 General Election, 'Keynes has been rejected, Beveridge has not.'

The opposition parties and many political scientists have argued, on the basis of polling evidence, that the electorate overwhelmingly rejects Thatcherite values – and that its degree of rejection has increased during the 1980s. A question regularly asked by Gallup about the priority of cutting taxes versus extending Government services such as health, education and welfare showed an even balance among those polled (37/37) between the two options when the Conservatives were elected in May 1979, but by the 1987 General Election there was a decisive margin (12/61) in favour of increased services even if it meant some increase in taxes.

Yet, paradoxically, the allegedly non-Thatcherite option has been exactly what has happened for most of the Thatcher era. Spending on public services has risen substantially, and until 1987–8 the percentage of income paid in direct taxes was higher than in the last Labour year in office for those on or below average earnings. From 1987–8 on, not only did spending on social provision increase but taxes were cut substantially as well, to below the 1978–9 level in relative terms. Table 7.1 shows the rise in the spending of the 'welfare state' departments (the Departments of Education and Science, Health and Social Security, and the housing budget of the Department of the Environment). These figures not only understate the scale of spending by excluding the separate budgets of the Scottish, Welsh and Northern Ireland Offices which include substantial social expenditure, but underestimate the size of the increase since the housing figure is net of sales of assets which have risen substantially during the 1980s. The figures show a large increase both in real terms and as a share of total public spending.

Table 7.1 Welfare state spending: £ billion in real terms at 1987–8 prices

	1978–9	1983–4	1988–9	1989–90 (plans)
Housing	7.3	3.8	1.9	1.5
Education	15.9	16.2	17.4	17.5
Health	15.2	17.7	20.5	20.8
Social Security	33.7	42.4	44.8	45.7
Total of above	72.1	80.1	84.6	85.5
As per cent of planning total	53.4	55.2	58.5	57.1

Source: Treasury statements

The Government has been acting in line with the public's wish for increased social provision – contrary to what its critics have claimed to be its priorities. But the Conservatives have received no credit for this; rather the reverse is true. A Marplan survey for Channel Four's *Week in Politics* programme showed that on a series of questions about the welfare state a clear majority of the public thought that conditons had got worse 'over the past few years.' Two-thirds of the sample thought that health provision had got worse, 44 per cent thought that state schools had got worse, and 50 per cent believed that the living standards of poor families had deteriorated. Nor was there any expectation of much improvement. Social issues such as health and pensions were among the few where Labour has been consistently rated well ahead of the Tories in the polls.

Yet the public's doubts have not been entirely misconceived, even if they have reflected a failure to appreciate the scale of the overall increase in spending. The Government's low political rating on the welfare state has resulted from its frequently ambivalent attitude. Ministers have tried, and failed, to resolve the dilemma between their desire to control spending on social provision and their political reluctance, in face of strong public opposition, to dismantle or privatize the structure of the welfare state. At various stages far-reaching proposals have been put forward by advisers to replace major parts of the 1940s framework, only for public outcry, including Tory MPs and ministers, to force a rapid retreat. This occurred, for example, in autumn 1982 after the leaking of a report from the Think Tank (the Central Policy Review Staff) outlining suggestions including private health insurance, removing the inflation-proofing or indexation of many benefits, and ending state funding for all institutions of higher education. After immediate protests, the report was shelved amid assurances from, amongst others, Mrs Thatcher, that 'the National Health Service is safe with us.' Pledges were made limiting the scope for substantial cutbacks in expenditure. Similarly, the wide-ranging series of social security reviews of 1984–5 led to big changes in discretionary payments but did not affect the main pledged benefits such as retirement pensions and produced few overall savings. The review of the NHS of 1988–9 also left intact the basic taxpayer funded service provided free at the point of use.

Instead of the mass privatization that was carried out on the state industries, the Government has sought to achieve savings at the margin by reducing entitlements to social security benefits (in aggregate quite significant for those affected) and by encouraging efficiency drives and increased private provision of services such as pensions, occupational health insurance and, particularly, housing. As a result, much to ministers' frustration and annoyance, these measures have widely been seen as implying cuts in these services, even though total spending on the main social areas, apart from housing, has been rising steadily. The Government has suffered the wrath of the losers from changes, whether those on social security or those affected by the closure of an old hospital, and it has received little appreciation from those who have benefited. Ministers have been caught in the dilemma of wanting to contain overall spending on the welfare state, yet being politically unwilling and unable to take the steps which would limit that provision. The public has therefore doubted the sincerity of ministerial commitments, and blamed the Government for not being prepared to meet the obligations it could not shed. Voters have suspected that the Government has wanted a welfare state on the cheap. This is hardly surprising in view of the regular leaks of proposals for more radical options. These were anyway publicly urged by a variety of free market groups with close links to Downing Street like the Centre for Policy Studies, the Institute of Economic Affairs, the Adam Smith Institute, and the No Turning Back group of younger Tory MPs (mainly elected in 1983, many of whom were ministers by the late 1980s). Just as some commentators described the Labour Government's attitude towards monetary targets in the late 1970s as 'unbelieving monetarism', so the repeated Conservative commitments to the welfare state at times lacked credibility.

Britain has not been alone in facing problems with the welfare state. First, most of the population are directly affected, either potentially (as future pensioners), or currently (in hospital or with children at school), and, as noted above, there has been considerable public attachment to the patterns of collective provision created in the late 1940s. Secondly, the services are generally demand-led in response to need, and the price mechanism plays little part. The distribution of illness is unrelated to ability to pay, and, in some cases, is in inverse relation to income, given the health needs of large, poor families and the elderly. A report produced by the Organisation for Economic Co-operation and Development in 1988 noted, for example, that the proportion of the population aged over 65 is projected to rise steeply after the year 2000 in all developed countries

From about 15 per cent at present in the UK, the proportion is expected to rise to nearly 19 per cent by the year 2020 (including, God willing, the author of this book) and up to 29 per cent by 2050. This implies a major shift in the balance between earners and those needing support from the rest of the community. For instance, health spending on the over-65s is over four times as high per head as for those aged under 65, and is nearly six times higher for the over 75s.

In the UK, with predominantly public rather than private sector provision, there has been no easy solution. The Government's initial response was to apply a squeeze without altering the fundamental structure – in the process maximizing political aggravation without dealing with the basic problem. As a result the growth of welfare spending, which is still rising faster than most other areas of public expenditure, has slowed relative to total national income. While social expenditure as a proportion of Gross Domestic Product had jumped from 12.4 per cent in 1960 to 19.6 per cent in 1975, it rose to only 20 per cent in 1980, and 20.9 per cent in 1985. The relative share of other programmes has, however, contracted. Over the industrialized world as a whole, the growth of social spending slowed from 8 per cent a year in real terms in the 1950s, 1960s, and early 1970s to 4 per cent in the second half of the 1970s, and down to 2.5 per cent in the first half of the 1980s.

In many countries, including the UK, there has been a marked change in the pattern of spending. Some areas have faced a significant squeeze – accounting for the protests over cuts – while other programmes such as income support have risen sharply in response to the big increase in unemployment and the growing number of pensioners. These needs have been financed in part by reductions in previous planned levels of spending on education, justified by the sharp fall in school rolls in the 1980s, and by tighter financial targets in the health service. Housing expenditure has fallen substantially in both absolute and relative terms as subsidies to council tenants and new public sector house building were cut. However, the cost of mortgage interest tax relief (which is not counted as part of public expenditure) rose substantially – roughly trebling to a peak of £4.75 billion in 1987–8 before falling slightly as a result of the cut in the higher rates of tax.

While these measures succeeded in reducing the overall rate of growth of social expenditure, they did not satisfy either voters or the

Treasury. The former complained about hospital waiting lists, while the latter saw the rising, and in part inescapable, demands of the welfare state as an obstacle to its public expenditure targets. However, from the beginning of Mrs Thatcher's second term in 1983 and particularly after her third election victory in 1987, there were increasing moves to boost private provision and to introduce greater financial disciplines into the remaining areas within the public sector. The managerial phase which started in the early 1980s had to be taken further and structures had to be changed, according to the free-market school. In each case there was an acceptance – by most ministers, though not all advisers – that basic provision of education, health and social security, should be available regardless of income. With important exceptions like medical tests and examinations, it was agreed that provision should be free at the point of use. Beyond the starting point of a basic state provision, or safety-net, such as the retirement pension, ministers agreed that people should be encouraged to seek provision for themselves such as occupational and portable pensions and private health insurance. There has consequently been increased talk of targeting.

Secondly, ministers have argued that, while the state would continue to provide the bulk of the financing for the welfare state, the public sector did not necessarily have to provide the services. This has involved the encouragement both of services being contracted out to the private sector by competitive tender and also a revival of the nineteenth century tradition of voluntary provision. Indeed, in the many cases where Government departments have given grants to independent charities there have been moves to shift the balance of activities towards providing services rather than primarily acting as pressure groups on behalf of their various interests, such as the disabled or the mentally ill. For instance, in 1987 the Government handed £10 million over to the Haemophiliac Society to pay out in benefits to haemophiliacs infected by Aids, while the Government has given money to the Independent Living Foundation, a charitable trust which tops up social security payments. Some of these organizations may be better placed than the state to distribute such benefits, though even mainstream leaders of charities have complained that the state has been trying to force the disabled to beg for charity. Housing associations have been encouraged to provide low rent accommodation, increasingly as a substitute for, rather than just a complement to, local authorities. This stimulus to the private and voluntary sectors tied in with the idea of the active citizen, which will be discussed in the next chapter.

Alternatively, the Government has challenged the long-established quasi-monopoly of local education authorities and local health authorities. This has been contrary to the post-war view that decisions on such provision should be collective. These have involved changes in the running of health authorities to permit greater competition in the provision of services, so as to hold down costs, and the legislation to allow schools to opt out of local authority control to be directly funded by Whitehall.

All this has added up to a view of the welfare state in which the Government acts as a basic provider, increasingly targeting help at those most in need, with growing private and voluntary sector involvement. There are tighter managerial controls and increased competitive pressures to replicate the market system. In this way it has been hoped to square the circle of ever rising demands and constrained resources. The remainder of this chapter discusses how this evolving approach has been achieved in the four major areas of the welfare state: social security, health, education and housing.

Social Security

Spending on social security has risen by nearly two-fifths in real, inflation-adjusted, terms during the 1980s. Table 7.2 shows changes in the number of beneficiaries.

There has been a shift with a steady rise in the number of retirement pensioners, offset in numbers (though not cost) by a decline in the number of children eligible for child benefit. The numbers receiving unemployment benefit – a figure which is far from the same as those counted as unemployed – rose sharply until the mid-1980s, before declining. Over the decade there was a sharp rise in those receiving other non-contributory benefits such as supplementary allowance and housing benefit. The numbers are not dependent on objective circumstances but on the application of varying rules. Thus the drop of 1.3 million between 1987–8 and 1988–9 in the number expected to receive rate rebates reflected policy changes and the reorganization of April 1988, rather than a change in demand.

The Government has sought to achieve savings where possible

Table 7.2   Numbers receiving benefits (in thousands)

	1978–9	1983–4	1988–9
Retirement pensioners	8,530	9,210	9,735
Unemployment benefit	570	1,020	755
Child benefit – numbers of children	13,480	12,600	12,015
Housing benefit – short-term rate	925	2,120	
Supplementary allowance – rent rebates	1,210	3,605	
Rate rebates	3,055	6,855	

Note: Comparisons are complicated by major changes in the system in 1982–3 and 1988–9, but the number of supplementary allowance beneficiaries rose by a tenth between 1983–4 and 1988–9, with the number of housing benefit recipients broadly stable

Source: Public Expenditure White Papers

within the constraints of its election pledges. This has involved big changes at the margin – for instance, an end to the linking of rates of long-term benefits, such as pensions, to the movement of earnings and prices, whichever was the larger of the two, and instead just linking these benefits to prices. Other, mainly short-term, benefits have at times been uprated by less than the rate of inflation. By 1983 these changes had already produced savings, that is lower benefits, worth £2 billion a year (according to Bull and Wilding, 1983).

The row in autumn 1982 over the leaked Think Tank options led to a gradualist approach. Norman Fowler, Social Services Secretary from 1981 until 1987, instituted reviews into the main areas of social security spending, with the exception of disability. In line with the Government's practice these were internal, rather than of the semi-independent Royal Commission type. It soon became clear that big savings could not be achieved. Indeed, the original Green Paper proposal to scrap the state-earnings related pension scheme was dropped. Instead, the long-term cost of the scheme – that is in 2033 – was to be halved to around £13 billion (at constant 1985 prices) as a result changing the formula of payments from 25 per cent of the best 20 years of a working-life to 20 per cent of average income for the whole of a working-life. The pensions of people retiring this century were to be unaffected. The most radical short-term changes affected income support. Supplementary benefit was replaced by income support and family income supplement by family credit, with a comprehensive overhaul of housing benefit. There was general agreement on the need for simplification, and on a substantial reduction in the poverty trap whereby families had lost more than a pound for each additional pound they had earned.

The key was the level of benefits set. The Policy Studies Institute challenged the Government's claims about concentrating help on those most in need. It argued that the changes would fail to deliver resources to the families suffering most hardship, would fail to iron out the disincentive effects of the overlapping tax and social security systems, and would fail to provide a reliable safety net for those with special needs. In particular, while total social security expenditure was rising because of more claimants, the changes would cut more than £500 million from the total in 1988–9. The institute maintained that the increased spending on family credit and income support would be more than offset by cuts in spending on housing benefit and by the freezing of child benefit. As a result the Government was forced to introduce modifications to alleviate the impact on a number of housing benefit recipients and pensioners.

Overall, some of the Government's more radical supporters regarded the Fowler reforms as a wasted opportunity. They believed that big changes should be introduced at some stage, probably in the 1990s after a fourth Thatcher election victory. This was not just, or even primarily, to do with public expenditure, since in the late 1980s enough money was available to finance an improved structure of benefits. Indeed, falling unemployment permitted a sizeable reduction below previously planned levels for social security in 1988–9 – amounting to 2 per cent of the total – though the overall social security budget was still rising in real terms.

Instead, there was a growing debate about the dependency culture, partly prompted by the arguments of some US sociologists that too extensive a benefit system would remove work incentives and make people too dependent on the state. Several ministers visited the US to see experiments there in, for example, workfare, whereby people are required to work on various state-sponsored schemes in order to receive benefits. The Centre for Policy Studies also sponsored a seminar and meetings in London with US critics of welfare such as Charles Murray of the Manhattan Institute for Policy Research. He has challenged the idea of entitlements and maintained that the problems of the underclass have been largely a response to welfare programmes. British ministers have not gone that far, though from

September 1988 unemployed 16 and 17 year olds who refused a place on the Youth Training Scheme would not be able to claim benefits. However, officially commissioned research has shown that less than 1 per cent of school-leavers prefer unemployment to a job, while those most affected by the change are those using benefits to support part-time study at a College of Further Education. Further changes along the same lines to encourage people to take jobs or training places have been introduced with the adult training scheme.

Similarly, there has been increased discussion of the targeting of benefits. Ministers have justified the continued freezing of child benefit in cash terms by saying that additional resources have been aimed at the poor families via family credit and family income support. Consequently, these targeted groups have been given more than they would have received from a universal increase in child benefit which would have mainly helped the better-off. The same point was at the heart of the row in early November 1988 after Nigel Lawson gave a briefing to Sunday journalists which was interpreted as implying means-testing of some pensioners' benefits. What was meant was that, beyond the basic inflation-proofed pension, help would be concentrated on poorer pensioners rather than all. Ministers fairly pointed out, for example, that the state pension represented only about half a pensioner's net income, which in turn had risen on average by a fifth in real terms during the 1980s. Pensioners have increasingly benefited from occupational schemes and from savings. But this still does not remove the charge of meanness in the Government's attitude to the nearly-poor without such sources of income. The distributional consequences are discussed in the next chapter.

Moreover, the change in the Government's approach to social security – while proceeding in gradual steps – has amounted to a fundamental challenge to the post-war belief in universal provision. Defenders of such benefits argue that they are cheaper to administer and, crucially, that the take-up rate for universal payments is nearly total, while only between a half and three-quarters of those qualified have taken up means-tested benefits such as family credit. Such selective benefits, while undoubtedly targeting help, also create incentive problems. There is also the contrast that tax allowances, such as relief for mortgage tax payments and occupational pension contributions, disproportionately benefit those with higher incomes – a curious asymmetry of selectivity. But that is all part of the challenge to the post-war welfare settlement.

Health

Britain's health record has, in many ways, been impressive during the Thatcher years. Spending in real, inflation adjusted, terms has risen by more than a third over the decade, and from about 4.8 per cent of Gross Domestic Product to over 5.5 per cent. There have also been increases in 'front-line' staff, that is nurses, doctors and medical and professional workers, of more than 18 per cent over the decade. As table 7.2 indicates, several key performance indicators show big improvements.

The figures suggest that the National Health Service has been doing its job in ways measurable other than just by the level of

Table 7.2   Performance of the National Health Service

(a) Numbers of patients treated (in thousands)

	1978	1986
In-patients	6,435	7,687
Out-patients	39,653	44,305
Day-patients	668	1,259

(b) Number of operations

	1978	Mid-to-late 1980s
Hips	31,090	44,036 (1985)
Cataracts	53,360	69,450 (1985)
Kidney transplants	849	1,485 (1987)

(c) Health prevention (in thousands)

	1978	1986
Sight tests	9,000	12,100
Dental treatments	30,800	36,800 (1987)
Cervical smear tests	2,840	4,270
Percentage of children vaccinated against polio, diptheria and tetanus	78	85

Sources: Public Expenditure White Papers and Department of Health statistics

spending. There have been clear efficiency gains with cost improvements averaging 1.2 to 1.5 per cent of budgets a year. The average cost per case has been reduced, with, for example, the length of stay per patient reduced from 9.4 to 7.3 days. The cross-party social services committee of the Commons noted in its report on 'The Future of the National Health Services' (Fifth Report,1987–8):

Looking at international league tables prepared by OECD, it is clear that overall, the UK compares reasonably well with the major western countries in terms of mortality and life expectancy and that the NHS is cheaper than some other systems. It is also clear that there is no direct demonstrable connection between the per capita amount spent on health services and the healthiness of the population as measured by the conventional indicator of mortality. There is plenty of evidence that the population is healthier in the 1980s than it was in the 1940s and that it lives longer ... Paradoxically, the improvements in health of the population have been accompanied by ever increasing demands for health services – and by an ever growing ability of doctors and other health professionals to treat or alleviate hitherto intractable complaints. Significantly, the measures used by government to chart the success of the health services are, almost exclusively, measures of increased activity – it is ironic that the 'success' of the health service is measured in terms of its ability to treat more people, not by the outcome of that treatment.

Yet, as the report pointed out, there has been a widespread view that the system established in 1948 needs major changes. The committee's own inquiry reflected the MPs' worries about whether the original objectives of the NHS were being met: 'that it should provide a comprehensive health service for every man, woman and child in the country; that it should be equitable in the sense of offering equal service for equal need; that it should offer equality of access to health care when needed and that it should be free in the sense that access to the service should not depend on patients' ability to pay.' As so often, the Government's decision to launch a fundamental review of the NHS – announced somewhat bizarrely by Mrs Thatcher in a *Panorama* television interview in January 1988 – was in response to a crisis. Ministers had originally argued that a fundamental review of the NHS should be a matter for the 1991–2 election manifesto, for action in a Conservative fourth term. However, that winter there had been only the latest in a series of protests about the level of funding of the NHS with highly publicized cases of wards being closed and life-saving operations for children having to be postponed because of shortages of nurses. There were two separate issues – one to do with nurses' pay structure, and the other to do with the underlying level of funding. The former was dealt with, clumsily, and with many nurses still dissatisfied, during the course of 1988 by a restructuring to reward staff who had particular skills and were in short supply. This followed the Government's acceptance of the recommendations of the independent pay review body.

The underlying problem of the funding of the NHS took much longer to tackle. The social services committee had been involved in a lengthy series of disputes with the Government (in its First, Second and Third Reports, 1987–8) over the scale of under-funding. The committee claimed that a £1.9 billion shortfall could be identified and called for investment of £1 billion over two years, plus a commitment to funding which would permit a 2 per cent rise in services. John Moore, the then Social Services Secretary, dismissed the £1 billion figure as arbitrary, but in the event Kenneth Clarke, the new Health Secretary, after the splitting of the old Department of Health and Social Security in July 1988, secured an extra £1.46 billion for 1989–90.

Yet, while these sums alleviated immediate problems, they could not tackle the basic issue of how to respond to an apparently infinite demand. More practically, the 2 per cent annual growth in services the Government accepted was needed to keep pace with developments in medical technology, to meet the additional health needs of an ageing population and to make improvements in the services offered. In funding terms, this was before allowing for a faster growth in NHS costs, including pay, than prices generally. One response has been to treat these figures as a benchmark – with money from cost improvement programmes and income generation projects (selling NHS services to outsiders) regarded as bonuses which will not of themselves generate enough revenue to ensure a sufficient growth in services without increased Government funding in real terms.

The announcement of the review generated a flood of proposals from health administrators and professionals as well as from the free-market think tanks – even though the inquiry itself was conducted entirely within Whitehall by a small ministerial group chaired by the Prime Minister. Indeed, as with the similar education debate of 1986–7, the pressures of an initially financial and staffing crisis brought out into public discussion options which would previously have been regarded as politically unacceptable. The Centre for Policy Studies under David Willetts and the Institute of Economic Affairs under Graham Mather produced a flood of ideas aimed at increasing patient choice and introducing market disciplines. Among the ideas floated (amongst others by the British Medical Association, the King's Fund, the Institute of Health Services Management, the No Turning Back group of Conservative MPs, and the Adam Smith Institute) were:

1   A dedicated health tax, as opposed to the present predominant, 80 per cent plus funding out of general taxation.
2   Social insurance schemes, with provision for opting out.
3   Further incentives to expand the private sector, which has already doubled from 5 to about 10 per cent during the 1980s. Among proposals would be to allow individuals to offset cost of private health care against personal tax liabilities.
4   Increasing patient charges for seeing doctors and 'hotel' payments towards staying in hospital, and charges for non-medical services. Charges, principally prescriptions and other tests, have been equivalent to nearly 4 per cent of NHS income.
5   Expanding income generation schemes by selling ancillary services such as shops and banks on hospital sites, by selling clinical services such as pay beds to private patients and to the private sector.
6   Creation of internal markets within NHS by allowing district health authorities to buy and sell services between each other, facilitating transfer of patients to where there is spare capacity or lower costs, thus reducing waiting lists.
7   Establishing health maintenance organizations on US lines offering voluntarily enrolled subscribers comprehensive health care for a periodic fixed payment in advance. Suggested British variants of managed health care organizations (Goldsmith and Willetts, 1988), funded by taxpayers to purchase comprehensive health care services for enrollees, and health management units (Pirie and Butler, 1988) under which consumers would register with a general practitioner of their choice who would then affiliate to a unit, rather than vice versa.

As the debate developed during 1988, there was, as the social services committee noted, a fascinating convergence of the many different ideas. There was a broad acceptance, even by the free-market advocates, of the virtues of retaining a National Health Service funded by some form of national taxation – either via income tax, a hypothecated health tax or a universal social insurance system. Similarly, there was general agreement that any changes should be evolutionary. This was reflected in a shift of ministerial rhetoric towards proclaiming the virtues of the NHS. It became clear that any changes would build on the present structure of the taxpayer funded service.

The eventual proposals – foreshadowing legislation in the 1989–90 parliamentary session – were based on the idea of increasing choice within the context of largely free at the point of use provision, financed by taxpayers. Hence there will be an internal market allowing resources to be shifted between local health districts – for instance, allowing patients to go where queues are shorter, or where costs are lower. The general practitioner is to be placed at the centre of the changes, being allocated budgets to buy health care for patients, including non-emergency operations. The aim is to allow doctors to determine where the money goes, rewarding more efficient hospitals. More radically, roughly 300 larger hospitals are to be allowed to opt out of health authority control – remaining in the NHS as independent self-governing bodies, called NHS hospital trusts, selling services to both private patients and hospitals and to regional health authorities which would pay for NHS patients treated. As with education, the aim has been not to remove the principles of universal taxpayer financed provision, but to challenge the quasi-monopoly role of local health authorities.

Critics questioned whether these managerial changes would be enough without continual extra funding. They were also concerned that the further extension of charges – most controversially to dental and eye tests – and the encouragement of private provision would create a two-tier structure; the better-off would increasingly seek private health insurance while the core NHS would be squeezed. Labour's shadow Health Minister, Robin Cook, was worried that allowing hospitals to opt out would increase inequalities in provision since some opted-out hospitals might not want to provide certain types of expensive treatment. The proposals were opposed by all the medical professions, notably general practitioners. Yet, as with other parts of the welfare state, the Thatcher years have seen the basic principles of the NHS remaining largely intact, even if there is an increasing challenge from the private sector.

Education

Ever since Prime Minister (now Lord) James Callaghan launched a great debate on education in a much discussed speech at Ruskin College, Oxford, in October 1976, it has been commonly agreed in British politics that something should be done to raise standards and to increase the accountability of teachers. For ten years, under both Labour and Conservative Education Secretaries, little of substance happened.

Moreover, with the size of the school population falling the Treasury saw an opportunity to achieve savings in the education budget. The March 1980 education White Paper projected a decline in spending on this programme of nearly 7 per cent in real, inflation adjusted, terms during 1978–9 and 1982–3. The outcome was only a drop of just over 1 per cent as local authorities maintained higher levels of spending than the Treasury planned. One result was that more teachers were employed than originally intended, and pupil: teacher ratios fell further than expected. The squeeze on the education budget produced serious problems, since while a sizeable number of schools were closed, there were diseconomies of scale associated with contraction. Where schools could not be closed, savings were achieved by cutting expenditure on books and on various ancillary services. The key features of the education scene in schools in the 1980s are in table 7.3.

Table 7.3   Shrinking schools (figures for England)

	1979–80	1983–4	1988–9
Total school population (thousands)	8,397	7,574	6,967
Percent of pupils under five in schools	39.0	41.4	43.8
Percent of pupils over school leaving age in school	19.4	21.3	20.0
Teachers (full-time equivalents)	438	411	397
Pupil:teacher ratios	18.7:1	18.9:1	17.0:1

Source: Public Expenditure White Papers

Discontent rumbled on until simmering disagreements over teachers' pay boiled over in a series of disruptive actions over the 1984–6 period as negotiations between the teaching unions and their local authority employers on the Burnham committee failed to reach agreement. The Government initially took a restrictive line. The dispute and the greater public discussion over shortcomings in the school system led to growing pressure within the Government for more radical action, encouraged by the various free-market think tanks and the Downing Street Policy Unit.

Lord (formerly Sir Keith) Joseph, the Education Secretary from 1981 until 1986, had recognized the problem. He launched some important initiatives to raise standards – by, for example, publishing the reports of Her Majesty's Inspectors, by requiring schools to provide more information about their performance, by sharpening up the curriculum, and by increasing the role of parents on more free-standing governing bodies, with the role of local education authorities reduced. Vocational training was strengthened and new examinations and methods of assessing children's performances were introduced. Lord Joseph put forward proposals in a 1985 White Paper, 'Better Schools'. Some of this was reflected in legislation in 1986. Yet, Lord Joseph lacked the political will, and the Cabinet's support, for radical changes in face of the opposition of frequently Labour controlled local education authorities and the power of the competing teachers' unions.

Mrs Thatcher underlined the priority she placed on education by appointing the highly ambitious Kenneth Baker to succeed Lord Joseph in May 1986. His brief was to produce radical proposals ahead of the coming general election. Mr Baker's first task was to end the disruption in schools which he did by obtaining more money from the Treasury to announce a 16.4 per cent pay and conditions package for the teachers – an approach followed in the settlement of the nurses dispute two years later. He followed this by dissolving the Burnham negotiating machinery and instead imposed the pay award with the assistance of an advisory committee. Teachers' pay was restructured to reward those with above average responsibilities and who performed well.

Mr Baker then produced a series of radical proposals which were included in the Conservatives' 1987 election manifesto and became legislation in the 1987–8 session. This measure was as far-reaching in its effects as the 1944 Butler Act. The main proposals affecting schools were:

1   Allowing parents to vote on whether to take their schools out of local authority control at the initiation of governors, with opted-out schools to be financed by a direct Whitehall grant.
2   A national curriculum of 10 foundation subjects, with English, mathematics and science at the core. Nationally agreed attainment targets and assessment arrangements at ages of 7, 11, 14 and 16.
3   Parents will be able to enrol their children at any school that physically has capacity for them, provided this is appropriate for the age and aptitude of the child.
4   All secondary schools and primary schools with more than 200 pupils will receive budgets from local authorities, which they will be free to spend as they wish, including staff costs.
5   During the passage of the bill through Parliament, Mr Baker bowed to a skilful backbench campaign led by those allies in mischief, Norman Tebbit and Michael Heseltine, and agreed to the immediate abolition of the Inner London Education Authority in 1990, rather than allowing gradual opting-out by boroughs, as originally proposed.

The effect of these changes will be to undermine significantly the position of local authorities, not only by allowing schools to opt out but also by switching power and responsibilities for schools which remain inside the system to governing bodies, on which parental representation has been strengthened. The future pattern will depend considerably on uncertainties of implementation – how many schools opt out, and how the core curriculum works out. The Government will also need the co-operation of teachers, particularly with the new curriculum and shortly after a big shake-up of the examination system with the General Certificate of Secondary Education replacing GCE O-levels and CSE. All this has involved more money. The education budget fell slightly in real terms from 1978–9 to 1985–6, down from £15.9 billion to £15.7 billion (at constant 1987–8 prices). Then, under Mr Baker's influence and the teachers' pay award, spending rose to £16.5 billion, with a total of £17.5 billion planned for 1989–90.

Potentially, the system could change significantly with a variety of competing types of school – including the industry-sponsored City

Technology Colleges in the inner cities. Launched by Mr Baker with the aim of stimulating technical and other education, these colleges had a slow start, partly because of local authority opposition. The overall changes are a classic illustration of the middle-class welfare state at work. Only a small minority of parents have been able to afford private education, and the majority of children of Conservative supporters are in the state sector. So the Government has responded to their concerns by offering them some of the independence of the private sector, though at the taxpayers' expense.

The Government has also faced considerable problems with the highly articulate lobby of the universities. Ministers have pointed to a rise in the proportion of 18 and 19 year olds entering higher education from 12.4 to 14.2 per cent between 1979 and 1986. Moreover, expenditure on higher education has risen in real terms. Yet the Government has come under consistent heavy fire from the universities, particularly about the level of funding of research. However, the Government responded to criticism about cutbacks in the funding of science (which has been discussed in chapter 4) by announcing big increases in the budget for the late 1980s – a 13 per cent rise for 1989–90 alone. Yet that followed an earlier period when resources were squeezed in real terms and when there was a small decline in the number of publications by British scientists.

The Government has also been accused of being unconcerned with academic freedom and of wanting to tie the universities too closely to industry. There is something in all these charges, though the economics of established tenure – and the resulting inflexibility – have ensured that the squeeze in spending experienced by the whole public sector during the 1980s has resulted in maximum dislocation in the universities. These institutions with their semi-independent professorial and departmental baronies are, almost by definition, slow to adapt, with the result that some cherished departments had to be closed. In November 1986 the Government agreed with the University Grants Committee and the Committee of Vice-Chancellors a programme to ensure greater selectivity in research funding, the rationalization (that is closure and merger) of small departments, better financial management and closer assessment of standards of teaching. As a result, as the Government intended, the universities have had to increase their proportion of income raised from non-exchequer sources, notably industry on tied projects, from 37 per cent in 1979–80 to well over 45 per cent by 1987–8.

Mr Baker sought to take the shift in university funding further in his education reform bill in 1987–8. This proposed that the polytechnics and similar colleges should be taken away from local authority control and that academic tenure should be abolished – to give more flexibility in handling staff. The bill also provided for the establishment of a Universities Funding Council to replace the University Grants Committee as the way of distributing Government money. The key change was that instead of the previous block grants which universities had, they were given, within certain limits, freedom to spend as they wished, and the new council would impose contracts with conditions as to performance in certain detailed respects. This was modified during the passage of the bill in the House of Lords by a powerful lobby from the University vice-chancellors to limit the Education Secretary's power to intervene in relation to any university. Nonetheless, the change in funding was seen by some as in effect a nationalization of the universities. Indeed, not only the universities, but also some free-market critics, had grave reservations about these aspects of the bill.

Proposals were soon circulating for a more market-based system, in particular from Robert Jackson, the Higher Education Minister. The general philosophy was that provision should be based on national assessments of the need for staff in business and industry. This would contrast with the Robbins principle that all who are qualified were entitled to a place. One option is that free higher education should be abandoned and replaced by fee-paying and a voucher system, funded by the taxpayer, which could be topped up by a loan. Ministers have anyway been attracted by the idea of shifting the balance of funding towards the student who would select the university of his or her choice. As a short-term measure, proposals have also been developed to change the system of student grants by freezing the subsistence element and introducing top-up loans. This plan produced strong hostility from the National Union of Students and considerable scepticism from the university authorities and the financial institutions which would be involved. The Government's proposals led to concern that moves to a market-based system would restrict access – returning, in the words of Labour spokesman Jack Straw, to the pre-war days 'when there were a few scholarships for the brightest and courses were only available to the rest if their parents could afford it'.

More generally, Mr Baker has created a whole series of powers for himself and his successors as Education Secretary. These powers include directly funding schools, and more closely controlling university funding. The results of the Baker Act in terms of educational standards will only be seen in the 1990s, but politically they represent a further illustration of the Government's instinctive centralism and disregard for local authorities.

Housing

The housing market is discussed more fully in chapters 3 and 6, while the social consequences are considered in chapter 8. This dispersed treatment reflects the importance of housing to so many other issues. Housing has been a classic example of the Thatcherite welfare state in action. Central Government subsidies to local authorities for their current housing expenditure have fallen substantially during the 1980s – down from between £1.2 billion to £1.4 billion at the beginning of the decade to between £450 and £500 million on average by the end of the 1980s. By contrast, the cost of mortgage interest tax relief started from roughly the same point but broadly trebled in size during the decade. The cut in council house subsidies resulted in a sharp rise in council rents in real, inflation-adjusted, terms. Rents rose from being equivalent to about 6.5 per cent of average earnings at the start of the decade to a peak of 8.8 per cent in 1983, and then around 8 per cent, or slightly less, as earnings grew more rapidly than rents in the late 1980s. However, this increase in rents was, in part, a catching-up process after the period of heavy subsidy during the 1970s when council rents were still below comparable private sector levels. The Government's policy was to limit these subsidies even further, by, for instance, ring-fencing housing revenue accounts to prevent cross-subsidization from general rate funds.

Tenants were not only encouraged to buy their own homes, but also to transfer away from local authority control to new landlords who would be approved by the Housing Corporation, whether in the private sector or by housing associations. Under the 1988 Housing Act special Housing Action Trusts were set up to take over some of the worst council estates from local authorities and to improve them. The Government expressed repeated doubts about whether local authorities should continue to own and manage housing on a large scale, apart from special property for the old and disabled, and as a result Whitehall support for new public housebuilding was cut substantially. Instead, the emphasis was on improvement and renovation, which was partly financed by continuing large-scale sales of property – and receipts were boosted by the late 1980s boom in prices.

The quality of the housing stock improved during the decade, with more homes having central heating and loft insulation. However, the English House Conditions Survey in 1986–7 found about 900,000 homes in England, nearly 5 per cent of the total, which were unfit to live in. While the proportion lacking basic amenities fell between 1981 and 1986 from 5 to 3 per cent of the total, the number of homes in serious disrepair remained broadly the same at around 6 per cent.

The big gap was the private rented sector which continued to decline for most of the decade as a result of the discouragement to landlords from rent controls. The sector accounted for less than 8 per cent of the housing stock, compared with nearly a third in the early 1960s. The experiment of assured tenancies introduced in 1980 made little overall impact on the problem, and the Government was cautious about taking more radical steps for fear of alarming tenants. But the 1988 Act provided for deregulation of new private rents in the hope of encouraging new investment. This involved a choice of an assured tenancy, under which landlord and tenant would be free to agree a rent at market levels, with the right to a new tenancy when the old one ended, or a shorthold under which the landlord would have the right of possession at the end of a fixed term letting but the rent would be registered and fixed to give a reasonable rate of return. The choice would be between security of tenancy with market rents or the right of repossession for the landlord with registered rents. In addition, in the 1988 Budget, the scope of Business Expansion Scheme tax relief was broadened to cover companies specializing in the letting of housing on assured tenancies, with limits on the value of the property. The early response was larger than expected, though all agreed that it would take a long time to reverse the 60-year long decline in the private rented sector.

8

A Divided Nation

We need to ensure that all our people have a share in that growing prosperity. We could take no pride in the rebuilding of a prosperity that remained the privilege of a few.

Norman Fowler, Social Services Secretary, Conservative Party conference,
Blackpool, 8 October 1985

It is arguable that rich and poor, suburb and inner city, privileged and deprived, have been becoming more sharply separate from each other for many years, and that the impoverished minority has become increasingly cut off from the mainstream of our national life.

Faith in the City, The Report of the Archbishop of Canterbury's
Commission on Urban Priority Areas, December 1985

One of the strongest and most frequent charges against the Thatcher Government is that Britain has become a more divided society since 1979. There has been much talk of Two Nations, reviving Disraeli's image of economic, social, geographic and political cleavage.

The existence of growing divisions within Britain since 1979 is indisputable. Yet that broad conclusion masks several questions. First, what are the types of division – in the distribution of income, wealth, employment, health, education, between and within regions, or politically? Secondly, how far have the changes been relative rather than absolute – in terms of the comparative rates of growth and job opportunities? Thirdly, how far can increased divisions be attributed to the actions of the Government itself, as opposed to underlying long-term trends?

Some of the changes are the intended result of Government policy. During the Conservative policy re-think of the second half of the 1970s, Lord (then Sir Keith) Joseph, Mrs Thatcher's ideological conscience, made the rejection of egalitarianism a central plank of his counter-revolution. In the book he co-authored with Jonathan Sumption, *Equality* (1978), Joseph challenged the social and economic priorities of the post-war era and the terms of the Beveridge settlement. He rejected the linking of poverty with loss of freedom or with the belief that the state has a role in redistributing wealth. In their fascinating survey of free market thought on both sides of the Atlantic, Hoover and Plant (1988) argued that a defence of inequality has been fundamental to the conservative-capitalist argument. In dismissing the view that factors such as merit or fairness can play any part, Joseph maintained that 'the working of a free economy depends upon differentials at every level.' In practical terms this was linked to a rejection of the then current incomes policies which in his view had led to a distortion of the labour market.

Joseph went further in his rejection of egalitarianism. He disputed the social democratic belief that the definition of levels of poverty should be related to the standards of income and of living of the time, and that therefore social provision should be explicitly linked to earnings. Joseph defined a minimum standard as 'an absolute standard of means defined by reference to the actual needs of the poor and not by reference to the expenditure of those who are not poor.' These assertions became tied in with the view expressed on both sides of the Atlantic that the post-war welfare state had created an attitude of dependence upon the state among the poor which reduced the sense of initiative and the incentive to work.

The New Right's counter-revolution provided the theoretical underpinning for the less high-flown political desire of Mrs Thatcher and her supporters to challenge the limited egalitarianism of the Wilson and Callaghan governments of the 1974–9 period. This meant the end of formal pay, price, dividend and rent controls. These restrictions had had the effect of squeezing income differentials, though also of encouraging hidden payments of various kinds. More significant was the change in attitudes in the early 1980s. It was all right for companies to reward directors and top executives; salaries in six figures became commonplace during the 1980s, especially as companies substantially increased their profits. Bourgeois guilt was definitely out. It is revealing that Lord Young, who has perhaps been less affected by such guilt than his colleagues who have faced the electorate, has drawn the comparison with the rise in standards of living in the nineteenth century as a consequence of successful entrepreneurs. 'So in looking at the generation of Victorian entrepreneurs and at the results of their achievement, we need not feel guilty that their success was at the expense of the poor' (quoted in Walker and Walker, 1987). As Mrs Thatcher put it equally bluntly in 1985 'you are not doing anything against the poor by seeing that top people are paid well.'

The combination of the end of incomes policies, a sharp recovery in profits and changes in the political climate led to a big increase in the pre-tax pay of top earners. According to Government figures, the gross earnings of the top 10 per cent increased by 22 per cent in real terms between 1979 and 1986, double the median rise. By contrast, the pre-tax earnings of the bottom 10 per cent rose by less than 4 per cent in real terms over the period. In 1976 the lowest paid worker in the top 10 per cent was paid 2.5 times more than the highest paid worker in the bottom 10 per cent of the range. By 1986 the ratio had increased to 2.6 for women and 3 for men – a 20 per cent widening in the spread of male earnings.

There has not just been an increase in inequality at the extremes, but also an improvement in the position of large groups of white-collar, non-manual workers compared to manual workers. An analysis in the monthly *Employment Gazette* in February 1988 showed that, while average male earnings rose by 15.7 per cent in real, inflation-adjusted terms between 1979 and 1986, manual workers enjoyed a rise of only 5.7 per cent. By contrast, the real pay of white-collar employees rose by 22.4 per cent, with that of professional workers in management and administration up by nearly 29 per cent. The different experience between industrial sectors was shown by real increases of just 3 per cent for those employed in construction, mining, painting and assembling. These figures suggest that highly-paid workers have sought to reverse the relative decline in earnings experienced as a result of the incomes policies of the 1970s, while the sharp rise in unemployment in the early 1980s disproportionately affected workers in manufacturing and construction.

These contrasts reflect a specific Government wages policy with two parallel and sharply contrasting attitudes, according to Dominic Byrne (in Walker and Walker, 1988):

The first is a laissez-faire approach towards, and in some cases active encouragement of, rapid growth in the earnings of the high paid and many in the middle income brackets. On the other hand, the earnings of the low paid workers in the public sector, have been held down through a combination of deregulation of employment and wage protection, job schemes linked to low pay, public sector cash limits, and the straight-forward fear of unemployment.

There is something in this analysis. The opening up of the private sector labour market to more competitive pressures and sustained downward pressure on public sector wages (after the impact of the Clegg awards of 1979 had worked through) has served to limit wage rises for the low paid. This has been associated with a large-scale shift in the balance of the workforce with the decline of manufacturing and the growth of private sector services, especially those offering part-time jobs for women. Moreover, as ministers pointed out, there has to some extent been a trade-off between the level of wages and the provision of jobs.

So, to an unquantifiable extent, some of the increase in employment since 1983 may have been associated with a widening of pay differentials. The increase in pay inequalities has been marked. The pay of the poorest 10 per cent of workers relative to national average incomes reached a record low. There has been a growing contrast between the majority of securely employed full-time workers in occupational pension schemes and with fringe benefits, and a substantial minority of part-time workers without such security and entitlements who exist on the margins of the labour market.

These contrasts have been further increased by Government tax policy. The cuts in income tax since 1979 have been heavily biased towards the better-off. Indeed, it was not until after the 1987 and 1988 Budgets that the reduction in the basic rate of income tax ensured that those on average earnings and just above paid less of their incomes in income tax and national insurance contributions than in the last Labour year of 1978–9. However, following the near doubling of Value Added Tax in the 1979 Budget the average earner paid more in indirect tax, and his or her total tax bill relative to income was 45.7 per cent in total in 1988–9, against 45.5 per cent a decade earlier. Yet the 1988 Budget with the slashing of the top rate of income tax to 40 per cent from 60 per cent (down from 75 per cent before 1979) left the better-off still by far the largest gainers. These are, of course, relative calculations, taking no account of the sharp rise in real, inflation adjusted, incomes for most of those in work. These contrasts are shown by the following points:

1 Taking the Thatcher decade as a whole a single person on half average earnings gained £6.22 week (at 1988–9 income levels) from income tax cuts over and above the indexation of allowances to inflation. A single person on average male earnings (£244.70 a week) gained £16. However, someone on five times average earnings gained £270 a week.
2 In aggregate the top 10 per cent of the income range enjoyed a £9.3 billion reduction in payments compared with an indexed 1978–9 regime, compared with a £400 million cut for the bottom 10 per cent.

The distributional impact is shown in table 8.1.

However, Treasury ministers eagerly pointed out that tax revenue paid by top earners rose sharply in spite of these cuts in tax rates, as was discussed in chapter 4. Moreover, the income tax due from the top 2.5 per cent in 1978–9 (groups then liable to the higher rates of above 40 per cent) was £3.4 billion. This was equivalent to £7.1 billion at 1988–9 prices after adjusting for inflation. But this top 2.5 per cent actually paid about £9 billion in taxes and higher personal allowances. Ministers claimed that this showed the incentive effects of lower taxes, but as important may have been the explosion in pre-tax pay of top earners noted above.

Table 8.1 Share of gross income paid in tax: income tax and national insurance as a percentage of gross earnings

	Multiple of average earnings			
Single person	½	⅔	1	5
1978–9	23.6	27.5	31.5	52.2
1988–9	23.8	26.3	28.9	36.1

Married couple with 2 children and part-time working spouse (as adjusted for child benefit)

	½	⅔	1	5
1978–9	1.9	10.4	19.2	46.7
1988–9	4.8	11.4	18.0	33.8

Source: Parliamentary written answer

Table 8.2   Changes in real net earnings from 1978–9 to 1988–9: per cent rise after income tax and national insurance

Multiples of average earnings	⅔	1	2	5
Single person	28.3	31	33	68.8
Married couple	26.1	29.4	32.8	65.3

Source: Parliamentary written answer

When the impact of these pay rises and tax cuts are taken together there has been a substantial increase in inequality in the distribution of take-home pay. Even when the equalizing effects of social security benefits are taken into account, the share of final income of the bottom fifth of households dropped from around 7 to 6.3 per cent during the 1980s, while the share of the top fifth rose from 38 to 42 per cent. These trends are underlined in tables 8.2 and 8.3.

It is more difficult to assess changes in the distribution of wealth, partly because of the absence of up-to-date statistics. However, the combination of tax changes in severely restricting the scope of various capital taxes, the long climb of share prices (even after the shake-out of 1987–8), and the boom in house prices has dispropor-tionately benefited the already well-off. The long-term, slow decline in the share of wealth of the best-off seems to have been halted. According to Inland Revenue statistics, the share of marketable wealth (houses, stocks and shares) of the top 5 per cent which had dropped from more than 50 per cent during the 1970s, held steady at just under 40 per cent during the 1980s. The considerable existing inequalities were perpetuated, and may have widened for the wealthiest.

Overall, there has not been a split just into two groups, but into three, as John Rentoul has argued (1987). 'There are now Three Nations, not Two, and the Thatcher Government has pampered not just the rich but even more that other, discreet Nation, the super-rich. The Three Nations are the haves, the have nots, and the have lots.' The haves are perhaps better described not as the rich but as the comfortably off majority – homeowners with jobs, including many skilled workers, with whom Mrs Thatcher has identified and who have sustained her parliamentary majority.

Government policies have directly affected the position of the poor, both those in and out of work. This has partly been a result of changes in social security policy – in the level of benefits and

Table 8.3   *Income shares: pre-tax figures, with post-tax in brackets (per cent)*

	1978–9	1983–4	1988–9
Top 1 per cent	5 (3.4)	5.6 (4.2)	6.6 (5.4)
Top 5 per cent	14.6 (12.2)	16.3 (14.1)	17.5 (15.5)
Top 10 per cent	23.6 (20.9)	25.9 (23.4)	27.1 (24.9)
Top 50 per cent	70.6 (68)	72 (69.6)	73.1 (71.1)
Bottom 25 per cent	11.1 (12.8)	10.8 (12.3)	10.3 (11.4)

Source: Parliamentary answers based on information reported to tax offices and collected through annual surveys of personal incomes

entitlements (as discussed in chapter 7), and partly because the poor have suffered most from the rise in unemployment. For instance, while the level of supplementary benefit increased slightly in real terms until it was replaced in the April 1988 reorganization of social security, its uprating lagged well behind the rise in earnings – falling from 61 per cent of average personal disposable income in 1978 to 53 per cent in 1987. Moreover, for all the ministerial talk of reducing dependency on social security, the number of recipients has increased substantially, largely as a result of the increase in unemployment.

Whatever the cause, the results have been devastating. According to the official Family Expenditure Survey those in the bottom tenth suffered a drop in real incomes of 9.7 per cent between 1979 and 1985. These figures differ from the earlier figures on gross earnings by including those dependent on social security and not just the much smaller number liable to income tax. There have, however, been considerable disputes between the Government and the poverty lobby over the exact figures, partly because of major changes in the nature and coverage of the statistics. A new series covering low incomes produced in 1988 indicated that the average incomes of people in the bottom tenth rose by 8.3 per cent between 1981 and 1985, compared with a national average rise of 6.4 per cent. This followed an earlier period of decline when unemployment was rising sharply. Over the 1980s as a whole the real disposable incomes of most groups improved in absolute terms, though there were marked exceptions within the poorest groups, such as the single unemployed.

Nevertheless, in the 1979 to 1985 period the number of people with an income at or below the officially defined poverty line (the supplementary benefit level) rose by 55 per cent to 9.4 million (or 17 per cent of the population). This included 2.4 million below the poverty line. Despite cutbacks in entitlements, the number of children taking free school meals rose between 1979 and 1986 from 12 to 18 per cent of all pupils. There was a marked shift in the burden of poverty away from pensioners to people below pension age, again in part a reflection of the incidence of higher unemployment.

Within this general picture both women and ethnic minorities have suffered particularly. Unemployment among women rose more rapidly than for men during the 1980s. Changes in the social security system – ranging from the April 1988 shake-up to the freezing of child benefit – have had a disproportionate effect on women. The unemployment rate for black men and women has been twice that of whites of similar ages, and black people are likely to remain unemployed for twice as long as white. This has reinforced the increased segregation of blacks in sections of certain cities which have experienced worse deprivation and violence, as reflected in the riots of the summer of 1981 and early autumn of 1985.

The alienation of these communities was increased by successive acts tightening up immigration controls and the practical application of these rules for relatives of those living in the UK. The Asian and Afro-Caribbean communities regarded the Government's approach as racist and the effect of the British Nationality Act of 1981 was to ensure that virtually only whites with close ties to the UK had an automatic right of entry and settlement. Total acceptances for settlement from the New Commonwealth and Pakistan fell from more than 40,000 a year in the late 1970s to just over 20,000 a year a decade later. These issues produced considerable tensions with some Commonwealth countries and with ethnic minorities in the inner cities, though the numbers involved were small, and generally much less than the scale of emigration.

There has been not just a widening of relative differences of income, but also a rise in absolute levels of suffering for many households. Well over 8 million people were dependent on income support in the late 1980s and there was a hard core of poor of 1.5 million claimants who had been drawing benefits for more than five years. Even if some increase in inequality has been an inevitable price for greater economic dynamism, the extent of the change and the associated growth in poverty could have been mitigated by different government actions. In particular, the frequently expressed

Conservative commitment to be the party of the family has been contradicted by the freezing of child benefit since the uprating of April 1987. Child benefit, which is paid to the mother, has been widely regarded as the most effective way of helping poor families with children. Since it is not means-tested nor taxed, it does not throw up any of the disincentive problems which existed with other benefits before the April 1988 changes. Yet the freezing of the benefit and the subsequent debate about its future after a 1991–2 election has raised questions about how far such universal benefits will continue to be paid.

Under Treasury pressure to produce savings, the Government's response has been to argue that help should be targeted. This was the philosophy of the April 1988 changes which introduced a much greater measure of selective assistance. Yet that has been at the expense of cutbacks in housing benefit for around 1.5 million households over four years. There has been an increase in help for the very poorest, partly paid for by the not quite so poor. Similarly, the community charge, or poll tax, being introduced in Scotland in April 1989 and in England and Wales in April 1990, will penalize those just above the bottom of the income scale. While the scope of rebates has been extended more broadly than originally envisaged, the level of income support is related to a 20 per cent contribution based on average rate/charge levels, irrespective of the actual level. Therefore it hits those living in inner city areas of high local government expenditure and high relative levels of charges.

The Child Poverty Action Group has argued that this general approach has represented 'horizontal redistribution between relatively poor people rather than vertical redistribution from rich to poor.' Fran Bennett, the group's director, has argued (in Walker and Walker, 1987) that this means that:

On the one hand, the better-off will benefit from tax relief on their private pension schemes (and mortgages and other savings schemes etc). On the other, the poor will be more reliant on poor relief from means-tested benefits, the social fund and charities. We will be retreating even further from Beveridge's aim of a benefits system 'for all citizens without distinction of rich and poor,' providing 'security against want without a means test'. We will be advancing even further towards a divided Britain.

The increased inequalities of the 1980s have been not just financial but also social. For instance, the stark inequalities in standards of health between different income groups revealed by Sir Douglas Black's report in 1980 have worsened during the subsequent decade. His analysis was anyway largely based on evidence up to 1970–72 and it highlighted big differences in overall death rates, early deaths and infant deaths between social classes. Sir Douglas concluded that 'a child born to professional parents, if he or she is not socially mobile, can expect to spend over five years more as a living person than a child born to an unskilled manual household'. A more recent study published in the *Lancet* of August 1986 suggested that, while mortality in 1979–83 fell in both non-manual and manual groups for both men and women, 'the social gradient has widened: mortality has declined more rapidly among non-manual than manual groups'. There are no certain or definite causal relationships but there are commonsense grounds for believing that increases in strains and pressures resulting from increased unemployment and poverty have been significant contributory factors. For instance, a survey of the health and life styles of more than 9,000 people conducted by the Health Promotion Research Trust showed that a third of unskilled manual workers reported ill-health compared with a twelfth of those in professional and managerial jobs. Unemployed middle-aged men also reported high rates of psychiatric symptoms – depression, anxiety, difficulties in relationships with other people and suicidal wishes.

Inequalities in housing provision have also grown with a sharp increase in homelessness. The number of households accepted as homeless rose from around 50,000 in the late 1950s to more than 120,000 a decade later. This is equivalent to around 370,000 people, according to Shelter, the housing pressure group, which has suggested that the true figure may have been nearly twice as large. The problem has got worse in part because of the Government's cutback in new money for housebuilding. So while needs have been rising, the stock of available low cost housing has fallen and increasing amounts of money have had to be spent on bed and breakfast and other temporary accommodation.

These inequalities have been matched, and in many respects magnified, by geographical divisions. The 1979–81 recession and the subsequent recovery have had an unequal impact through the UK. The south and east have prospered, while the north and west have lagged behind. All the main indicators – population change,

Table 8.4 Regional differences in main economic indicators

(a) Total output per head as per cent of UK average

	S. East	E. Ang.	S. West	W. Mid.	E. Mid.	Y&H[a]	N. West	North	Wales	Scotland
1979	112.2	94.7	90.8	98.1	96.0	94.0	96.4	95.6	89.6	98.6
1987	118.5	99.8	94.0	91.6	95.1	92.8	92.8	88.9	82.3	94.5

[a] Yorkshire and Humberside
Northern Ireland has fallen from 81 to 77.4 per cent

(b) Average earnings as percentage of South East earnings

	E. Ang.	S. West	W. Mid.	E. Mid.	Y&H	N. West	North	Wales	Scotland
1979	88.4	85.2	90.4	89.5	91.3	91.4	91.9	90.0	93.3
1986	83.8	82.9	83.3	82.0	83.0	85.2	82.8	81.8	86.5

levels of output and unemployment, low pay, dependence on social security, and health – have shown marked regional contrasts which have generally increased during the 1980s. For instance, in 1987 the rate of infant mortality, deaths under one year per 1,000 live births, varied from 10.1 in Yorkshire to 7.8 in East Anglia. The following lists and table 8.4 show variations in the main and economic indicators.

Changes in total employment 1979–87, in per cent

East Anglia +17.8
South West +7.2
South East +4.4
East Midlands +2.8
UK as a whole −1.6
Yorkshire and Humberside −4.9
West Midlands −5.1
Northern Ireland −6.6
Scotland −8.1
North −9.6
North West −12.1
Wales −12.6

Changes in total investment in real terms 1979–87, in per cent

South East +10
North West +4
East Anglia +2
UK as a whole −2
East Midlands −8
West Midlands −12
North −14
South West −15
Yorkshire and Humberside −15
Scotland −17
Wales −23
Northern Ireland −31

The figures show that the South East, East Anglia and, to a lesser extent, the South West have not only enjoyed more favourable economic conditions than the rest of the country, but have in most cases increased their lead. Even after the long upswing of the late

1980s, there was a big contrast in unemployment rates between Northern Ireland, the North, and Scotland – all still above 10 per cent – and the South East and East Anglia at below 5 per cent. However, the pattern is more complicated than just a North/South divide, since there are major differences within regions which are often as important as those between them. Most striking of all is the contrast between big cities and smaller towns. A key feature of the 1980s has been the decline of manufacturing which has tended to be concentrated in many of the larger cities and single industry towns of the north and west of England, Scotland and Wales. Growth has been focused on the new technology industries, distribution, and private sector services which have been more concentrated in the South East and East Anglia. A paper for an Institute of British Geographers' conference ranked 280 'travel to work areas' according to an index of 10 economic indicators. The top 35 areas all lay below a line from the Severn Estuary to Lincolnshire, while towns in the north, Scotland and Wales were concentrated in the bottom half of the table. The net job gain between 1983 and 1987 was just 1 per cent in the north, but more than 6 per cent in the south.

But there was not a uniform picture. Some poor areas were in the south and some prosperous places in the north. A report published by Warwick University (1988) showed that since the late 1960s there had been a shift of population and wealth from the larger cities to the country and smaller towns. Towns such as Macclesfield, Kendal and Penrith in the north all benefited as places offering a higher quality of life. Affluent, growing towns in the north-east and north-west have been alongside declining shipbuilding, steel and port cities. Similarly, there have been areas of high unemployment and deprivation in London, notably to the north and west of the City and docklands, and in Bristol and other southern cities.

There has also been growing evidence of very wide differences of income and employment within regions. This has partly been because wages of low paid manual workers in, for example, the public sector, have been broadly similar between regions, while the pay of non-manual workers and executives has varied considerably. Executives have been paid much more in London than in Newcastle and their salaries have risen more sharply during the 1980s. Consequently, the gap between the top and bottom has been higher in the South East than in other regions.

Nevertheless, the problems of decline and deprivation have been mainly concentrated in the large urban areas of northern England, Scotland and Wales. As Lewis and Townsend have pointed out (1989), the lower average figures in the north show that better conditions in a few places have been outweighed by worse conditions in poorer areas. At the same time, the rapid growth of small towns south and west of London has created problems of congestion and intensive arguments over planning controls on further development. The Government has pursued a variety of policies to counter this imbalance. Most of the regional inequalities have been longstanding and can only be attributed to specific Government policies to the extent to which the strong pound of 1979–81 squeezed manufacturing and therefore hit the north more than the south.

However, the Conservatives have come to reject a specifically regional approach in shifting most of Government help away from the previous blanket subsidies for capital investment in areas of high unemployment towards more selective assistance and to a series of initiatives to revive the depressed inner cities. The previous approach of automatic help for new manufacturing plants in the regions often financed large capital intensive projects employing few new workers and which might anyway have gone ahead. This approach was substantially modified in November 1984 with limits on the availability of assistance and an extension of regional development grants to include some service operations such as data processing and software development. In January 1988 the system of regional development grants was scrapped and replaced by a framework of discretionary selective assistance related to the number of jobs expected to be created or safeguarded.

Critics of previous regional policy such as John McEnery, a former Department of Trade and Industry civil servant, argued (1988) that these changes, while welcome, still missed the basic problem of the imbalance of services, rather than manufacturing, employment and self-employment. He argued that services, employing two-thirds of the workforce, were biased towards the South East. In particular, he wrote, 'the cancer debilitating the rest of the country is the concentration of company headquarters in the London area, whether in manufacturing or service industry. It is those headquarters, themselves autonomous services that in turn spawn the vast range of ancillary services in the south-east and cause the national imbalance in service employment (and in house prices).' Yet the Government's monopolies and mergers policy, focusing almost entirely on competition, has ignored regional factors in considering takeovers of companies with head offices outside London. It was no thanks to Government decisions that the conglomerate BTR in January 1987 withdrew its takeover bid for glassmakers Pilkington, based in St Helens in Lancashire. The decision reflected both the cross-party outcry in the north-west and the sensitive political timing ahead of the imminent general election. Indeed, little more than a year later, after the election, a similar level of protest in Yorkshire did not preserve the independence of the York-based Rowntree chocolate group, which was taken over by Nestlé of Switzerland. As with the Pilkington takeover the Government stood aside.

It is significant that one of the few British cities outside the south showing evidence of revival has been Glasgow where the head offices of several leading groups are sited. Moreover, the local authorities, of both the city and the Strathclyde region, have been closely involved in this regeneration, along with the taxpayer-financed Scottish Development Agency. Their activities have attracted considerable private sector investment in the renewal project in the east of the city. However, for all the euphoria surrounding the Garden Festival, Glasgow has continued to have serious problems of poor housing and poverty. In spite of the problems caused by the decline of the shipbuilding, steel, motor and other manufacturing industries, Scotland's economy has been helped by having its own banking system and locally based financial institutions – unlike, say, Birmingham and Liverpool. This is similar to the pattern in the US, where, partly thanks to the federal structure and laws against retail banks operating across state boundaries, there has been a tradition of independent political, business and financial centres across the country. A strong sense of local community and business/local authority links have aided the regeneration of cities such as Baltimore, Atlanta and Cleveland. The same pattern of locally based financial and political institutions has also applied in West Germany. By contrast, England, though not Scotland, has lacked such independent centres which are able to resist the pull of the capital. Moreover, these examples of successful local revival have also been dependent on substantial initial public sector investment in infrastructure.

The Government's regional and linked inner cities policies have been aimed at creating a climate for self-sustaining growth led by the private sector. Unlike the example of Glasgow, the Government has sought to by pass the largely Labour-controlled local authorities. The

Tories' first idea was to set up small enterprise zones, free of planning and other Government controls and taxes. Eventually 25 were established and led to successful development in areas like the Isle of Dogs in London's docklands, Corby in the east Midlands (the site of a closed steel works) and Swansea. But there were complaints that these developments diverted activity and jobs from neighbouring areas at considerable expense. The total cost was around £300 million by the end of 1986. Doubts were expressed by the Public Accounts Committee of the Commons in summer 1986 about the effectiveness of the experiment. It noted evidence that, while between 4 and 12 per cent of wholly new firms might not have started but for the zones, about 75 to 85 per cent of incoming firms would have been operating in the same country or region even if there had been no zones. The committee said arrangements for monitoring enterprise zones had lacked completeness and consistency and argued that special attention should be paid to establishing the adverse effects of enterprise zones on other areas. After arguing that employment in the zones had more than doubled, the Government decided in December 1987 not to extend the number of zones, arguing that other measures would be more cost effective.

Later, in the mid-1980s, a more ambitious initiative was attempted involving Government pump-priming money, though on a smaller scale than in Glasgow. Rundown and derelict areas were designated to be taken over by centrally appointed urban development corporations with planning and compulsory purchase powers. These corporations – set up, for example, in Teesside, Tyne and Wear, and Trafford Park in Manchester – were based on the initial London docklands and Merseyside corporations. Following an earlier stalemate among the mainly Labour-run councils, the London corporation succeeded in stimulating private sector investment (at a ratio of over 5:1 to public support) in offices, such as the Canary Wharf financial complex, and in homes. However, long-established residents complained that the corporation was undemocratic and that the character of the area had been changed with the main beneficiaries being well-off yuppies rather than locals. But the overall impact was to open up a whole, previously rundown, area of London. Moreover, the London example was exceptional since other factors, notably location, were so favourable to development. The Government has also sought to by pass local authorities in its housing and education policies on the similar view that Town Halls have inhibited the rights and choice of tenants and parents.

There is only limited evidence that these and other public/private sector initiatives have so far reversed, or significantly checked, these inequalities. The £3 billion Action for Cities programme covered a wide range of projects in 57 inner city areas, though the earlier impact had been marred by squabbling between Government departments. Some development has been stimulated. London docklands aside, the most successful examples have tended to be where local authorities and businesses have worked together, as in Glasgow, Birmingham and Newcastle. There remain contradictions between the Government's desire to see private sector regeneration and its mergers policy which has allowed the takeover of companies with regionally-based head offices. Moreover, while in some cases it may have been necessary to avoid obstructive local councils, the amounts of money in the expanded urban programme have been less than the cuts in Treasury rate support grant for the same areas. Local enterprise agencies have lacked the resources to make much impact. This raises doubts as to how far such top-down solutions can generate a self-sustaining revival without local co-operation.

The Government's policy remains balanced between stimulating private sector development in areas of high unemployment and allowing market forces full play. So far there have been a number of limited initiatives to increase pay flexibility between regions by encouraging regionally-based deals, as discussed in chapter 3. A related problem is the restriction of choice imposed by the decline of the private rented housing sector and the inflexibility of the council rented sector – which the Government has been seeking to remedy.

The main barrier to migration has been the regional house price gap with prices in Greater London twice as high as in the north-west, the north, and Yorkshire and Humberside. Houseowners in the latter areas therefore have had insufficient equity to move south. For most of the 1980s there was little evidence of manual workers following the advice offered to the unemployed in 1981 by then Employment Secretary Norman Tebbit that should copy his father by getting on their bikes to look for work as he did in the 1930s. Manual workers have, in general, been immobile in response to unemployment. Despite strong local Conservative pressures against further development in southern England, the Government has been torn between allowing further expansion where businesses have wanted to go and restricting construction to push up house prices and wages, so as to divert activity northwards.

Overall, Britain has undoubtedly become a more divided country during the 1980s. The recession and subsequent recovery have had unequal economic, social and geographic effects. While there is not a simple North/South divide and prosperity has spread northwards during the second half of the 1980s to the east Midlands and smaller towns in the north, there remain clear geographical divisions. This has been brought out starkly in recent general elections. Outside London the Conservatives held all but three seats south of Coventry in England at both the 1983 and 1987 elections, while Tory MPs won many smaller towns in northern England, like Darlington, Hyndburn, two in Bury and two out of three in Bolton. Labour predominated in the North. John Curtice and Michael Steed have pointed out (in Butler and Kavanagh, 1988) that the Tory share of the vote rose by 1.2 percentage points between the 1983 and 1987 elections in south and east Britain, but fell by 2.7 points in north and west Britain. By contrast, the Labour share rose by just 1.6 points in the former, but by 6.5 points in the latter. Johnston, Pattie and Allsopp (1988) have argued that relative social and economic conditions are not the whole explanation. There has also been what they have described as a neighbourhood effect. People living in predominantly Labour areas have been more inclined to vote Labour, and vice versa – a clear reflection of a Two Nations attitude. For instance, an unskilled manual worker in the north was in 1987 13 per cent more likely to vote Labour than his counterpart in the south; in 1979 there was a 4 point gap. The Tory effect appears to have spread to the Midlands.

More fundamentally, there have been signs of what sociologist Professor A.H. Halsey has called a polarization between 'a majority in secure attachment to a still prosperous country and a minority in marginal social and economic conditions'. The hard-core of the poor and unemployed black youngsters in the big cities form an emerging under-class alienated from the successful majority and their values. The result has not only been increases in violent crime and drug-taking, but also a greater feeling of social malaise. This unease has not been just in the under-class, as will be discussed in the next chapter.

The increased inequalities and social strains of Britain during the 1980s have represented both a significant qualification to claims of national revival and a series of major problems which the Government has begun to tackle only belatedly and clumsily. Yet, politically, the Conservatives, like Republican presidential candidates in the US, have been able to survive and prosper with the votes of the affluent majority, without needing those of the poor minority.

9

State of the Nation

It is not the creation of wealth that is wrong but love of money for its own sake. The spiritual dimension comes in deciding what one does with the wealth.

Mrs Margaret Thatcher, Address to the General Assembly of the Church of Scotland, 21 May 1988

The fruits of economic success could turn sour unless we can bring back greater social cohesion to our country. Social cohesion is quite different from social equality: indeed the two are ultimately incompatible. But social cohesion alongside the creation of wealth through private enterprise: these are the two conditions of our future progress.

Douglas Hurd, Home Secretary, Peel Society Dinner, Tamworth, 5 February 1988

The trigger of today's outburst of crime and violence lies in the era and attitudes of post-war funk which gave birth to the 'Permissive Society' which, in turn, generated today's violent society ... Family life was derided as an outdated bourgeois concept. Criminals deserved as much sympathy as their victims.

Norman Tebbit, chairman of the Conservative Party, First Disraeli Lecture, 13 November 1985

The far-reaching economic and industrial changes of the 1980s have raised fundamental questions about the social health and cohesion of Britain. Not only has the country become more divided, economically and geographically, as discussed in the last chapter, but there has been increasing concern about crime and a loss of community. This has been allied with a debate about whether the Thatcher Government has become authoritarian, and so caused an erosion of civil liberties.

During the second half of the 1980s the costs of Thatcherism have been debated more and more. Even those who have welcomed the economic changes have felt that the emphasis should shift more to the social area – though naturally the prescriptions have varied. The sense of unease is conveyed by the quotation at the beginning of this chapter from Douglas Hurd, Home Secretary from September 1985, who, in his public service and attitudes, has epitomized the One Nation tradition of Tory paternalism. In a series of speeches and interviews in 1987–8, he expressed concern over the threats to social cohesion – a call echoed by other Tories as well as by opposition politicians.

The extent of the problem has been underlined by the crime figures. During most of the 1980s the number of notifiable offences, particularly violent crime and robbery, rose sharply, at an annual rate of over 5 per cent between 1980 and 1987, even allowing for all the necessary caveats about possible changes in the proportion of crimes notified to the police. Admittedly, this growth continued a long-established trend, both domestically and internationally. The rate of increase of overall crime accelerated during the early 1980s, but Home Office ministers highlighted signs of a stabilization, in the late 1980s, with a drop in recorded offences of nearly 5 per cent between 1987 and 1988. There was a fall in notifiable offences in London, Greater Manchester, Merseyside and the West Midlands. But a noticeable drop in property related offences, such as burglaries, and thefts from cars and from shops, was partially offset by a further sharp rise in the already record number of violent crimes, such as assaults and sexual offences. These have remained a small proportion of the total but have naturally been worrying for the public.

None the less, the trend over the 1980s presented a tricky internal party problem for the Conservatives as the self-proclaimed party of law and order. The annual debate on the subject at the Conservative Party conference was an even more difficult exercise than usual for successive Home Secretaries faced with the vocal demands of the rank-and-file for even tougher action and instant solutions. The Government could, and did, point to the substantial extra resources devoted to the police and to crime prevention. The Home Office budget, primarily devoted to law and order, rose by more than 55 per cent in real, inflation adjusted, terms in the decade to 1988–9, with further sizeable increases planned for the following three years. Over the decade total staff available to the police rose by a fifth. There were also improvements in police pay and conditions, in training and in resources.

The courts were given powers to increase sentences, with a much-publicized regime of 'short, sharp shocks' for young offenders. Among the changes were the maximum sentence for carrying firearms during a crime, which was raised from 14 years to life imprisonment, while those sentenced to over five years in prison for violent and drug-related offences were in future not normally eligible for parole. To meet public concern over allegedly too low sentences, a right was introduced to go to the Court of Appeal when sentences passed in Crown Courts were seen as unduly lenient, with the provision that the Court of Appeal could increase as well as reduce any custodial term. As a result of these and other changes, including the guidance given to judges, the average sentence for serious violence against the person rose by 20 per cent in the 1983–8 period.

These changes posed serious problems for the prison service. The combination of a rise of around a quarter in the number, though not the proportion, of offences cleared up by the police, the increase in average sentences, and a sharp rise in the number of people in prison awaiting trial has resulted in a deterioration in already overcrowded prison conditions. This has been only partially alleviated by efforts to ensure that some groups of non-violent adult offenders do not go to prison. Recently there has been an increased emphasis on what has become known as punishment in the community, providing non-custodial community service orders for young offenders, more intensive forms of probation and surveillance devices such as electronic tagging. The average number of prisoners rose by around 12 per cent during the 1980s, which was broadly equivalent to the extent of overcrowding in the prisons. A big prison building programme was launched – aimed at providing 26 new establishments, of which eight were open by early 1989. The target was over 25,000 new places in existing or wholly new prisons between 1988 and 1995, on top of 6,000 new places provided between 1979 and 1988. While this acceleration of prison building was welcome, it was overdue. The Government was still having to run fast even to prevent prison conditions from becoming even worse.

The uncompromising commitment in the Tories' 1979 election manifesto to give 'the right priority to the fight against crime' was fulfilled in terms of increased expenditure and powers of punishment, but only partially in terms of results. In spite of one or two hopeful signs in the late 1980s in the crime figures, the level of offences, particularly of violence, was substantially higher than a decade earlier and remained one of the public's main worries. As it became clear that more police and tougher sentences were not sufficient in themselves, the debate broadened out to focus on the social roots of crime. To Mrs Thatcher and her allies the problem lay in the permissive 1960s – in the breakdown of standards, discipline and respect for authority. This concern was expressed most cogently by Norman Tebbit, the Conservative Party chairman from 1985 to 1987, whose outlook was neatly summed up by the title of his autobiography, *Upwardly Mobile* (1988). To him, everything represented by the liberal/progressive establishment was anathema. He vividly argued that the self-delusion about the economy of the 1960s reflected 'a shallow optimism about human nature.' The legislation of that era – changes in the law on capital punishment, homosexuality, abortion, divorce and censorship – had created 'the impression that there was no need for restraint at all.' Yet, significantly, none of this legislation was reversed during the 1980s.

Similarly, for Mrs Thatcher, while the criminal was to blame for each crime committed, 'if anyone else is to blame it is the professional progressives among broadcasters, social workers and politicians who have created a fog of excuses in which the muggers and burglars operate' (speech to Conservative Central Council, Buxton, March 1988). She argued that 'a culture of excuses' had been created for criminals. 'The threat of crime will only recede when we re-establish a code of conduct that condemns crime plainly and without exception.' To Mrs Thatcher and Mr Tebbit, the answer lay in increasing discipline and personal responsibility exercised by parents, teachers and individuals. In a memorable phrase in a *Woman's Own* interview Mrs Thatcher said, 'There is no such thing as society. There are only individual men and women, and there are families.'

A contrasting emphasis came in the call for social cohesion from Mr Hurd. He fully welcomed the gains of the enterprise economy and the greater emphasis on wealth creation. But in a speech to the Peel Society in February 1988 quoted above, he went on to argue that 'the enrichment of the individual and his or her family is only part of the Conservative agenda for the 1990s.' He maintained that, 'the amazing social cohesion of England, formed under Peel and the Victorians, is in need of repair.' To him the answer lay in active citizenship – 'the active businessman can help to stimulate the arts or to create employment in discouraged areas. The active citizen can make sense of a Neighbourhood Watch scheme or a crime prevention panel. The active parent will under our reforms have much greater opportunities in shaping the education of his or her child.' In a challenge to the prevailing philosophy of putting profit and success first, Mr Hurd urged more companies to be committed to wider social responsibilities in the community, as well as to shareholders, employees and customers. He hoped that 'the day is not long off when the selection panels, considering appointments to a company board or to a senior management post, will routinely take into account not only the commercial experience and expertise of the various candidates (although that will clearly be of prime import-ance), but also the candidates' record of public service'. Yet Mr Hurd's own broadcasting proposals removed the social obligation on the independent radio companies to provide time for charity appeals since this would continue on the BBC.

Kenneth Baker, the Education Secretary from 1986, and like Mr Hurd formerly a close aide of Edward Heath, offered a similar vision, summed up in the phrase 'a community of individuals'. He argued that the task for the Government was to pass power from the hub of the wheel towards the rim by, for example, encouraging parents and local communities to take greater responsibility in running schools. Referring to the large cuts in direct taxation in the 1988 Budget, Mr Baker said in a speech in April 1988 that a challenge had been issued: 'from those who have much, much is expected. The dispersal of the ownership of wealth and power carries with it an obligation for people to respond to the challenge of enhanced responsibility ... It is now up to the many who have benefited from the reductions in taxation to increase their personal contribution to the charities and good causes of their own choice.'

Developing his view of the active citizen, Mr Hurd offered a portrait of crime. He noted that the peak age for committing offences was 15, that a quarter of all crimes are committed by juveniles, and nearly half by young people aged under 21. On his view this showed that parents, teachers and broadcasters had tremendous powers to shape a child's moral development. Home Office ministers believe that their emphasis on active citizenship is already showing signs of success with the spread of the Neighbourhood Watch scheme from two in 1982 to over 60,000 by the end of 1988, covering 750,000 people. These schemes involve residents in small communities working in close collaboration with the police on crime prevention, and they have encouraged local people to re-create a sense of community. There may have been some link between the spread of such schemes and the drop in recorded crime in the big cities. The decline in crime figures in 1987–8 was most marked for domestic burglary, stealing of motor vehicles and theft. These are precisely the sort of offences which Neighbourhood Watch, crime prevention panels, better designed homes, more effective locks and bolts and several other joint police/industry/local community initiatives might be expected to influence.

Yet if a greater emphasis on crime prevention has offered a sensible way of containing rising crime, it is unlikely of itself to reverse a trend so long established, both in the UK and overseas. While Mrs Thatcher and Mr Tebbit may have been right to trace one of the causes of the rise in crime to the progressive ideas and practices in the 1960s, the values of the 1980s have also played a part. For much of the period there was an emphasis on individualism with little regard for wider social responsibilities and interests.

Not surprisingly, the opposition put much of the blame on Mrs Thatcher and her values. Labour politicians pointed both to a number of well-publicized violent incidents involving British thugs at football matches overseas which led to the continued banning of English clubs from international competitions, and to a series of outbreaks of violence at weekends at affluent market towns in southern England. The criminals involved were not the products of unemployment and discrimination. Many of the football hooligans and rural thugs, commonly known as lager louts, were well-dressed and well-paid. Indeed in 1988 a new sub-group was discovered of young City workers going on drunken brawls at commuter stations. Roy Hattersley, Labour's Shadow Home Secretary, described these thugs as 'Thatcher's children' – whose delinquency was 'the by-product of their affluence, combined with their rejection of any sort of responsibility for their neighbours and their neighbours' welfare'. He condemned the selfishness, greed and lack of social responsibility of Mrs Thatcher's Britain:

The young thugs who rampage through our towns are encouraged by an ethos which urges the individual to get on at the expense of others and the expense of the community. Greed and individual gain are the gods which they are urged to worship.

The materialism which the Thatcher years helped to create has undoubtedly contributed to what Mr Hurd described after visits to market towns where there had been violence: 'You do not find much poverty or social deprivation there. What you do find are too many young people with too much money in their pockets, too many pints inside them, but too little self-discipline and too little notion of the care and responsibilities which they owe to others.' The parents of these young people were the children of the 1960s. Their children are the children of the 1980s, of the Thatcher decade.

Against this background, the idea of the active citizen may be desirable, but it will take a long time to achieve. The increased violence and general slovenliness have not been the product of any one government, and cannot be reversed by any single government. But that task is perhaps even more difficult for any administration which has spent so much time challenging long-established institutions. Professor Ralf Dahrendorf, one of the leading centrist academic sceptics about Thatcherism, argued in a *Weekend World* television interview in 1988 that the Government's drive to encourage individualism and enterprise had broken down traditional solidarities of class, groups and institutions. But, according to the Professor, having done this, the Government now recognized that individualism was not enough, and something was missing in social terms and for people's well-being. There was now, he said, 'a widespread sense that perhaps a little more community was necessary – very hard to do by the same people who have first broken those institutions'. Similarly, Professor Eric Hobsbawm, a Marxist, has argued that, 'almost every bit of the moral consensus governing Britain for an awful long time has been deliberately outraged: the sense of fairness, the sense of noblesse oblige on the part of the upper classes, the sense that ordinary people can deserve something, and above all the sense that the community and the state have social responsibilities.'

The Tory view of the active citizen has been challenged as inadequate by many on the centre and left of British politics. To them the Tory definition of the citizen is too narrow since it is primarily to do with individual duties and social responsibilities and not with rights. To these critics, who include the Social and Liberal Democrats as well as Labour politicians, a full definition of citizenship must be broad enough to cover a range of entitlements – not only basic civil liberties and the accountability of the executive, but also the right of all to good quality education, health and welfare, environmental protection and employment opportunities. The opposition parties have argued that their definition of citizenship is diametrically at odds with the Tory vision based on social duties and a view of the citizen primarily as a consumer and taxpayer. Describing citizenship in terms of entitlements and life chances, Professor Dahrendorf argued (in Holme and Elliott, 1988) that Thatcherism had been a decade without citizenship: 'a decade obsessed with provisions and oblivious of entitlements'.

The debate over citizenship was partly linked with reflections on the 300th anniversary of the 'Glorious Revolution' of 1688. This led to renewed calls for constitutional reform in Britain. The argument was that Britain had become increasingly authoritarian, notably since the election of the Thatcher Government. This concern was illustrated by a movement entitled 'Charter 88' launched by the *New Statesman and Society* magazine and by the Constitutional Reform Centre (a nominally cross-party but largely centrist pressure group). This argued that:

A process is underway which endangers many of the freedoms we have had. Only in part deliberate, it began before 1979 and is now gathering momentum. Scotland is governed like a province from Whitehall. More generally, the government has eroded a number of important civil freedoms: for example, the universal rights to habeas corpus, to peaceful assembly, to freedom of information, to freedom of expression, to membership of a trade union, to local government, to freedom of movement, even to the birth-right itself. By taking these rights from some, the government puts them at risk for all.

The suggested new constitutional settlement included:

1 a Bill of Rights to enshrine various civil liberties such as the right to peaceful assembly, freedom of association and of expression;
2 subjecting executive powers and prerogatives to the rule of law;
3 establishing freedom of information and open government;
4 creating a fair electoral system of proportional representation;
5 reforming the upper house to establish a democratic non-hereditary second chamber;
6 ensuring the independence of a reformed judiciary;
7 providing legal remedies for all abuses of power by the state and its officials;

8   guaranteeing an equitable distribution of power between local,
    regional and national government;
9   drawing up a written constitution anchored in the idea of
    universal citizenship.

In political terms, the statement was interesting as an indication of
the frustration and short-term pessimism of a large number of those
opposed to Thatcherism – not just politicians but also the many
academics, bishops, writers, artists, lawyers and actors among the
initial signatories. The charter's support quickly ran to over 10,000
and ranged across the centre and the non-aligned left, as well as very
large numbers of people with no specific political alignment. The
Labour leadership was opposed to the document, partly because of
its advocacy of proportional representation. A more fundamental
objection of Conservative and Labour leaders alike was that the
document rejected the absolute sovereignty of parliament – the
ability of one government to undo the work of another through a
majority in the House of Commons. The Conservative leadership
naturally saw the virtues of the present structure, while Labour
leaders, though concerned about an erosion of civil liberties, regarded the call for a written constitution as, in Roy Hattersley's
words, 'a badly thought-out counsel of despair'. They still believed
they could win power under the present system. But some of the
supporters of the charter argued that only cross-party co-operation
could defeat the Tories. While the Labour leadership remained cool
to any talk of electoral pacts and reform of the voting system, some
influential Labour MPs were urging that these options should be
considered if their party was to have any hope of even sharing in
power. The opening-up of such a discussion within the Labour Party
was anyway the short-term aim of the centrist backers of the charter.
    Yet, aside from the political implications, many of the assertions in
the charter were challenged as being exaggerated, both in detail and
in total. Conservative commentators regarded the choice of the title
Charter 88 and the associated newsletter Samizdat as an absurd echo
of the Charter 77 human rights group in Czechoslovakia (despite the
latter's support for the UK charter) and of the underground papers in
the Soviet Union. Conservatives argued that it was offensive to
compare conditions in Britain with those of genuinely oppressed
Czech and Soviet dissidents. The writers of the Charter 88 argued
that Britain had become significantly more authoritarian during the

Thatcher years. For all the somewhat pretentious tone adopted by some of the charter's sponsors, there was evidence of centralization and of an erosion of civil liberties for some people, a concern shared by a few independent-minded Tory MPs like Jonathan Aitken and Richard Shepherd as well as opposition members. A number of examples can be given of these trends:

(1) *Local Government.* Roughly 50 separate acts have been passed since 1979 aimed at reducing the independence of local authorities. The primary motive – to restrain expenditure and rate increases within Treasury targets – was soon followed by a further tightening of controls. This involved, over time, financial penalties, including the withholding of central Government grants, rate-capping, and the abolition of the Greater London Council and the six metropolitan county authorities. After the 1987 Election there was an overhaul of the whole system of local authority finance, involving the replacement of domestic rates by the flat-rate community charge, or poll tax, together with a uniform national business rate. Also, from the mid-1980s onwards, a series of measures were introduced to encourage contracting out to the private sector of local authority manual services, to reduce housing subsidies to push up the council rents and to encourage tenants to switch to a different landlord (whether private sector or a housing association), and to allow schools to opt out of local authority control.

As a result, both the independence and the duties of local authorities were substantially reduced. In a House of Lords debate in March 1988, revealingly entitled 'The Executive Power of Government', Lord Jenkins of Hillhead complained: 'throughout the 1980s the Government used every weakness of local government as a reason for making it weaker still and every act of political extravagance committed by a few local authorities as an excuse for also penalising the responsible ones and transferring still more power to the centre. The result of that policy has been a degree of civic degradation which it would be difficult to imagine being imposed in any other democratic country. London is unique among capitals in not now being allowed a unified voice.' The Government's view was that the successive changes were necessary to prevent abuse of power by local authorities which, ministers alleged, in many cases were in practice unaccountable to their residents. However, critics, including a number of shire county Tories, regarded the Government as fundamentally out of sympathy with the ethos of local government, and, especially in the second half of the 1980s, determined to make them marginal organizers of communal services, generally provided by the private sector.

(2) *Civil liberties*. Examples of alleged erosion include: extensions of police powers; removal of right to silence for the accused; curbs on public protests as a result of additional official powers to require a week's notice of any demonstration and to change the venue; the ban on local authorities intentionally promoting homosexuality; and the banning of any television or radio interviews with supporters of terrorist organizations. To critics, these moves have represented a serious erosion of personal liberty and of freedom to dissent, yet ministers have maintained that each of the moves was necessary to protect ordinary people from violent or offensive behaviour. In most cases, these issues produced little passion among the public generally, which, according to most polls, on balance supported the Government's stance.

(3) *Official secrets*. The Government has consistently prosecuted and pursued alleged breaches of official secrets legislation – winning against Sarah Tisdall (a civil service clerk who leaked a memo about cruise missiles), losing against Clive Ponting (a Ministry of Defence official who leaked embarassing evidence about Whitehall attitudes to the row over the sinking of the Argentine cruiser *Belgrano* in the Falklands War), and stumbling unsuccessfully through the lengthy and often farcical attempt to ban *Spycatcher*, the memoirs of Peter Wright, an obsessive former MI5 officer. As Peter Hennessy argued (1989), the result in early 1988 was to plunge Whitehall once more 'into protracted convulsions in another attempt to deliver a secrecy settlement which would command respect. The Spycatcher story, and its spin-offs in the guise of injunctions preventing the press from publishing reports or extracts, plus further spin-offs in the form of contempt of court actions, had produced a situation which was recognised as unsatisfactory all round.' The Government finally lost its bid to stop press reporting of the Spycatcher allegations in a House of Lords ruling in October 1988, though the judgement upheld the life-time duty of confidentiality imposed on MI5 officers. The Government also applied pressure on the broadcasters not to show programmes on the IRA (*Real Lives* in 1986) and a

subsequently abandoned secret intelligence satellite (*Zircon*, 1987). In both cases, when the slightly modified programmes were ultimately shown, they appeared innocuous.

The problem was to balance the perfectly legitimate necessity to ensure secrecy for the operations and personnel of the intelligence services – with the need for adequate surveillance and accountability to ensure that these services are not abusing their powers. In autumn 1988 the Government produced a twin-track legislative approach with proposals to put MI5, the security service, on a legal footing for the first time and also authorizing operations like burglary and bugging by MI5 (though it still did not officially recognize the existence of MI6, the secret intelligence service operating overseas). Separate legislation reformed the 1911 Official Secrets Act by limiting the application of the Act primarily to disclosures involving national security, intelligence, defence, foreign relations, crime, wiretapping and interception. Critics argued that the measures still failed to provide reassurance about proper surveillance of the intelligence services by, for example, a parliamentary oversight committee as happens with the US Congress and in many Commonwealth countries. Moreover, the official secrets legislation still left the initiative with the Government in seeking press-gagging injunctions, and provided no public interest defence for disclosure. Mrs Thatcher's instinct remained on the side of the prevailing culture of secrecy in Whitehall, and against disclosure and public interest.

(4) *Broadcasting*. Mrs Thatcher and her allies (notably Norman Tebbit in his book *Upwardly Mobile*) have seldom been able to disguise their dislike of the broadcasters, and particularly the BBC for alleged left-wing bias and for encouraging collectivist and permissive attitudes. The attacks on the BBC came in protests over individual programmes, the coverage of the Falklands War in 1982, and the extraordinary episode in which Mr Tebbit was involved in lengthy exchanges with the board of governors over the corporation's coverage of the US bombing of Libya in April 1986. There was little evidence of general bias, but more of complacency and a lack of professionalism in some of the news and current affairs coverage, which was belatedly remedied in 1987–8. However, the upheavals of the period, including the resignation of Alisdair Milne, the director-general, in January 1987, had their effect in making some of the coverage safety-first with executives always having to

look over their shoulder at the Government. Moreover, the BBC faced a declining income from licence fees in real terms, with the prospect of having to raise revenue from subscriptions from viewers.

The BBC and ITV duopoly was ripe for challenge from technological changes such as cable and particularly satellite, in which those rival purveyors of prejudice and bad taste, Rupert Murdoch and Robert Maxwell, had large investments. The Government was committed to deregulation with a loose supervisory oversight after the abolition of the Independent Broadcasting Authority. Yet Mrs Thatcher and her colleagues combined this free-market approach with a continuing paternalism in attitudes towards standards. A Broadcasting Standards Council was established under the chairmanship of the High Tory Lord Rees-Mogg to examine fictional material, delivering verdicts on the suitability of individual programmes which have to be broadcast. The council reflected the Tories' concern about violence and pornography. They appeared less worried about other standards of the kind that have earned British television its worldwide reputation for excellence. The combination of nannying and deregulation, with increased commercial competitive pressures, has been widely seen as a threat to the standards of public service broadcasting. However, some of the changes, such as the increased use of independent producers, have offered the prospect of more imaginative and varied programmes, as the successful record of Channel Four showed following its launch in 1982.

Whether all these changes add up to a significant threat to long-established British liberties is debatable. There have been clear tendencies towards centralism and an instinctive belief in authority rather than freedom of dissent and of expression. Ministers have put the interests of the state ahead of freedom of the press. Moreover, the weakness of the parliamentary opposition has allowed ministers to take powers in, for instance, education (where ministers control the curriculum and teachers' pay), which they would undoubtedly been reluctant to see in the hands of their opponents in office. But the liberties and freedoms of the ordinary citizen have not been altered dramatically. Few would go to the stake for the Greater London Council, and few noticed much difference to their lives with its abolition. Moreover, the curbing of trade union power and the widening of choice for parents, council tenants and consumers has increased economic freedom and liberty. Many of the other changes, such as those against potential terrorists, have been in line with public feeling.

Mrs Thatcher's determination to fight terrorism – understandable after the assassination of her close friends by the IRA and her own attempted murder in October 1984 in the Brighton bombing – has led her to take a tough stand on this issue in relation to the broadcasters. She has brushed aside the worries of the civil libertarians on questions like, for example, the shooting of three IRA terrorists by British forces in Gibraltar in 1988. Her view has been 'you are either with us of against us.' There is no room for honest questioning. Nevertheless, Mrs Thatcher was persuaded to agree to a joint approach with the Irish Republic to the problems of Northern Ireland via the Anglo-Irish agreement of November 1985, which also ensured political and financial support from the US. The agreement infuriated the Ulster Unionists. Despite close ministerial contacts, it has been sorely tested because of IRA outrages and Mrs Thatcher's widely shared, though scarcely diplomatic, impatience with the failure of the Republic to extradite suspected terrorists. Yet for all the mutual suspicions the agreement has survived.

More generally, some of the critics have confused Mrs Thatcher's dominant style with the substance of her policies. Many in the literary, artistic and academic elites have vehemently disliked Mrs Thatcher in part because of her style. She and her government have been regarded not only as illiberal but also as philistine and hostile to the universities and academic freedom – as was reflected when members of her former university, Oxford, voted against granting her an honorary degree.

Mrs Thatcher and her allies have certainly been intolerant of criticism, and particularly intolerant of institutions and vested interests, such as the BBC, the Foreign Office and the Church of England. This has led to a for-us or against-us attitude, in, for example, some appointments to quasi-independent bodies. There has been concern about a possible politicization of the civil service with advancement being dictated by enthusiasm for the cause. There is a danger here of confusing the promotion of people for having 'acceptable' views, of which there is little evidence, and of Mrs Thatcher picking civil servants for top posts whom she believes will energetically implement the Government's priorities, of which there have been several examples. In particular, Sir Robin Butler, the Cabinet Secretary from January 1989, is the model of a non-partisan civil servant – praised and respected equally by Harold Wilson, Edward Heath and Mrs Thatcher. There have, however, been a number of incidents which have tested the non-political character of the civil service – these range from the involvement of officials in highly controversial campaigns on behalf of Government policies (and also against it, in for instance the Campaign for Nuclear Disarmament) to the role of civil servants in the bitter in-fighting of the Westland affair. Lord (formerly Sir Robert) Armstrong, Sir Robin Butler's predecessor, got in the unusual and unsatisfactory position of being the Government's spokesman during the Westland affair (before a Commons select committee) and in giving evidence to an Australian court over *Spycatcher*.

Much of this is the result of a Prime Minister – and a Government – being in power for a very long time. Mrs Thatcher has towered over her Cabinet – seeing off ministers who were initially her equals, such as Lords Carrington and Whitelaw; those who were her rivals, such as Lords Prior and Pym; and her previous allies, like Norman Tebbit and John Biffen. Her dominant style, and unwillingness to allow full debates in Cabinet and Cabinet committees, helped fuel the Westland crisis of 1985–6 by increasing the irritation of Michael Heseltine and leading to his remarkable resignation from the Cabinet in January 1986. The Westland affair, with its leaking and counter-leaking by Mr Heseltine and Sir Leon Brittan, reflected little credit on any of the participants. It was a murky, shabby episode in which Mrs Thatcher and some of her closest advisers breached the normal standards of public conduct in trying to discredit Mr Heseltine. This and other episodes led Tam Dalyell, that indominatable Labour member of the parliamentary awkward squad, to describe her (1987) as deceitful, power-hungry and lacking in common political integrity. But Westland had little lasting political impact for the Tories – perhaps voters expected such rows and dirty-dealing at the top and were more concerned with rising living standards. Overall, the power and dominance displayed by Mrs Thatcher since 1979 go with her personality, rather than any fundamental change in the powers of the Prime Minister, and will probably not survive her.

The overall balance sheet of the Government's home record is more chequered than its economic and industrial performance. The stress on materialism and individualism has further weakened the already loose bonds of community and social responsibility. The active citizen has not yet been reconciled with the enterprise culture.

Moreover, the divisions of the opposition parties and their weakness in parliament have allowed the Government to ride roughshod over dissent and cut down the power and influence of previously independent institutions such as those in local government or the broadcasting authorities. This does not mean that Britain has become an irreversibly authoritarian society. Pluralism is battered, but not destroyed. Instead, the absence of the usual political checks and balances has allowed Mrs Thatcher and her Government to behave at times in a high-handed way, disregarding rather than eliminating traditional liberties.

10

Britain's Place in the World

Since Ernest Bevin made his plea a generation ago for more coal to give weight to his foreign policy our economic decline has been such as to sap the foundations of our diplomacy. Conversely, I believe that, during the same period, much of our foreign policy has been such as to contribute to that decline.

Sir Nicholas Henderson, Valedictory Despatch, March 1979

I believe that Britain's role and standing in the world have increased immeasurably as we have succeeded in overcoming our problems at home, getting our economy right, and proving ourselves a staunch ally. We are now able once again to exercise the leadership and influence which we have historically shown.

Mrs Margaret Thatcher, Speech to Foreign Press Association,
13 January 1988

Nowhere is it more difficult to assess the changes since 1979 than in respect of Britain's place in the world. At one level, ministers have frequently claimed a transformation – 'an end to retreat', 'a new found self-confidence', and 'Great Britain is great again' – in the phrases favoured in Mrs Thatcher's speeches. So much of Britain's international position in the 1980s has been bound up with Mrs Thatcher's personality and achievements that it is next to impossible to disentangle changes in Britain's underlying influence. Personalities do matter in building up, and extending, the role of even a medium-ranking power like Britain, as Ernest Bevin showed as a masterly Foreign Secretary in the late 1940s.

The strength of Mrs Thatcher's character – and increasingly her longevity – have given Britain more say, or at least more recognition, than her predecessors achieved in the 1970s. Her name crops up frequently in the comments of fellow world leaders and foreign ministers, often in exasperated tones and double-edged compliments. For instance, President Mitterand has allegedly remarked that 'she has the eyes of Caligula and the mouth of Marilyn Monroe.' Her close personal relationship with President Reagan mattered on some crucial occasions. Similarly, her meetings with Mikhail Gorbachev have resulted in the closest contact between Britain and Soviet leaders since Churchill and Stalin in the 1940s. The question is less how she has exploited these contacts, as why have the leaders of the super-powers given her such access and time?

There is no doubt that Mrs Thatcher's personal contribution has been immense. Partly because she was the first woman political leader of a leading western country, partly because of her uncompromising style, and notably because of her determination and success during the Falklands War in 1982, she has become a symbol of a revived Britain − Boadicea with a handbag. From personal observation Mrs Thatcher has a considerable international appeal. When she addressed a joint session of Congress in February 1985 one of the sights was the young Republican senators staring adoringly up at her. Similarly, on her visit to the Soviet Union in March 1987 Mrs Thatcher was mobbed by enthusiastic crowds. In Tbilisi in Georgia, outside the former seminary from which Stalin was expelled for his revolutionary activities, women kissed her hand. In short, Mrs Thatcher is a star. She attracts interest partly because she has become so well-known.

But what lies behind this remarkable performance? How much is dependent on her personally and how far did her relationship with President Reagan gloss over increasing tension and differences between Europe and the US? Also, how far have her personal Atlanticism and combative style reinforced illusions of a worldwide role and held back British influence in Europe? Or, for all Mrs Thatcher's rhetoric and the conscious comparisons with the late President de Gaulle, can the 1980s be seen as the period when Britain finally came to terms with playing a positive role within the European Community?

The background is the years of British decline and pessimism of the late 1970s. This was epitomized by Sir Nicholas Henderson's famous valedictory despatch as British Ambassador in Paris in March 1979, which was leaked in the *Economist* later that year (Henderson, 1987). He argued that the economic weaknesses of the 1970s had undermined British foreign policy, reducing Britain's role as Washington's European partner in relations with Germany and

France, and weakening the UK's role within the community, where the Government's commitment was anyway less than wholehearted.

After more than two terms in office even that prosaic practitioner of Thatcherism, Sir Geoffrey Howe, could claim that Britain had recaptured her leading position in world affairs. Britain, he said in December 1987, was 'setting the pace and mapping out a route forward' on arms control, on East-West affairs, in the European Community, the North Atlantic Alliance and the United Nations Security Council. 'We are pulling our weight internationally, and thanks to our domestic and foreign policies Britain's weight is greater than it has been for many years.' His case started with the economy – a steady growth of output and productivity, fewer strikes, low inflation and the start of new businesses – all of which, he said, had been watched abroad with increasing interest and respect. Sir Geoffrey argued in May 1987 that the economic turnround since the 1970s represented 'the solid foundation of our influence in Europe and the wider world'. He then claimed that Britain had adopted a more positive attitude towards the European Community which had given it a leading role in, for example, promoting political co-operation and the liberalization of internal markets. Similarly, he pointed to improved prestige elsewhere, notably following the Falklands conflict, but also as reflected in Mrs Thatcher's Moscow visit in 1987.

Yet if economic recovery has been the necessary condition for a revival of Britain's international standing during the 1980s, the practical application of that influence has borne the personal stamp of Mrs Thatcher – at times in conflict with the caution of the Foreign Office. She has rightly been seen as a nationalist – defending 'our money' and 'our boys', but this is not the Little Englandism of an isolationist. Her approach is rooted in a belief in the primacy of the North Atlantic Alliance and, in particular, on the special relationship with the US. As she pointed out in her address to the US Congress in February 1985, she shares Churchill's vision of the union of mind and purpose betwen the English-speaking peoples. She admires the US approach to enterprise and there has been a regular traffic of ministers across the Atlantic to study initiatives for reviving the inner cities, health care, education, the prisons, private sector electricity, and so on.

Mrs Thatcher has at all times sought to avoid public conflict with the US, even though she has often revelled in confrontation with other European countries. Sir Anthony Parsons, the British Ambassador at the United Nations during the Falklands War and later her personal foreign policy adviser in Downing Street, has summed up her view (Young and Sloman, 1986):

I think the Prime Minister believes very strongly that the United States is absolutely vital to us, and that obviously one of the cardinal planks of our policy must be the best possible relations with the United States. By the same token, I think she believes we can only hope to influence the United States in private and affect their judgements over various issues where we may disagree, if the basic relationship is extremely good. I think she has demonstrated with the Reagan administration a feel for how to achieve all these objectives.

This influence was cemented by her close personal relationship with President Reagan. Despite their contrasting temperaments and styles – and by all accounts some vigorous private interventions from her on occasion – there was mutual admiration and a recognition of shared values. The President saw her as an ideological soul-mate in their joint battle against socialism and communism. And this gave her special access, and at times influence, such as when she successfully pressed the President to halt the US Justice Department's legal action against British Airways which was holding up its privatization.

The most striking result of the relationship was the flow of intelligence and supplies from the US during the Falklands War which was invaluable to the British effort. This reflected the close working links between the two defence departments and the two navies. Yet the US delayed for a month coming out in public support of Britain and there remained strong counter-voices in the Reagan administration. Even after the task force landed back on the Falklands there were US calls for the UK to stop short of inflicting an overwhelming military defeat on the Argentine because of the implications for the Reagan administration's policies in South America, as Sir Nicholas Henderson, then the British Ambassador in Washington, has noted (1987). He has concluded that American support was not inevitable and could have been lost at any time had Britain shown complete intransigence in negotiation. However, Sir Nicholas has recorded the repeated promises by then Secretary of State Alexander Haig that there would be no repeat of Suez, when US opposition forced Britain and France to halt their operation halfway. Britain could not have succeeded in retaking the Falklands without US support.

Critics have argued that the relationship has been one-sided. They have pointed, for example, to the Reagan administration's failure to consult Mrs Thatcher over the US invasion in 1983 of Grenada, which was a Commonwealth country. Both sides now regard this as an unfortunate episode, a one-off embarrassment. But this incident underlines that the US is far more important to Britain than vice versa. The failure to consult over Grenada was not an accident. US national interests came first. It was the same story, an absence of prior discussion, with the launch of Star Wars, the Strategic Defence Initiative, in 1983. Later, in April 1986, the Thatcher Government suffered considerably temporary unpopularity at home when alone in Europe it agreed to the use by the US Air Force of its F-111 bases in Britain to attack Tripoli in Libya. This was primarily a demonstration of political support for the US and also a repayment of the services provided by the US during the Falklands conflict. It would, Mrs Thatcher said, have been 'inconceivable' for Britain to have refused, an illustration of her desire publicly to support Britain's closest ally. However, the extent of domestic British hostility meant that the exercise could not be repeated and it opened Mrs Thatcher to opposition charges that she was President Reagan's 'poodle'.

The nature of any special relationship, as well as Mrs Thatcher's claims to have influence, was tested by the erratic progress of the nuclear arms talks during the 1980s. Up to 1982–3 Mrs Thatcher echoed the strident anti-Soviet rhetoric of the Reagan administration, the type of language which had earned her the 'Iron Lady' tag from one Soviet paper when she was Leader of the Opposition. In 1983, after her re-election and the appointment of Sir Geoffrey Howe as Foreign Secretary, the British approach began to change. Sir Geoffrey himself apparently played a key role in persuading Mrs Thatcher of the need for a new policy. The result was an acceptance of the need for closer discussions and for negotiations, though without any dropping of the guard.

In parallel with US moves to resume discussions with the Soviet Union, the British Government began to increase contacts at a ministerial level with the Warsaw Pact countries. First, Mrs Thatcher went to Hungary in February 1984 and then there was the extended visit to Britain by Mr Gorbachev shortly before he became Soviet leader. This, and later British/Soviet contacts culminated in her pre-election visit to Moscow in spring 1987 and his brief stopover in Britain on his way to the US in December of that year – followed by a further longer visit in April 1989. The warmth of Mr Gorbachev's welcome and the length of the meetings in Moscow reflected the Soviet belief not only that Mrs Thatcher would be re-elected but that she exercised influence over the US, particularly over President Reagan. Despite the naive flattering headlines of the British tabloid and Tory press, Mrs Thatcher was in no sense speaking on behalf of the west, or acting as a negotiator, but she was someone whose view would be heard where it mattered.

The evidence for special British influence over the US in arms control came first in December 1984 over the Star Wars (SDI) project, and then, two years later, following the ill-prepared Reykjavik summit. British policy-makers – and especially Sir Geoffrey Howe in a highly critical speech in March 1985 – were sceptical about the feasibility of SDI and were worried about its implications for the existing deterrence strategy. Howe warned of creating 'a Maginot Line in the sky'. Mrs Thatcher pursued her characteristic policy of giving public support to the President – as a counter to Soviet resistance in this area – while seeking to safeguard European, and especially British, interests. In December 1984 she flew to the US and secured the so-called Camp David pacts which said that the US would not seek nuclear superiority over the Soviet Union but would maintain the balance between the super powers, and that any movement from research to deployment of the new system would have to be a matter for negotiation. The Camp David accord reconfirmed the 1972 Anti-Ballistic Missile Treaty. These guidelines were much resented by the opponents of arms control in the Pentagon who sought to circumvent them in arguments about the definitions implied by the ABM treaty. In the event, the slow progress on the SDI project mainly reflected the inherent scientific problems and spending curbs imposed by Congress. Moreover, the promise of sizeable SDI research contracts for the UK failed to materialize. This was seen as another illustration of the imbalance in UK/US defence and procurement work, a point underlined by later criticism of the inadequacy of the offset contracts promised to Britain by Boeing for the Awacs airborne early warning project.

Mrs Thatcher also intervened in autumn 1986 after US and Soviet leaders had discussed far-reaching proposals for the reduction and elimination of certain classes of nuclear weapon in Europe. This was in line with President Reagan's belief in the eventual total elmination of nuclear weapons, as reflected in some of his more starry-eyed descriptions of SDI. The discussions at Reykjavik proved abortive but set alarm bells off throughout western Europe about the prospect of the reduction, and even possible removal, of the US nuclear umbrella from Europe. This would leave the Warsaw Pact with the advantage of its large superiority in conventional weapons in Europe. Mrs Thatcher went over to the US, and, to the satisfaction not only of many European leaders, but also key US advisers, secured reassurance from the President. This showed that she and Britain were at their most effective when there were divisions within the US administration and her special access to the President could be used in alliance with one side or another in the debate. The final statement supported an intermediate-range missile deal and a 50 per cent cut in strategic weapons, but also, crucially, confirmed the existing Nato strategy of nuclear deterrence, the modernization of Britain's deterrent with Trident, and the elimination of chemical weapons.

The negotiations leading to the signing of the INF Treaty in Washington in December 1987 were publicly supported by Mrs Thatcher. This was seen as a vindication of the highly controversial decision in the early 1980s to deploy Cruise and Pershing missiles on the ground in response to the Soviet's SS20 missiles. But Mrs Thatcher was cautious about further moves, publicly supporting the President's desire for a strategic arms limitation treaty, but constantly warning against the delusion of a nuclear-free Europe and stressing the need to modernize existing weapons and deal with the conventional imbalance.

Britain appeared to be left aside in new developments in Nato – not only by US priorities on arms control but also by closer Franco-German moves, such as the creation of a joint brigade, which Mrs Thatcher dismissed with irritation as a sub-structure. For all the talk of building up the European pillar of Nato, Mrs Thatcher herself remained sceptical about Europe-based solutions.

Moreover, the dramatic initiative of Mikhail Gorbachev at the United Nations in December 1988 in proposing a unilateral reduction in conventional weapons in Europe changed the political climate. The move appeared to offer an end to confrontation via a genuine substantial reduction in armaments, and hence possibly a turning-point in post-war international relations. Mrs Thatcher was careful to welcome the move and in November 1988 she had even talked of an end to the cold war. But her instincts were sceptical and she was in danger of being left behind by a shift in public and political opinion. Mr Gorbachev proved to be a brilliant international political operator, playing very weak domestic cards with skill and style – leaving the west to respond rather than initiate.

This shift and the potential isolation of Britain were vividly illustrated in the early summer of 1989. Political pressures in West Germany forced, first, the postponement (and probable abandonment) of a decision to modernize short-range nuclear missiles, and, second, a commitment to eventual negotiations over their future. Admittedly, the agreement at the Nato summit in Brussels in May 1989 specifically linked such talks to substantial progress, including implementation, of a reduction in conventional force imbalances in Europe, while the total elimination of such missiles was ruled out. But the communique none the less reflected some, initially reluctant, concessions by Mrs Thatcher from her prior insistence on modernization and no negotiations. Moreover, the US sought a compromise in order to help the political position of Chancellor Helmut Kohl of West Germany, with President Bush describing Mrs Thatcher's role somewhat dismissively as 'an anchor to windward'.

As President Reagan neared the end of his Presidency, David Dimbleby and David Reynolds pointed out in a comprehensive survey (1988) that there were questions about whether Britain was wise to rely so heavily on the US. They concluded:

It would be unwise to assume that the relationship between Britain and America will continue indefinitely in its present form. Close personal friendships alone will not insulate traditional policies against changing international realities. In the 1980s the rapport between Ronald Reagan and Margaret Thatcher has been as close as any in Anglo-American history, but it cannot conceal the signs, apparent since the early 1970s, that the interests of the two countries are growing further apart and the imbalance in their power is becoming more pronounced.

The election of George Bush as US President promised a continuation of previous close contacts. He had known Mrs Thatcher well for many years and they shared a similar world view. Yet the close personal relations which Mrs Thatcher enjoyed with President Reagan were unlikely to be repeated. She could not treat the well-briefed, and at times prickly, Mr Bush in the direct, almost patronizing, way she dealt with his predecessor. While Mrs Thatcher enjoyed a special personal standing in the US, that should not be confused with Britain's position as one of a number of important US allies in Europe.

Mrs Thatcher's Atlanticist preferences have also affected her attitude towards the European Community. There has been no question of withdrawal but her vision has been a practical one of ensuring a fair budgetary deal for Britain, presented in national rather than community terms. Her instincts have been invariably critical – regarding Brussels as a wasteful bureaucracy needing to be tamed, and watchful for any erosion of British sovereignty. However, paradoxically, her toughness, irritating though it has often been to other European leaders and to the Foreign Office, ensured that the question of whether or not Britain should be a member of the community disappeared from the domestic political agenda after the 1983 General Election. The Labour leadership then in practice shifted its policy to one of making the best of membership in alliance with European socialist parties. In the House of Commons the fiercest criticism of Government policy came from 15 to 20 diehard Conservative opponents of membership. By symbolizing the generally wary, unenthusiastic and pragmatic attitude of the British people towards the community, Mrs Thatcher neutralized opposition to membership.

The question has been rather whether Mrs Thatcher's approach, successful as it has been domestically, has hindered Britain's interests within the community. There is no doubt that in the late 1970s Britain appeared to be at best a reluctant participant, critical about the community's finances, opposed to new initiatives and unwilling to join the European Monetary System when it was launched in 1978–9. During the Thatcher Government's first term and up to the Fontainebleau budget settlement in 1984, the British tone was essentially negative. Mrs Thatcher's behaviour at the Dublin summit in November 1979 infuriated other community leaders like Chancellor Helmut Schmidt of West Germany. The Foreign Office and the pro-Europeans argued that she should have been more accommodating. Mrs Thatcher only very reluctantly agreed to back the deal agreed in May 1980 following a furious row with Foreign Office ministers Lord Carrington and Sir Ian Gilmour. The system of rebates to compensate for Britain's excessive contributions proved to be a temporary expedient and arguments over the community budget were renewed in 1982 and 1983, becoming a dominant topic at summits. Nevertheless, partly owing to unforeseen favourable factors, notably the drop in world prices, the 1980 deal ensured that the UK net contributions were much lower than they would otherwise have been. Budget refunds to Britain totalled £4.32 billion for the 1980–5 period.

After the 1983 General Election, with the forthcoming entry of Spain and Portugal into the community, the debate was re-opened. After tough negotiations an agreement was reached at the Fontainebleau summit in June 1984. Again it was a matter of Mrs Thatcher accepting less than she wanted but having to compromise with the realities. This deal was presented as a lasting solution to the problems of Britain's inequitable contributions to the community budget, while, crucially, also promising guidelines on spending to ensure that outlays on agriculture rose more slowly than the total. Partly for external reasons to do with world food prices, expenditure on the Common Agricultural Policy did fall from 75.5 per cent of total community spending in 1979 to 65.7 per cent in 1986. However, as the critics feared, the new budgetary disciplines turned out to be less than watertight and a further crisis appeared in 1987 – leading to yet another package of measures at the Brussels heads of government summit in February 1988. This retained the UK's rebate but involved an increase in the community's overall resources, and hence Britain's net contributions. Yet again the UK claimed to have achieved tight constraints on agricultural spending with binding agreements aimed at reducing production and curbing the prices of surplus commodities such as milk, beef and cereals.

Some progress was achieved but it was a slow process. It involved the political problem for Britain of being at odds with its community partners in lengthy negotiations – arguing at first that there was no case for an increase in the community's resources, then making concessions leading to such an increase, in order to achieve any advance on curbing agricultural spending. It was a messy and negative procedure.

Yet the Fontainebleau agreement in 1984 could fairly be seen as a turning point in Britain's relations with the rest of the community. British policy shifted from the preoccupation with budgetary matters of the previous decade to adopting a more positive role, notably during the British presidency of the council of ministers in the second half of 1986. For instance, in December 1985, the British Government agreed upon a far-reaching series of objectives for community initiatives which were embodied in the Single European Act. This extended qualified majority voting on decisions except where the vital national interest of a member state was invoked. This was criticized as a further erosion of British sovereignty by the small, but vocal, group of parliamentary opponents of the community. But in the British Government's eyes the Act gave increased impetus to securing a single common internal market for goods and services by the end of 1992, to encouraging collaboration in research and technological development, and to enhancing co-operation in foreign policy. In practice, the British Government was cautious about the scale of its participation in a number of community-wide techno-logical programmes. After the 1987 General Election, the Govern-ment launched an extensive advertising campaign to increase business awareness of the changes in the internal market – for instance, removing barriers to the movement of capital and financial business, harmonizing standards and regulations, and so on. Critics were concerned about whether the Government was doing enough to ensure that Britain would be in a position to compete.

Indeed, the debate about the implications of the creation of the single European market in 1992 highlighted large underlying differ-ences of view about the direction of the community. These surfaced after Jacques Delors, the French President of the Commission, suggested in the summer of 1988 that by 1992 national parliaments must give way to the embryo of a European Government, with 80 per cent of national decisions by community members being taken on a Europe-wide basis within a decade. Such talk was dismissed by Mrs Thatcher as 'wrong', 'over the top', and 'quite absurd'. Identifying herself with de Gaulle, she said that 'this is a Europe of separate countries working together,' and she dismissed 'airy fairy' ideas about European union. Mrs Thatcher argued that instead of general talk about European economic and monetary union, Britain had taken practical steps to remove controls of capital movements and was 'streets ahead' of most other EC countries in this respect. These differences emerged in a series of arguments about the practical implications of the 1992 single market – such as Britain's desire to retain border checks to combat terrorism and drug-trafficking. Critics, such as Lord Jenkins of Hillhead, the President of the

Commission from 1977 to 1981, saw a paradox in her position (Jenkins, 1988):

'She wishes British industry to have the benefit of a large, single market, and would like to exercise a political leadership role within it. But her self-righteousness and instinctive nationalism makes it difficult for her to see that these objectives can only be achieved on a basis of give and take and respect for both the legitimate self-interest and the European idealism of others.'

For all the talk of the pro-Europeans about Britain having a leadership role alongside France and Germany, the key axis remained that between Bonn and Paris. This was underlined by the long saga of the European Monetary System. The Callaghan administration decided in autumn 1978 to stay out of the exchange rate mechanism and this position was maintained by the Thatcher Government despite the gradual conversion of, first, Sir Geoffrey Howe, and then Nigel Lawson to a belief that EMS offered a hope of greater overall exchange rate stability. But, backed by advisers such as Professor Alan Walters and Professor Brian Griffiths, Mrs Thatcher stood out for the flexibility provided by free-floating against the views of the Treasury, the Foreign Office and the Bank of England. Sir Geoffrey and Mr Lawson's argument that Britain would enter the system when the time was ripe appeared to be an indefinitely postponable date in the eyes of Mrs Thatcher. Her attitude irritated Britain's community partners and confirmed their suspicions of the half-heartedness of her European commitment.

Overall, there was still a sense of Britain as a nation apart. Although one result of the Thatcher administration was to have cemented Britain's membership of the community, Mrs Thatcher herself treated the rest of Europe differently from the way she regarded the US. Her minimalist view, underlined in her Bruges speech of September 1988, led to increasing divisions within her own party.

European affairs have been a classic illustration of Mrs Thatcher's approach to foreign policy. This has involved a mixture of a vigorous statement of an instinctive belief (some would say prejudice) followed by lengthy internal arguments, persuasion by the Foreign Office, and finally a compromise. She and her advisers have had a suspicion of the Foreign Office's apparent detachment and desire always to be on friendly and harmonious terms with other countries. This view led Normal Tebbit, in characteristically populist style, to talk of a ministry for foreigners. There were tensions, particularly in Mrs Thatcher's first term – initially with the experienced team of Lord Carrington and Sir Ian Gilmour (until the former resigned over the Falklands in 1982 and the latter was sacked in 1981) and then with Francis Pym, with whom relations were always cool. There were fewer open problems after 1983 – partly because of the more accommodating character of Sir Geoffrey Howe, though her own greater interest in, and experience of, foreign affairs issues produced considerable tensions.

The classic examples of her distinctive, and abrasive, approach to foreign policy, with both its pluses and minuses, have been southern Africa, the Falklands, and Hong Kong. The Rhodesia/Zimbabwe independence talks were the peak of Foreign Office influence in the Carrington era. At the time of her election in May 1979 Mrs Thatcher was sympathetic with the internal settlement devised by Ian Smith and Bishop Abel Muzorewa, as she publicly hinted. The Foreign Office believed that such a settlement would not work and argued that it was necessary to involve all groups, including the Patriotic Front of Robert Mugabe. Any other approach might lead to a damaging public split with the then Carter administration in the US. Lord Carrington then embarked on the lengthy task of persuading Mrs Thatcher. He warned her at one stage that maintaining her view 'would be disastrous to the interests of the west in general and Britain in particular'. As so often on major issues, Mrs Thatcher listened, argued, was persuaded, and modified her instincts. She then flew to the Commonwealth heads of government conference in Lusaka to push her new approach with vigour. The eventual settlement, reflecting the skill of Lord Carrington and his team, may have left many serious problems in Zimbabwe, but these were common to the neighbouring states. The overall result, ending nearly 15 years of stalemate and violence, was probably the best possible deal in the circumstances.

The later arguments, in 1985–6, over South Africa showed Mrs Thatcher at her most characteristic. As the internal situation in South Africa deteriorated, with increasing violence and repressive legislation and actions, there were calls from Commonwealth countries to put pressure on the Pretoria regime, notably via sanctions. Repeatedly stating its opposition to apartheid, the British Government argued that the right way to secure peaceful change was by political and diplomatic pressure and contact. In its view economic sanctions could make the South African government even more intransigent and repressive. Mrs Thatcher argued that trade sanctions would not work and would be evaded, while if the South African economy was damaged it would increase unemployment among blacks and in the neighbouring states, while also threatening jobs in Britain. However, at the Commonwealth Conference in Nassau in October 1985 Mrs Thatcher faced considerable pressure to agree to wide-ranging sanctions. But she resisted and agreed only to minimal measures as a psychological signal to Pretoria – such as banning the import of Krugerrands, ending new government loans to the South African Government and its agencies, and stopping trade missions. Her emphasis on how tiny the sanctions were infuriated other Commonwealth members.

The Nassau meeting agreed to set up the Eminent Persons Group consisting of prominent Commonwealth politicians, including Lord Barber, the former Conservative Chancellor of the Exchequer. They had a series of meetings in South Africa and produced a pessimistic and moving analysis of the prospects for peaceful change. The report (Commonwealth Eminent Persons Group, 1986) called for further measures, arguing that their absence, and Pretoria's belief that they need not be feared, deferred change. The report led to renewed demands for sanctions, and a further heated meeting of Commonwealth leaders was held early in August 1986. This produced an agreement to differ with all but Britain backing sanctions. A parallel mission by Sir Geoffrey Howe, as chairman of the European council of ministers, led that September to a limited community package of measures, involving a ban on the import of iron, steel and Krugerrands and on new investment in South Africa. The subsequent failure of most Commonwealth and Black African states to impose general economic sanctions was seen by Mrs Thatcher as a vindication of her position and the controversy then died down, apart from a brief but bitter recurrence at the Commonwealth Conference in Vancouver in October 1987.

Yet, while Mrs Thatcher could claim to be acting rationally, with the western supporters of sanctions behaving hypocritically, her approach was out of tune with world opinion most of the time, both in the Commonwealth and in the US outside the Reagan White House. She appeared not to appreciate the need at times for symbolic actions, albeit ineffective ones. Thus, by seeking consistency and being impatient with diplomatic gestures, Mrs Thatcher alienated large sections of Third World opinion which accused her of appeasing apartheid. Indeed, while her policy gave her some standing with the Pretoria regime, it was not an influence which produced any apparent results.

The Falklands War will be remembered for the single-minded leadership of Mrs Thatcher, which made her international reputation; it will also be remembered for the courage and professionalism of the British forces which re-took the islands in a hazardous campaign. Yet the future of the islands in the South Atlantic has represented, in the words of Sir Nicholas Henderson (1987), one of 'the residual problems of empire (along with Gibraltar and Hong Kong) which are central to our responsibilities but peripheral to our long-term interests, except in so far as our handling of them affects our standing in the world.' The official report under Lord Franks concluded (1983) in rather generous terms that the Argentine invasion in April 1982 could not have been foreseen and that no blame could be attached to the British Government. Yet the accompanying evidence recorded the combination of failures of policy and intelligence appraisal, as well as an unwillingness by the Foreign Office to confront ministers collectively with the implications of where events might lead in face of strong protests by a small pro-Falklands lobby in the Commons. Misleading signals were then sent to the junta in Buenos Aires about British intentions, notably with the announcement of the withdrawal of the survey ship HMS *Endurance* from the South Atlantic, and later in the immediate run-up to the invasion after the breakdown of bilateral talks. As with so many domestic problems facing the Thatcher Government, like Westland during 1985, the Falklands was treated for a long time as an irritant which did not require immediate attention. But when the crisis appeared the Government responded with skill and determination, being prepared to take risks and back service advisers when faced with a threat to the task force, as over the decision to order the sinking of the Argentine cruiser *Belgrano*. After the end of the war Mrs Thatcher firmly ruled out talks with the Argentine about the sovereignty of the islands. She was prepared to support the cost of defending and reinforcing the islands, thus ensuring not only continued frosty relations with the Argentine but also coolness with much of the rest of South America. It was a problem not solved but deferred.

The negotiations with China over the future of Hong Kong started off badly with a visit to Peking by Mrs Thatcher at her most insensitive which ruffled the host government's susceptibilities and threatened the success of any deal. However, the patient diplomacy of Sir Geoffrey Howe secured a joint declaration in late 1984, stating that British sovereignty would end in 1997. This was combined with agreement on a high level of Hong Kong's autonomy from China in economic, financial, and monetary fields. There was considerable concern within the colony about the nature of these assurances but the agreement was widely welcomed, domestically and internationally, as an example of quiet effective diplomacy. The Hong Kong deal was probably the only one available, for all the potential difficulties of later mass emigration from the colony – fears underlined by the brutal Chinese crackdown on protesters in June 1989.

The central question raised by Britain's foreign policy since 1979 has been whether the personal pyrotechnics of Mrs Thatcher have re-created delusions of a grander international role than can be sustained after her departure. The very success of her international visits – and a parliamentary recess hardly ever passed by without one – may have inflated expectations about Britain's influence. In particular, the closeness of Mrs Thatcher's relations with President Reagan may have put too much emphasis on a residuary, though real, special relationship with the US, to the detriment of European commitments. Mrs Thatcher has been a world figure but that does not mean that Britain is a world power. Yet, under Mrs Thatcher, Britain retained substantial foreign policy and defence commitments outside the main Nato area in Europe and the North Atlantic.

Crucially, the Conservative Government decided to remain a nuclear power, albeit one heavily dependent on the US operationally and for the provision of supplies. The Callaghan administration was, at its end, moving towards accepting the need for the modernization of the deterrent in the 1990s after Polaris went out of service, though without any formal commitment. The then Foreign Secretary Dr David Owen argued at the time, and subsequently, against Trident, and in favour of a non-ballistic system, such as sea-launched Cruise, which, he argued, would offer a minimum deterrent. This view was rejected by the incoming Thatcher administration and its advisers. Consequently, four Trident submarines were ordered, initially with the C-4 missile system, and later the more powerful D-5, even though they would be potentially much more destructive than Polaris. The

Thatcher Government decided, with apparently no internal dissent, to go ahead on the grounds that it was necessary to retain a nuclear component as long as the risk of war in Europe remained. The Government also wanted to retain the capacity to threaten major Soviet cities which had been offered by Polaris when ordered: the so-called Moscow criterion in British strategic objectives. If Britain was retaining a world role, then it would have to remain as a nuclear power.

This approach has posed the familiar, but fundamental, question of whether Britain has been over-extending itself, particularly in relation to defence spending. The Conservative Government came into office pledged to reverse the cutbacks in defence spending of its predecessor. In 1979 it initially accepted the Nato plan for a 3 per cent annual increase in defence spending in real (inflation adjusted) terms. So, even excluding the spending for the defence of the Falklands, the defence budget in 1985–6 was 28 per cent higher in real (inflation adjusted) terms than in 1978–9. However, these increases were ended in 1986 as a result of pressure from the Treasury and other spending departments which were concerned that the Ministry of Defence was absorbing too many resources. From then on, defence spending was held down and indeed fell in real terms. The extent of the decline depends on what assumptions are made about inflation – notably the tendency for the cost of defence equipment to rise faster than prices generally.

Increases in defence spending resulting from the 1987 and 1988 expenditure rounds partially offset a higher than expected rate of price increases, so as to limit the decline in real terms. After a peak of £19.7 billion in 1984–5, the total dropped to £18.2 billion in 1988–9 (all figures at constant 1987–8 prices). A total of £18 billion was projected for 1989–90, with rises to £18.3 billion and £18.6 billion projected for the following two years. Defence Secretary George Younger claimed that these plans would ensure that, on a three-year sliding scale, a downward slope in the defence budget would be followed by a small upward slope. Nevertheless, the large rises in the early 1980s ensured that defence spending in the late 1980s was roughly a fifth higher in real terms than a decade earlier.

Concern was expressed by, amongst others, the Defence Select Committee of the Commons, who pointed out that, since the late 1980s would be the period of peak spending on the Trident project, there might be a severe squeeze on other areas of the defence budget.

Commenting on the 1988 defence estimates, the committee warned (1988) that even with level funding

difficult choices cannot be avoided. The scale of some forthcoming procurement decisions suggests that it will not be easy to keep changes to the margin of the defence programme; and even those at the margin will have some effect on capability. The Government has made clear its commitment to maintain all the UK's major defence roles. The question is not whether this can be done, but how well it can be done. Only if the ministry maintains the effectiveness of British defence will it be demonstrated that no fundamental review of defence priorities is required.

Other commentators were certain that a major defence review would be needed to reconcile expenditure and commitments. They were worried by the impact not only of the decline in total spending but also by cost overruns on projects such as the Type 23 frigate fire control systems and the Tornado F3 Foxhunter radar, let alone new commitments like the Boeing Awacs airborne early warning aircraft and the European Fighter Aircraft. Consequently, Sir Frank Kitson, a former commander in chief of UK land forces and noted writer on defence matters, argued in 1987: 'it is absolutely necessary to make a major reassessment of tri-service defence commitments within the next few years.' The same view was taken by leading academic specialists such as David Greenwood who maintained that in the early 1990s there would be a sizeable gap, of several billion pounds, between what is needed to fulfil existing commitments and planned spending totals. Similarly, Robin Laird and David Robertson argued that 'the military budget would be in trouble even without Trident or the European Fighter Aircraft. With these two programmes, there is no possibility of reaching the UK's stated defence goals.'

Successive defence secretaries were adamant that such a far-reaching review was unnecessary, even though tough decisions would have to be taken on spending priorities. They were reluctant to go down this route remembering the major controversy over the 1981 review when Defence Secretary Sir John Nott decided, to the navy's anger, in favour of some contradiction of the surface fleet compared with home defence and Britain's land contribution in West Germany. Indeed after the 1988 spending round, George Younger claimed that the real increases projected for the 1990 to 1992 period disposed 'of any talk of the need for a defence review.'

The fulfilment of existing commitments was broadly achieved during the second half of the 1980s, though not without problems. This reflected a combination of small increases in the budget (as in 1987 and 1988), favourable trends in the cost estimates for Trident, a drive to produce savings in defence procurement by more competitive contract procedures and by deferment of certain programmes. Contrary to previous experience with large contracts, the cost of Trident was steadily revised downwards in real terms – by £1.05 billion, or a tenth, between the original 1982 estimate and early 1989, to produce a figure of £9.09 billion. This reflected efficiency savings and favourable exchange rate movements, leaving aside the impact of the decision to transfer servicing of the submarines to the US. This was despite delays, and considerable cost overruns, in the Trident warhead programme. Over the whole procurement period the costs of Trident were expected to amount to 3 per cent of the defence budget, and even at the peak only 11 per cent of procurement expenditure, compared with 18 per cent at one stage of the Tornado aircraft project.

The other major development was the effort to improve value for money, notably associated with the appointment in 1984, as chief of defence procurement, of Sir Peter Levene, who had been running a successful supplier. He was behind a drive to extend competitive tendering to contain costs. This was reflected in claimed savings of over £250 million on six important equipment purchases costing £2 billion overall. The total value of contracts subject to competition rose from 38 per cent in 1983–4 to around 65 per cent in 1985–6, though with a decline to just over 50 per cent in the following two years because of the impact of the Trident and Awacs programmes, where there was no competition at the prime contractor level. The extent of the problems on the £9 billion a year procurement budget was underlined in spring 1988 by the disclosure of a report following the cancellation in late 1986 of the £880 million Nimrod project. Evidence to the House of Commons Public Accounts Committee showed that up to between £3 billion and £4 billion may have been absorbed by unforeseen increases in equipment costs over the whole defence budget and because of weaknesses in project management such as the requirement for expensive modifications. Sir Peter laid much of the blame on the old system of cost plus contracts and argued that competitive tendering and tight project management should produce greater efficiency.

In practice, the Ministry of Defence has also achieved savings by deferring orders for equipment from one year to the next under the familiar Whitehall principle of equal misery. This has applied especially to the pattern of ordering of new frigates. Predictably, there have been protests from the services, particularly the army, which accounted for less than a fifth of the procurement budget.

Despite these developments, the question remained how long it would be possible to maintain the balancing act between a constrained defence budget and the demands of the services for up-to-date equipment. The Government has been keen not only to maintain major commitments such as forward defence in West Germany, naval protection in the North Atlantic, air defence of the UK and the nuclear deterrent, but also out-of-area commitments such as the Persian Gulf (increased because of the Iran/Iraq war), Belize, Gibraltar, Hong Kong and the Falklands (though this last should be contained at just over £100 million a year with the completion of the airport and buildings for the garrison). Options may have to include a reduction in the size of the surface fleet from the current target of roughly 50 destroyers and frigates to the mid-40s and a reallocation of the army's role. With spending advancing rapidly on the Trident programme, this would be well past the stage when cancellation would make any sense in economic, let alone defence, terms by the time of a 1991–2 general election.

Mrs Thatcher showed no willingness to consider any reduction in Britain's worldwide commitments – no limitation to purely a Nato role. The Thatcher years may be seen in retrospect as an era when, thanks to strong leadership and a successful economy, Britain asserted itself in the world and regained respect and influence, while finally reconciling itself to an uneasy membership of the European Community. But how far will her charismatic style of leadership have a lasting influence? To some extent Mrs Thatcher's distinctive approach may have fostered illusions about the extent of Britain's role – and particularly its relations with the US – which may not be sustainable in the long-term after she has ceased being Prime Minister.

Conclusion

If people could be sure that we would never have another socialist government, increasing control of the state, increasing control of ownership, then I think the prospects for this country would be really bright. If only we could get rid of socialism as a second force and have two parties which fundamentally believed that political freedom had to be backed by economic freedom and that you can get the best out of people when you delegate power down.

Mrs Margaret Thatcher, interview with The Financial Times,
19 November 1986

People do not vote for Thatcherism because they believe in the small print. What Thatcherism does is address the fears, the anxieties and the lost identities of a people.

Professor Stuart Hall, The Hard Road to Renewal, 1988

Since 1983, when this series began, British public opinion has actually become more alienated from many of the goals of an 'enterprise culture'. To the extent that attitudes have moved, they have become less sympathetic to these central tenets of the 'Thatcher Revolution'.

'British Social Attitudes' – Fifth Report, 1988–89 Edition

Something has stirred in Britain during the 1980s. For all the reservations expressed in the preceding chapters about the gap between ministerial rhetoric and achievements in many areas, Britain is a very different society in the late 1980s from a decade earlier. It may not be a 'kinder gentler nation', to transfer President Bush's campaign refrain. In many respects Britain is a more divided, less secure and harsher society, but it is economically more competitive.

The Thatcher Government is responsible for helping to provide a powerful, and, in many respects, much-needed shock to British industry and society. The tripartite consensus approach had clearly failed in the 'winter of discontent' of 1978–9. Although the impact on the public was rather less than in the disputes of the early 1970s, the actions by public sector workers in hospitals and the like had a greater symbolic, and therefore political, importance. While many agreed at the time with Mrs Thatcher and her allies that the answer lay in a new approach – with a movement towards the free market – the main reaction by the electorate was negative, against what had happened. There were also many who doubted whether it would be possible to govern without the consent of the trade unions, though few would agree with the retrospective judgement of veteran centrist and political historian David Marquand (1987) that:

The corporatist experiments of the 1960s and 1970s failed not because they went too far but because they did not go far enough. The British version of corporatism is half-hearted, opaque and in a curious way, furtive. Similarly, the real problem with Britain's producer groups was that they were too narrow, too fragmented and too inward-looking.

Professor Marquand has rejected the widespread view that an over-ambitious state driven by excessive popular demands reached further than it could grasp and in doing so exacerbated problems it was trying to solve, notably via the steadily worsening inflation/unemployment trade-off of the 1970s. In his view the state became over-extended in the period of Keynesian social democracy not because it was over-ambitious but because it was the wrong kind of state. Consequently, he has seen the market approach as inherently flawed, since it has ignored the need for a sense of community and for a negotiated model of economic development. While some senior Tories have recently begun talking about active citizenship and mutual obligations, there is nothing in the events of the 1980s to suggest that an attempt to revive the corporatist approach would have worked. The trade unions were too much in need of reform to participate, and there have been clear benefits in abandoning corporatism through shifting responsibility for economic decisions away from the state to the market and to individual firms and workers.

The result has been a shake-up of established attitudes, with a greater willingness to adapt and change in British industry and, belatedly and partially, in the much-weakened trade unions. There has been undoubted evidence of improved productivity, of the creation of more businesses, of a reduced number of strikes, and of a higher quality of management, both in the public and the private sectors. There has been a change in the attitudes, at any rate of a crucial minority, towards the enterprise culture. This has been allied with a freeing up of markets and a reduction of subsidies, with important exceptions like Mrs Thatcher's attachment to mortgage interest tax relief. Even belatedly in the legal profession, Lord Mackay of Clashfern, potentially the most innovative Lord Chancellor of the century, has produced proposals for more competition in the provision of services, breaking down traditional barriers between barristers and solicitors. These ideas stimulated predictable outraged protests from his predecessor Lord Hailsham, a conservative rather than a Thatcherite radical, and from lawyers. The Government, however, faced the danger that in proposing radical changes to the legal profession, as well as to health and education, it might offend the interests, susceptibilities and votes of the middle-classes, who during the 1980s shifted away from the Tories towards the opposition parties.

Yet, while all these changes may have helped to check Britain's relative decline, they have not reversed it. Indeed, perhaps all that any government could reasonably have aspired to do was to induce a shock, or rather a series of shocks, which would halt the accelerating decline of the 1970s. For all the charismatic leadership style of Mrs Thatcher, the UK is still a medium-sized country lagging behind its main trading competitors in several key indicators, notably the reduction of inflation. The political problems posed by the unions may have been solved, but there remain considerable weaknesses in the structure of the labour market and inadequacies in training and education by international standards. Britain's general standing overseas may have improved during the 1980s, particularly as a result of Mrs Thatcher's efforts and reputation, but these external constraints remain. The tendency to regard 1979 as 'Year Zero' of the glorious revolution, or rather counter-revolution, is as misleading as talk of a subsequent economic miracle. There have been considerable continuities with the past, especially in the redirection of macro-economic policy, even though it has been in the interests of neither the government nor the opposition currently to admit as much.

Even within the Government's own terms, these main changes have not always been as favourable in their results as ministers have often liked to pretend. Privatization may have been the most striking and internationally influential policy innovation of the 1980s – with clear gains in terms of management drive and efficiency in breaking away from the embrace of Whitehall. Yet the form in which privatization has often occurred has been flawed. In too many cases in the core utilities like British Telecom and British Gas the interests of achieving a rapid sale and safeguarding the position of existing management has prevailed over those of the consumer. The option of increasing competition has been rejected and instead the regulator has had to take the strain. The planned electricity privatization has underlined the problem. While the widespread criticism of the earlier British Telecom and British Gas sales led to the introduction of competition, it has been in a highly qualified and highly regulated form. Because of the continuing need to subsidize nuclear power, electricity has turned out to be the most difficult industry in which to introduce competition. Overall, the boundaries between the public and the private sectors may have been shifted dramatically – with two-thirds of the state-owned commercial sector of 1979 in private hands by the 1991–2 election – this is only part of the story. Industrial structure matters as much as ownership.

Similarly, the much trumpeted spread of capital ownership has owed as much to the impact of past changes as to the specific initiatives of the Thatcher Government. By far the greatest influence on creating 'a nation of inheritors', in Nigel Lawson's phrase, has been the death of that generation of first-time home owners of the 1950s and 1960s. Their homes have been inherited by children, often in their 30s and 40s, who already own their own homes and there-fore receive a big increase in available capital. The sale of council houses, cuts in income and capital taxes and the inducements to individuals to buy shares in the main privatization flotations have naturally assisted the building-up of capital holdings by more people. But these moves have extended an existing trend rather than created a new one. Three qualifications have to be added. First, in a decade when the personal savings ratio has fallen substantially, enthusiasm about the creation of an enlarged group of capital owners needs to be tempered. Second, homes represent by far the largest proportion of personal wealth, and the extension of personal share ownership, while significant in its influence on attitudes, has been small in relative financial terms. Third, the extension of capital ownership, like many other changes during the 1980s, has benefited the existing middle class and some skilled workers, but has bypassed the substantial minority of the poor – thus reinforcing the impression of a two-thirds/one-third society. Nevertheless, there has been a steep move towards the goal of popular capitalism during the 1980s.

For all these qualifications the political and economic ground has clearly shifted in Britain since the late 1970s – noted as ever by those two most reflective practitioners of Thatcherism, Sir Geoffrey Howe and Nigel Lawson. Sir Geoffrey talked in a speech in 1985 of staking out 'the new common ground' – of establishing 'a post-nationalisation, post-trade union monopoly era'. In 1987 after the Conservatives' third successive election victory, he argued that:

The 1987 general election was the crucial step from a period when the reversal of the Conservative revolution always seemed possible, to one where it is almost inconceivable. It was a watershed between a party crusade for a property-owning democracy and the establishment of a new national common ground of politics. The foundations for national recovery have been firmly laid. The results are coming through. And there is no political, moral or intellectual challenge in sight to the liberalising Conservative policies which have released the spirit and the talent of our nation.

Nigel Lawson similarly argued in a lecture in July 1988:

The rehabilitation of market forces in the early 1980s was seen at first as an aberration from the post-war consensus, and one that was likely to be short-lived. But I have little doubt that, as a longer-term perspective develops, history will judge that intervention and planning were the aberration, and that the market economy is the normal, healthy way of life.

There is something in these claims. The political agenda has changed. The focus has shifted from the problems of producers and trade union obstruction to the freeing of the market and the extension of consumer choice – though familiar difficulties about high rates of wage settlement and inflation have not disappeared. Ideas like wholesale privatization, opting out from local control of schools and hospitals and the effective end of the closed shop were all regarded as politically impossible in the late 1970s, if raised at all outside the more zealous of free market New Right pamphlets. Yet they have since become common points of political debate. The extent of the change in thinking about the economy was noted even in March 1983 by Sir Douglas Wass in a retirement interview as Permanent Secretary of the Treasury:

I think the change in attitudes or behaviour towards overmanning in British industry and the discipline which has come into industry is something which I had not expected or thought possible even with three million odd unemployed .... My intellectual position then was that improvements in productivity, in manning levels and efficiency, had to be pursued by good management, by joint consultation, by bipartisanship between management and labour. What has emerged in shop floor behaviour through fear and anxiety is much greater than I think could have been secured by more co-operative methods.

The extent of the change in attitudes is brought out by comparing comments made nearly three years apart by the West German sceptic, Anglophile, and social and political scientist, Ralph Dahrendorf. In March 1985 he argued:

It is totally absurd to try to change a society 180 degrees. The point about Ronald Reagan's success is that he is reviving traditional American values and virtues. Mrs Thatcher is trying to do just the opposite – fighting all the traditional English values – and, in my view, she is doomed to failure. Britain is a society of many solidarities, totally averse to the spirit of competition between individuals. If you try to set one against the other, you get nowhere in Britain. America is exactly the opposite.

These solidarities have been tested during the 1980s. Individualism has been asserted strongly over collectivism, not least in the prosperous southern half of the country. Professor Dahrendorf reflected at the end of 1987 on returning to Britain that there had been 'a real change in people's values and attitudes' which he had not thought possible. He noted that 'the quick pound, the quick buck, seems to be very much on people's minds'.

The change in the political agenda has also been reflected in the shift of policies within the opposition parties. The dominance of the Conservatives – though at around 42–3 per cent with a smaller share of the total vote than they enjoyed during the 1950s and 1960s – has reflected the impact of a divided opposition and the first-past-the-post electoral system. These divisions have in part been because of a failure to produce a clear alternative to Thatcherism – with the appearance at times of defensive incoherence. So, after the 1983 and 1987 General Elections, Labour and to an extent the centre parties have all accepted parts of what the Thatcher Government has done, as was shown by the major shift in Labour economic and defence policies in its statement of May 1989. Council house sales have become common to all party platforms. Similarly, no one has seriously talked of returning to the 1979 boundaries between the public and the private sectors – though there has been a vigorous debate about how far central Government should control and/or regulate the utilities. Many, though not all, of the changes in trade union law – particularly the opening-up of internal elections to membership ballots – have been accepted by Labour, with a number of qualifications. The spread of share ownership has also become political common ground, though with more emphasis on employee involvement and participation and decision-making on the opposition side.

But this does not mean that we are all Thatcherites now. There remain whole areas of fierce political controversy – the clear minuses of the Thatcher decade – the increased social and economic divisions, the Government's ambiguity over the welfare state, the challenge to 'intermediating institutions' like local government, and the tendencies towards authoritarianism. There have been avoidable social costs. It is not just that macro-economic policy mistakes were made in 1979–81 which pushed up unemployment to a higher relative level than overseas, but, more persuasively, that the Government has been slow to deal with the continuing high level in the inner cities, in some areas of the north and west of Britain, and among ethnic minorities. Because the Tories have not needed the political support of these groups, the Government has reacted slowly to their problems and the solutions have placed too much emphasis on market forces rather than on local communities. The lessons of successful urban regeneration in the US are that the two need to go together.

The Government's record on the welfare state has been of steadily increased spending – not least because of the desire of many traditional, as well as new, Conservative supporters to retain the benefits of collective, free-at-the-point-of-use provision. This is in spite of the encouragement of growing private services at the margin. Yet pressures to contain the overall growth in public expenditure meant that for most of the 1980s the Government was seeking savings which produced maximum annoyance while not satisfying the limitless demand for services. Only in the late 1980s did the Government produce plans for education and health intended to replicate free market disciplines within a framework of collective taxpayer financed provision – in practice again mainly aimed at middle-class supporters. Perhaps not surprisingly, Central Statistical Office figures showed that benefits in kind – notably the National Health Service and education – averaged £1,510 per head for the poorest 20 per cent in 1986, but £1,700 for the top 20 per cent, the highest for any group. The difference was largely because far more children from better-off families stayed on in the sixth form of schools, another illustration of the fact that the middle classes are doing best out of the welfare state.

Another strand of controversy, at least among politicians, if not always among the public, has been the tendency towards authoritarianism. As discussed earlier in the book, this charge can be overstated. But Mrs Thatcher and her allies have had an attitude to criticism, and particularly towards freedom of information and discussion, which startles US and other foreign observers. The 'one of us' mentality has too often meant an intolerance of independent institutions and a concentration of power at the centre. Ministers have taken on powers which they might be horrified to see in the hands of their Labour opponents. But there has been a growing belief, particularly in the third term, that such centralization is all right since no one else will be in office for a long time. This has been the politics of hubris. Local government has had its faults – not least an unrepresentative character in many big cities because of the decline of local community involvement and a narrow financial base. There are merits in increasing the independence of schools and hospitals in relation to local authorities of various types. Parental, patient and customer power and choice ought to be encouraged in comparison with the previous unchallenged dictates of state bodies and producer-dominated authorities. But locally elected bodies have advantages in stimulating local enterprise and initiatives. For instance, many of the most creative and successful experiments in welfare provision in the US have come at the state level – from both Republican and Democrat Governors and legislatures. This is a source of independence and innovation at a local level which is increasingly absent in Britain.

Yet if ministers have often behaved as if Britain had become a one party state with the real debate only within the Conservative Party, how far have the British embraced Thatcherism? Is there a new consensus? This question has produced a fierce debate among political scientists. Professor Ivor Crewe has noted (in Skidelsky, 1988):

A strange alliance of Thatcherites, Owenites and *Marxism Today* Euro-communists regard the elections (of the 1980s) as more than a succession of landslides. They constitute an enduring transformation – social, ideological, and cultural – of the party system, the 'Great Moving Right Show' of Stuart Hall's nightmare. Parallels are drawn with Roosevelt's New Deal Democratic ascendancy in the 1930s, or de Gaulle's dominance in the 1960s. In each case there is a towering political leader; a sense of national renewal; a shift in the social balance of power; an alternation in the terms of political debate – and a twenty-year ascendancy for one party. To historically minded sceptics the three elections look more like a tremor than an earthquake. Normal political life has been temporarily disrupted, but the political landscape remains geologically intact.

Several social influences have undoubtedly worked in favour of Thatcherism and the Conservatives. In particular, there has been a decline in the size of the core working class of manual workers – down to just 45 per cent of the labour force by the late 1980s, or less than a third when the self-employed, foremen and supervisors are excluded. Moreover, policies introduced by the Thatcher Government – sales of council houses, the weakening of the position of local authorities and trade unions – and the decline of manufacturing industry have accelerated these social changes. There is a danger of a chicken-and-eggs train of causation here: Professor Crewe has suggested that 'house- and share-owners do not become Conservatives: rather Conservatives become house-owners and share-owners.' But ownership is likely to have reinforced a Conservative commitment. And, as the *Marxism Today* group have argued, these social changes have undermined and broken-up the traditional social and political bases of Labour support. Professor Crewe's own analysis of the BBC/Gallup election day survey in June 1987 highlighted the increasing social and regional divisions in Britain between a declining working class (living in the north, council tenants, union members and working in the public sector) who tend to support Labour, and expanding new working class (living in the south, owner occupiers, non-union and working in the private sector) who tend to support the Conservatives. Thatcherism has identified with the aspirations of the new and expanding group of foremen, supervisors, craftsmen and high technology workers. Labour's share of the skilled workers' vote has dropped from 45 to 34 per cent between 1979 and 1987. These social changes may have accounted for a switch in votes of 5 per cent from Labour to the Conservatives between the mid-1960s and the late 1980s.

Yet these social changes only provide a framework and do not predetermine people's voting. For instance, there has been a continuing shift of votes among the professional middle classes away from the Conservatives, mainly towards the centre parties. The advance and appeal of Thatcherism has been principally working class. Both Thatcherites and New Marxists believe, in Professor Crewe's words, that 'Thatcherism has a special appeal to the working class because it speaks to their actual experience in language (and, nowadays, accent). It understands about unwanted strikes, work dodging, welfare cheats and crime in the streets.' In short, Thatcherism strikes what is known in the US as 'cultural' chords – a blend of authoritarianism and patriotism.

The most frequently quoted polling evidence does not point to any ringing endorsement of Thatcherism. On issues such a pornography, respect for authority, progressive teaching and sexual equality, the electorate as a whole has become less conservative since 1979 – possibly reflecting the middle-class defection from the Tories. However, even in the late 1980s, more voters agreed than disagreed with Mrs Thatcher's general approach on these social/cultural questions. She was still speaking for Britain, or rather England, and at any rate enough of the country to sustain her in office when faced by a divided opposition.

The opposition parties and political scientists (notably in the annual British Social Attitudes reports) have made much of poll findings showing that voters have moved unambiguously away from a Thatcherite approach. On issues such as the priority of fighting inflation versus reducing unemployment, cutting taxes versus improving public services, the extent of the change during the 1980s in favour of the second options has been clear. Similarly, there has been strong opposition to a whole series of specifically Thatcherite policies such as privatization, even though this has not stopped large-scale public support for buying shares in most flotations. The 1988–9 British Social Attitudes report, quoted at the beginning of this chapter, argued that there had been an increasing alienation from the values of the enterprise culture. An analysis carried out by Market and Opinion Research International in June 1988 for *The Sunday*

Times and London Weekend Television pointed to more complicated cross currents of opinions between economic and social issues. The poll showed that only 18 per cent of voters backed four out of five core Thatcherite beliefs (capitalism, individualism, efficiency, personal reward and wealth creation), while 41 per cent backed three out of four of these propositions. Significantly, more voters thought that Britain had become Thatcherite on these core issues than would like it to be so.

Professor Crewe has concluded from these and similar findings that:

Conservative success remains a puzzle. Voters oppose the Government on the vast array of its specific policy initiatives. They say they prefer Labour on the issues that matter. Their economic values are solidly social democratic, their moral values only half-Thatcherite, and on both fronts they have edged to the left since 1979. There has been no ideological sea change. The economic record might account for 1987, but not 1983. The changing class structure explains only a fraction.

The puzzle can be explained in three ways. First, that the Government is well aware of the concern of voters with unemployment and with standards of public service, particularly health and education, and over the years it has sought to reduce the numbers out of work and has increased spending on welfare provision. The Government is not itself Thatcherite in the way it is often characterized. Secondly, elections and political preferences are not decided by abstract questions but by voters' sense of their personal and family well-being. The 1987 BBC/Gallup survey indicated that people think of public issues when answering survey questions, but they concentrate on their own affairs in the polling booth. The public believed that the Conservatives were more likely to provide prosperity – by a two-to-one margin.

Third, and most doubled-edged for the Tories, has been the Thatcher factor. Voters may have liked or, often, loathed her for being out of touch and divisive. A Gallup survey in April 1989 showed that 67 per cent disliked her, but 63 per cent respected her. Professor Anthony King commented that, 'the saloon bar view that she is more respected than liked turns out to be true.' Her leadership style has won respect. It has conveyed an impression of conviction, competence and decisiveness – of being a convincing Prime Minister. By contrast, Labour and its leaders have not persuaded voters that they would be strong leaders. On all measures of being a suitable Prime Minister, Mrs Thatcher has come out much more favourably than she and the Tories have on specific policies. When the Tories have looked wobbly in the polls, as in the mid-term years of 1981, 1985–6 and 1989, this has generally been because Mrs Thatcher has shown less than her usual sureness of touch, making mistakes and appearing indecisive.

There has been considerable discussion about the significance of the Falklands War in this respect. A group of Essex University academics have argued (Sanders et al., 1987) on the basis of a detailed regression analysis that the favourable effects of the Falklands War for the Government were small (probably no more than three per cent above the expected trend in the polls) and short-lived (not lasting more than three months). The study argued that the real reason for the large and sustained improvement in the Government's popularity in the summer of 1982 was an earlier improvement in the economy, and particularly the upturn in living standards. Apart from a number of statistical objections, this analysis ignores the basic political fact of the dominance of the Falklands campaign compared with all the other economic influences during this period. Moreover, as Professor Lawrence Freedman argued in the autumn 1987 issue of *Contemporary Record*: 'if the Government had failed to respond decisively to the Argentine invasion or had responded decisively but disastrously, then strength in the economy might not have been sufficient to save the Conservative Government.'

The Falklands War was also a striking symbol of the attempt by Mrs Thatcher and the Conservatives to arrest the decline of Britain. It may have been a far away place of which we knew little and many errors may have been made by the Foreign Office and by Parliament before the Argentine invasion, but the struggle to regain control of the islands did have a wider political significance for many in Britain as polls pointed out at the time. As Nigel Lawson noted (1988):

In our first term came, out of the blue, the Falklands experience, which finally laid the ghost of Suez. It also showed the world – and, even more important, ourselves – that Britain still possessed a patriotism and a moral fibre that many thought had gone forever.

My own view is that a central factor sustaining the Conservatives' political dominance has been Mrs Thatcher's leadership style – as demonstrated during the Falklands War and at other crises like the miners' strike and the Brighton bombing – coupled with the prosperity of the majority of the population (at least those in employment). Of course, the divided opposition has made her task easier, but that division has been partly because the Tories' have to split the working class.

Yet this does not mean there is necessarily anything permanent about Tories' dominance. Indeed, to the extent that the success of Thatcherism has been dependent on Mrs Thatcher herself, it may not be lasting. After all, Mrs Thatcher will go one day, voluntarily or involuntarily, and prosperity could well fade. She nearly slipped up in 1981–2 and in 1985–6, and the Tories' problems in 1989 – the feeling that this time 'she's gone too far' – could mark a turning point, rather than be followed by a pre-election recovery, as previously. Moreover, there has been a pattern in British politics that when long-lasting leaders eventually go, their coalitions of political support fracture and their immediate successors face serious problems and are often short-lived. This occurred after the departures of Liverpool in 1827, Salisbury in 1902 and Churchill in 1955. However, while seemingly impregnable governments do falter, they leave legacies. It is as misleading for Labour and the centre parties to believe that the dominance of Thatcherism is founded on a chimera – and therefore temporary – as it is for the Thatcherites and the *Marxism Today* group to proclaim an enduring transformation.

Would there have been Thatcherism without Mrs Thatcher? Both the changes in macro-economic policy starting in Britain in the mid-1970s and international developments during the 1980s suggest there would have been a shift away from collectivism towards individualism, at least in the economic sphere, with a greater emphasis on monetary and public spending restraint. The retreat from the post-war settlement would have occurred to some extent under any alternative Conservative leader. There might even have been a shift in policy under a re-elected Callaghan/Healey administration in 1979, though possibly the internal Labour strains were then so great that the party would have split and foundered in face of the already growing challenge of the Bennite fundamentalists. Mrs Thatcher's distinctive contribution has probably been to ensure that critical events – the 1981 Budget, the Falklands War in 1982 and the miners' strike of 1984–5 – that might have fatally weakened her Government were overcome. She has forced the pace of change and extended the free-market counter-revolution further than alternative Tory leaders might have done. Other prime ministers might also have been more responsive to the problems resulting from the 1979–81 shake-out – and the increased social divisions of the 1980s – and they might also have tempered her tendencies towards centralism and authoritarianism, and been more pro-European.

That most subtle of political commentators, Ferdinand Mount, the head of Mrs Thatcher's Policy Unit in Downing Street from 1982 to 1984, has put Thatcherism in the context of what he has called 'survivor regimes'. These are long-lasting governments, like the Democrats under Roosevelt in the 1930s and 1940s, the Swedish Social Democrats, and the Christian Democrats in West Germany in the first two decades of the post-war era. He has noted (1988) that

Survivor regimes do not usually arrive in office with any detailed set of plans stretching over years, or, if they do, the plans have speedily to be rewritten under the pressure of events (Roosevelt came to power promising to balance the budget). Their first needs are to communicate a sense of confidence and to establish stability. Characteristically, they will then develop a 'rolling agenda' which both expresses and renews a continuing sense of political purpose and builds on experience.

He has argued that many of the reforms known as Thatcherism had been a twinkle in Tory eyes for decades: 'What is remarkable is not their originality but their implementation ... There was no great intellectual difficulty in setting out a blueprint of this kind. The effort of will involved in carrying it out was immense.'

This reference to long-lasting regimes provides a hint of what may happen after Mrs Thatcher goes. The distinctive style of a Roosevelt, a de Gaulle or an Adenauer, quickly disappears, but the approach to policy which they fostered has a more enduring impact. In this respect the fact that many characteristically Thatcherite policies have been upopular when being introduced is less relevant than the fact that they have become part of the political landscape. Voters may have had reservations about a number of Mrs Thatcher's economic and social policies when proposed, but this does not mean they want a return to the 1970s. The political agenda has changed and any successor will have to operate in that context. A successor leader, either from Mrs Thatcher's own party or elsewhere, will have different priorities and a different style, but all these will function within the framework of what she has created, so incorporating Thatcherism. An illustration of what might happen has been provided in the US where the 22nd Amendment prevented President Reagan – much to his annoyance – from repeating Mrs Thatcher's achievement of being elected for three terms. President George Bush has deliberately changed his style from his boss of eight years – not only in being a more active executive but also in criticizing material-ism, praising public service and encouraging voluntary and commun-ity service. Yet there have been fewer changes in policy. The Bush administration has taken forward the approach of the Reagan years.

The post-Thatcher agenda in Britain will be concerned with facing up to the unsolved problems of the 1980s – reducing social divisions, responding to the growing concern over crime and a loss of commun-ity the environment (an issue Mrs Thatcher herself took up with alacrity in 1989), improving standards of education and training, reshaping the welfare state to cope with the greater number of old people, and regulating the privatized monopoly utilities. In addition, many familiar problems remain – notably the persistently high level of wage settlements and a rate of price inflation which is consequent-ly above the international average.

The Thatcher era, however long it lasts, will be remembered as a period of remarkable political convulsion – similar to the 1830s, the 1880s, the 1906–14 years, and the late 1940s. Each period compress-ed a series of underlying social and political changes which had a lasting impact long after their creators had left the political stage. The decade, or longer, of Mrs Thatcher's rule will be seen politically either as an interlude of unusually long single party dominance before the resumption of more traditional party alternation, or, less likely, the start of an era of one party rule similar to Japan – if Mrs Thatcher succeeds in her aim of eliminating socialism. The economic and social results of the Thatcher years have been less spectacular and more ambiguous than Mrs Thatcher and her allies have claimed. But British industry and society have been shaken up. To some extent the result has been a two-thirds/one-third society of winners and losers. But while the problems of decline remain, they are less acute than in the late 1970s.

Bibliography

Adeney, Martin and Lloyd, John 1986: *The Miners' Strike, 1984–85: Loss without Limit*. London, Routledge and Kegan Paul.

Autumn Statement 1983, Stationery Office, House of Commons paper 112.

Autumn Statement 1984, Stationery Office, House of Commons paper 12.

Autumn Statement 1985, Stationery Office, House of Commons paper 22.

Autumn Statement 1986, Stationery Office, House of Commons paper 14.

Autumn Statement 1987, Stationery Office, House of Commons paper 110.

Autumn Statement 1988, Stationery Office, House of Commons paper 695.

Baker, Kenneth 1988: The Community of Individuals, speech to the Bow Group Annual Dinner.

Bank of England 1988: Regional Labour Markets, *Quarterly Bulletin*, August 1988.

Barnett, Correlli 1972: *The Collapse of British Power*. London, Alan Sutton.

Barnett, Correlli 1986: *The Audit of War*. London, Macmillan.

Bassett, Philip 1986 and 1987: *Strike Free*. London, Macmillan.

Beer, Samuel H. 1982: *Britain Against Itself: The Political Contradictions of Collectivism*. London, Faber and Faber.

Britain's Post-War Industrial Decline: Symposium 1987: *Contemporary Record*, vol. 1, no. 2; Reply to Criticisms, vol. 1, no. 3, and vol. 1, no. 4. Oxford, Philip Allan Publishers.

British Social Attitudes, annual reports 1984 to 1988. Aldershot, Gower Publishing.

Brown, Professor William 1988: The Structure and Processes of Pay Determination in the Private Sector, 1979–86. London, Confederation of British Industry.

Bruce-Gardyne, Jock 1984: *Mrs Thatcher's First Administration: The Prophets Confounded*. London, Macmillan.

Building Businesses ... Not Barriers 1986: Stationery Office, command 9794.

Bull, David, and Wilding, Paul, eds 1983: *Thatcherism and the Poor*. London, Child Poverty Action Group.

Butler, David, and Kavanagh, Dennis 1980: *The British General Election of 1979*. London, Macmillan.

Butler, David, and Kavanagh, Dennis 1984: *The British General Election of 1983*. London, Macmillan.

Butler, David, and Kavanagh, Dennis 1988: *The British General Election of 1987*. London, Macmillan.

Butler, Dr Eamonn, ed. 1988: *The Mechanics of Privatisation, papers from an international conference organised by the Adam Smith Institute*. London, Adam Smith Institute.

Campaign Guide 1987, Conservative Research Department.

Civil Research and Development 1987: *Government Response to the First Report of the House of Lords Select Committee on Science and Technology, 1986–87 Session*. Stationery Office, command 185.

Clarke, Kenneth 1985: speech to Conservative Party conference, Blackpool, October 1985.

Clarke, Kenneth 1986: speech to Engineering Employers' Federation, London, May 1986.

Clarke, Kenneth 1987: speech to City University Business School, London, February 1987.

Cockle, Paul, ed. 1984: *Public Expenditure Policy, 1984–85*. London, Macmillan.

Cole, John 1987: *The Thatcher Years, A Decade of Revolution in British Politics*. London, BBC Books.

Commonwealth Eminent Persons Group 1986: *Mission to South Africa for Commonwealth Heads of Government*. London, Penguin.

Crewe, Ivor 1983: Why Labour Lost the British Election, *Public Opinion*, June/July, vol. 6, no. 3. Washington DC, American Enterprise Institute.

Crewe, Ivor 1987: What's left for Labour; An Analysis of Thatcher's Victory, *Public Opinion*, July/August, vol. 10, no. 2. Washington DC, American Enterprise Institute.

Dahrendorf, Ralph 1982: *On Britain*. London, BBC Books.

Dalyell, Tam 1986: *Patterns of Deceit*. London, Cecil Woolf.

Dalyell, Tam 1987: *Misrule. How Mrs Thatcher has Misled Parliament from the Sinking of the Belgrano to the Wright Affair*. London, Hamish Hamilton.

Davies, Gavyn 1985: *Governments Can Affect Employment*. London, Employment Institute.

Defence Committee, Sessions 1987–8, Seventh Report, Defence Estimates, House of Commons paper 495.

DTI – the Department for Enterprise 1988: *Government Statement on Objectives for Department of Trade and Industry*. Stationery Office, command 278.

Dilnot, Andrew, and Kell, Michael 1988: *Top-rate tax cuts and incentives. Fiscal Studies*, vol. 9, no. 4, November 1988. London, Institute for Fiscal Studies.

Dimbleby, David, and Reynolds, David 1988: *An Ocean Apart*. London, BBC Books and Hodder and Stoughton.

Economic Policy 1987: *A Special Report, The Conservative Revolution*. Cambridge, Cambridge University Press.

Edmonds, John 1986: interview in *Marxism Today*, vol. 30, no. 9, September 1986.

Employment, The Challenge for the Nation 1985: Department of Employment, March 1985. Stationery Office, command 9474.

Energy Committee 1987–8: Electricity Privatisation, Fourth Report, Session 1987–8, House of Commons paper 701.

Faith in the City, The Report of the Archbishop of Canterbury's Commission on Urban Priority Areas 1985: London, Church House Publishing.

Falklands Islands Review 1983: Report of a Committee of Privy Counsellors, chaired by Lord Franks. Stationery Office, command 8787.

Fforde, John 1983: Setting Monetary Objectives, *Bank of England Quarterly Bulletin*, June 1983.

Financial Statement and Budget Report 1984–85. Stationery Office, House of Commons paper 304.

Financial Statement and Budget Report 1985–86. Stationery Office, House of Commons paper 265.

Financial Statement and Budget Report 1986–87. Stationery Office, House of Commons paper 273.

Financial Statement and Budget Report 1987–88. Stationery Office, House of Commons paper 194.

Financial Statement and Budget Report 1988–89. Stationery Office, House of Commons paper 361.

Financial Statement and Budget Report 1989–90. Stationery Office, House of Commons paper 235.

Fowler, Norman 1987: speech to Conservative Trade Unionists' annual conference, Pudsey, November 1987.

Freedman, Professor Lawrence 1987: Controversy. The Falklands Factor, *Contemporary Record*, vol. 1, no. 3. Oxford, Philip Allan Publishers.

Gamble, Andrew 1988: *The Free Economy and the Strong State, The Politics of Thatcherism*. London, Macmillan Education.

Goldsmith, Michael, and Willetts, David 1988: *Managed Health Care: a New System for a Better Health Service*. London, Centre for Policy Studies.

Government's Expenditure Plans 1983–84 to 1985–86 1983: Stationery Office, commands 8789-1 and 8789-2.

Government's Expenditure Plans 1984–85 to 1986–87 1984: Stationery Office, commands 9143–1 and 9143–2.

Government's Expenditure Plans 1985–86 to 1987–88 1985: Stationery Office, commands 9428–1 and 9428–2.

Government's Expenditure Plans 1986–87 to 1988–89 1986: Stationery Office, commands 9702–1 and 9702–2.

Government's Expenditure Plans 1987–88 to 1989–90 1987: Stationery Office, commands 56–1 and 56–2.

Government's Expenditure Plans 1988–89 to 1990–91 1988: Stationery Office, commands 288–1 and 288–2.

Green, David G. 1988: *Everyone a Private Patient*, Hobart Paperback 27. London, Institute of Economic Affairs.

Green, David G. 1988: *Acceptable Inequalities? Essays on the pursuit of equality in health care*, IEA Health Unit Paper number 3. London, Institute of Economic Affairs.

Griffiths, Professor Brian 1983: *The Moral Basis of the Market Economy*. London, Conservative Political Centre.

Grimstone, Gerry 1987: Privatisation: The Unexpected Crusade, *Contemporary Record*, vol. 1, no. 1. Oxford, Philip Allan Publishers.

Grout, Professor Paul 1987: article on share ownership in August issue of *Fiscal Studies*. London, Institute for Fiscal Studies.

Hall, Stuart 1988: *The Hard Road to Renewal: Thatcherism and the Crisis of the Left*. London, Verso.

Hall, Stuart, and Jacques, Martin eds 1983: *The Politics of Thatcherism*. London, Lawrence and Wishart.

Hanson, Charles G., and Mather, Graham 1988: *Striking Out Strikes*. London, Institute of Economic Affairs, Hobart Paper 110.

Harris, Ralph, and Seldon, Arthur 1987: *Welfare without the State, A quarter-century of suppressed public choice*. London, Institute of Economic Affairs.

Harris, Kenneth 1988: *Thatcher*. London, Weidenfeld and Nicolson.

Hattersley, Roy 1988: Thatcher's Children, speech in Southwark, June 1988.

Heald, David 1987: UK: The End of Nationalisation, and Afterwards?, speech to conference on privatization at Nuffield College, Oxford.

Healey, Nigel M. 1987: From Monetary Restraint to Closet Keynesianism, *Economic Affairs*, April/May 1987. London, Institute of Economic Affairs.

Henderson, Nicholas 1987: *Channels and Tunnels, Reflections on Britain and Abroad*. London, Weidenfeld and Nicolson.

Hennessy, Peter 1989: *Whitehall*. London, Secker and Warburg.

Heseltine, Michael 1987: *Where There's A Will*. London, Hutchinson.

Holme, Richard, and Elliott, Michael eds 1988: *1688/1988, Time for a New Constitution*. London, Macmillan.

Holmes, Martin 1985: *The First Thatcher Government 1979–83, Contemporary Conservatism and Economic Change*. Brighton, Wheatsheaf Books.

Hoover, Kenneth, and Plant, Raymond 1988: *Conservative Capitalism in Britain and the United States*. London, Routledge.

Howe, Sir Geoffrey 1982: *Conservatism in the Eighties*. London, Conservative Political Centre.

Howe, Sir Geoffrey 1985: *The Choices Facing Britain*. London, Conservative Political Centre.

Howe, Sir Geoffrey 1986: *Britain's Agenda for the Future*. London, Conservative Political Centre.

Howe, Sir Geoffrey 1988: *The Conservative Revival of Britain*. London, Conservative Political Centre.

Hurd, Douglas 1988: speech to Peel Society Dinner, Tamworth, February 1988.

Hurd, Douglas 1988: Portrait of Crime, speech to English Speaking Union, Oxford, July 1988.

Jackson, Peter ed. 1985: *Implementing Government Policy Initiatives, The Thatcher Administration 1979–83*. London, Royal Institute of Public Administration.

Jenkins, Peter 1987: *Mrs Thatcher's Revolution*. London, Jonathan Cape.

Jessop, Bob, Bonnett, Kevin, Bromley, Simon, and Ling, Tom 1988: *Thatcherism*. Cambridge, Polity Press.

Johnston, R.J., Pattie, C.J., and Allsopp, J.G. 1988: *A Nation Dividing? The Electoral Map of Great Britain 1979–87*. London, Longman.

Joseph, Sir Keith, and Sumption, Jonathan 1978: *Equality*. London, John Murray.

Kavanagh, Dennis 1987: *Thatcherism and British Politics, The End of Consensus?* Oxford, Oxford University Press.

Kay, John, Mayer, Colin, and Thompson, David eds 1986: *Privatisation and Regulation – the UK Experience*. Oxford, Oxford University Press.

Kay, John, and Bishop, Matthew 1988: *Does Privatisation Work? Lessons from the UK*. London, London Business School, Centre for Business Strategy.

Kennedy, Paul 1988: *The Rise and Fall of the Great Powers*. London, Unwin Hyman.

King, Anthony 1985: Following the Leaders: How Ronald Reagan and Margaret Thatcher have Changed Public Opinion, *Public Opinion*, June/July, vol. 8, no. 3. Washington DC, American Enterprise Institute.

King, Anthony ed. 1985: *The British Prime Minister*, second edition London, Macmillan.

King, Desmond S. 1987: *The New Right, Politics, Markets and Citizenship*. London, Macmillan Education.

Krieger, Joel 1986: *Reagan, Thatcher and the Politics of Decline*. Cambridge, Polity Press.

Lamont, Norman 1987: speech on privatisation to the Bow Group.

Lawson, Nigel 1981: *Thatcherism in Practice, A Progress Report*, speech in Zurich, January 1981. London, Conservative Political Centre.

Lawson, Nigel 1981: *The New Conservatism*. London, Conservative Political Centre.

Lawson, Nigel 1982: *Financial Discipline Restored, The Road to Economic Recovery*. London, Conservative Political Centre.

Lawson, Nigel 1982: *What's Right with Britain?* London, Conservative Political Centre.

Lawson, Nigel 1985: *Britain's Economy, A Mid-Term Report*. London, Conservative Political Centre.

Lawson, Nigel 1984: *The British Experiment*, The Fifth Mais Lecture, City University Business School. London, June 1984.

Lawson, Nigel 1988: The Frontiers of Privatisation, speech to Adam Smith Institute conference on privatisation.

Lawson, Nigel 1988: *The New Britain, the tide of ideas from Attlee to Thatcher*. London, Centre for Policy Studies.

Layard, Richard 1986: *How to Beat Unemployment*. Oxford, Oxford University Press.

Letwin, Oliver 1988: *Privatising the World, A Study of International Privatisation in Theory and Practice*. London, Cassell.

Letwin, Oliver, and Redwood, John 1988: *Britain's Biggest Enterprise, Ideas for Radical Reform of the NHS*. London, Centre for Policy Studies.

Levitt, M.S. ed. 1987: *New Priorities in Public Spending*. Aldershot, Gower.

Lewis, Jim, and Townsend, Alan 1989: *The North–South Divide*. London, Paul Chapman.

MacGregor, Ian 1986: *The Enemies Within, The Story of the Miners' Strike 1984–85*. London, Collins.

MacInnes, John 1988: *Thatcherism at Work*. Milton Keynes, Open University Press.

Marquand, David 1988: *The Unprincipled Society, New Demands and Old Politics*. London, Jonathan Cape.

Maude, Angus, ed. 1977: *The Right Approach to the Economy, Outline of an Economic Strategy for the next Conservative Government*. London, Conservative Central Office.

Maynard, Geoffrey 1988: *The Economy under Mrs Thatcher*. Oxford, Basil Blackwell.

McEnery, John 1988: *Manufacturing Two Nations*. London, Institute of Economic Affairs.

Meade, Professor James 1986: *Different Forms of Share Economy*. London, Public Policy Centre.

Minford, Patrick, ed. 1987: *Monetarism and Macro-economics*. London, Institute of Economic Affairs.

Minogue, Kenneth, and Biddiss, Michael, eds 1987: *Thatcherism: Personality and Politics*. London, Macmillan.

Moore, John 1984: Privatisation Achievements, speech in London.

Moore, John 1985: The Success of Privatisation, speech to Hoare Govett.

Moore, John 1986: Ownership, speech at the National Association of Pension Funds annual conference.

Moore, John 1986: Privatisation in the UK, speech to Institute for International Research conference.

Moore, John 1987: Philosophy into Practice, speech on privatisation to conference in Indianapolis.

Moore, John 1987: *The Welfare State – The Way Ahead*. London, Conservative Political Centre.

Mount, Ferdinand 1988–9: Thatcher's Decade, *The National Interest*, no. 14. Washington DC.

Muellbauer, John 1986: How House Prices Fuel Wage Rises, *Financial Times*, 23 October 1986.

Muellbauer, John 1986: The Assessment: Productivity and Competitiveness in British Manufacturing, *Oxford Review of Economic Policy*, autumn 1986. Oxford, Oxford University Press.

National Institute Economic Review 1987: The British Economy since 1979, number 122, November 1987. London, National Institute of Economic and Social Research.

No Turning Back, A New Agenda from a Group of Conservative MPs 1985: London, Conservative Political Centre.

No Turning Back Group of Conservative MPs 1988: *The NHS: A Suitable Case for Treatment*. London, Conservative Political Centre.

Olson, Mancur 1982: *The Rise and Decline of Nations*. London, Yale University Press.

Overseas Trade, 9 1985: Report of House of Lords Select Committee, Session 1984–85. Stationery Office, House of Lords paper 238–1 and 238–2.

Oxford Review of Economic Policy, vol. 4, no. 1, articles by Geoffrey Meen and Nick Crafts. Oxford, Oxford University Press.

Pirie, Madsen, and Butler, Eamonn 1988: *Health Management Units: The Operation of an Internal Market within a National Health Service*. London, Adam Smith Institute.

Prior, James 1986: *A Balance of Power*. London, Hamish Hamilton.

Privatising Electricity 1988: Government proposals for the privatisation of the electricity supply industry in England and Wales. London, Stationery Office, command 322.

Public Accounts Committee of the Commons, Session 1985–6, *Thirty-fourth Report, Enterprise Zones*. Stationery Office, House of Commons paper 293.

Pym, Francis 1984: *The Politics of Consent*. London, Hamish Hamilton.

Redwood, John 1988: *Popular Capitalism*, London, Routledge.

Redwood, John 1988: *In Sickness and Health, Managing Change in the NHS*. London, Centre for Policy Studies.

Rentoul, John 1987: *The Rich Get Richer*. London, Unwin Paperbacks.

Rhodes James, Robert 1986: *Anthony Eden*. London, Weidenfeld and Nicolson.

Riddell, Peter 1983, updated 1985: *The Thatcher Government*. Oxford, Basil Blackwell.

Robinson, Professor Colin 1988: Competition in Power Supply?, *Institute of Economic Affairs Inquiry* 2. London, Institute of Economic Affairs.

Sanders, David, Ward, Hugh, and Marsh, David 1987: Government Popularity and the Falklands War: A Reassessment, *British Journal of Political Studies*, vol. 17.

Seldon, Arthur, ed. 1981: *The Emerging Consensus?* London, Institute of Economic Affairs.

Skidelsky, Robert, ed. 1988, *Thatcherism*. London, Chatto and Windus.

Smith, David 1987: *The Rise and Fall of Monetarism*. London, Penguin Books.

Social Services Committee of the Commons, Session 1987–88, *First Report, Resourcing the National Health Service: Short Term Issues*, House of Commons papers 264–1 and 264–2; *Second Report, Government Re-action to the First Report*, House of Commons paper 369; *Third Report, Resourcing the National Health Service: Prospects for 1988–89*, House of Commons paper 547; *Fifth Report, The Future of the National Health Service*, House of Commons paper 613.

Stephenson, Hugh 1980: *Mrs Thatcher's First Year*. London, Jill Norman.

Tebbit, Norman 1985: *Britain's Future, A Conservative Vision*, The First Disraeli Lecture. London, Conservative Political Centre.

Tebbit, Norman 1988: *Upwardly Mobile*. London, Weidenfeld and Nicolson.

Thatcher, Margaret 1968: *What's Wrong with Politics?* London, Conservative Political Centre.

The Thatcher Years, The Policies and the Prospects, A Balanced Appraisal by the Financial Times 1987: London, *Financial Times*.

Treasury 1988: Share Ownership in Britain, April issue of *Economic Progress Report*, number 195.

Treasury and Civil Service Committee, Session 1979–80 *Second Report, The Budget and the Government's Expenditure Plans 1980–81*. House of Commons paper 584.

Treasury and Civil Service Committee, Session 1980–81: *Fifth Report, The 1981 Budget and the Government's Expenditure Plans 1981–82 to 1983–84*.

Treasury and Civil Service Committee, Session 1981–82: *First Report, The Government's Economic Policy*, Autumn Statement, House of Commons paper 28.

Treasury and Civil Service Committee, Session 1982–83:*Third Report, The Government's Expenditure Plans 1983–84 to 1985–86*, House of Commons paper 204; *Fifth Report, The 1983 Budget*, House of Commons paper 286.

Treasury and Civil Service Committee, Session 1983–84: *First Report, The Government's Economic Policy*, Autumn Statement, House of Commons paper 170; *Third Report, The Government's Expenditure Plans 1984–85 to 1986–87, House of Commons paper 285: Fourth Report, The 1984 Budget*, House of Commons paper 341.

Treasury and Civil Service Committee, Session 1984–85: *First report, The Government's Economic Policy*, Autumn Statement, House of Commons paper 44; *Sixth Report, The Government's Expenditure Plans 1985–86*, House of Commons paper 213; *Eighth Report, the 1985 Budget*, House of Commons paper 306.

Treasury and Civil Service Committee, Session 1985–86: *Second Report, The Government's Economic Policy*, Autumn Statement, House of Commons paper 57; *Fourth Report, The 1986 Budget*, House of Commons paper 313.

Treasury and Civil Service Committee, Session 1986–87: *Second Report, The Government's Economic Policy*, Autumn Statement, House of Commons paper 27; *Third Report, The Government's Expenditure Plans 1987–88 to 1989–90*, House of Commons paper 153; *Sixth Report, the 1987 Budget*, House of Commons paper 293.

Treasury and Civil Service Committee, Session 1987–88: *First Report, The Government's Economic Policy*, Autumn Statement, House of Commons paper 197; *Second Report, The Government's Public Expenditure Plans 1988–89 to 1990–91*, House of Commons paper 292; *Fourth Report, The 1988 Budget*, House of Commons paper 400.

Treasury and Civil Service Committee, Session 1988–89, *First Report*, Autumn Statement 1988, House of Commons paper 89.

United Kingdom 1988: *Annual Report of the Organisation for Economic Cooperation and Development*, August 1988. Paris, OECD.

Veljanovski, Cento 1987: *Selling the State, Privatisation in Britain*. London, Weidenfeld and Nicolson.

Vickers, John, and Yarrow, George 1985: *Privatisation and the Natural Monopolies*. London, Public Policy Centre.

Vickers, John, and Yarrow, George 1988: *Privatisation: An Economic Analysis*. London, Massachusetts Institute of Technology.

Walker, Alan, and Walker, Carol, ed. 1987: *The Growing Divide, A Social Audit, 1979–87*. London, Child Poverty Action Group.

Walters, Alan 1986: *Britain's Economic Renaissance, Mrs Thatcher's Reforms 1979–84*. Oxford, Oxford University Press.

Whitehead, Philip 1985: *Writing on the Wall*. London, Michael Joseph.

Weiner, Martin J. 1981: *English Culture and the Decline of the Industrial Spirit 1850–1980*. Cambridge, Cambridge University Press.

Yassukovich, Stanislas 1987: speech to industrial policy seminar on privatisation at the London School of Economics.

Young, David 1985: *Enterprise Regained*. London, Conservative Political Centre.

Young, David 1986: *Enterprise*, Stockton lecture. London Business School, April 1986.

Young, Hugo, and Sloman, Anne 1986: *The Thatcher Phenomenon*. London, BBC Books.

Young, Hugo 1989: *One of Us*. London, Macmillan.

Index